The End of North Korea

The End of North Korea

Nicholas Eberstadt

The AEI Press

Publisher for the American Enterprise Institute

WASHINGTON, D.C.

1999

The American Enterprise Institute would like to thank the Korea Foundation for its support of this project.

To order call toll free 1-800-462-6420 or 1-717-794-3800. For all other inquiries please contact the AEI Press, 1150 Seventeenth Street, N.W., Washington, D.C. 20036 or call 1-800-862-5801.

Library of Congress Cataloging-in-Publication Data

Eberstadt, Nicholas, 1955–
    The end of North Korea / Nicholas Eberstadt.
       p.   cm.
    Includes bibliographical references and index.
    ISBN 0-8447-4087-X (cloth: alk. paper). — ISBN 0-8447-4088-8 (paper: alk. paper)
    1. Korea (North)—Economic conditions. 2. Korean reunification question (1945–)   I. Title.
    HC470.2.E25   1999
    330.95193—dc21   99-12628
                                                        CIP

1 3 5 7 9 10 8 6 4 2

THE AEI PRESS
Publisher for the American Enterprise Institute
1150 17th Street, N.W.
Washington, D.C. 20036

ISBN 978-0-8447-4088-1

TO THE MEMORY OF

ERIC MARC BREINDEL (1955–1998)

FALLEN FRIEND

GREATLY MISSED

Contents

Acknowledgments

I n ordinary life, prudent people are expected to avoid accumulating deep and diverse debts. In research and writing, the rules are very different. There, one is enriched by one's debts—and the more diverse the debts, the better. I have accumulated more than my fair share of debts over the course of my work on this volume. I am happy here to point to a few of the very deepest.

For nearly a decade and a half, the American Enterprise Institute for Public Policy Research has been my institutional home in Washington, D.C. For me, this association has been, and remains, both a privilege and a pleasure. A privilege because AEI looks after its scholars more wholeheartedly, and intelligently, than any other research institute I have ever come across; a pleasure because AEI is, to my knowledge, quite simply the most exciting "think tank" for any policy researcher in the world today. If AEI did not exist, I am not at all sure that such a place would be invented.

My other institutional home for the past two decades has been the Harvard University Center for Population and Development Studies in Cambridge, Massachusetts. The American academy, as its critics assert, may indeed be ever less tolerant of controversial research and less supportive of unfashionable thinking. But that cannot be proved from my experience with the Population Center. In that long and happy relationship, colleagues and friends at the center have demonstrated nothing but interest, encouragement, and support for the research I have shared with them—no matter what that research happened to be. Some of them, I imagine, must have thought that devoting so much time to the study of North Korean affairs was—well, eccentric. I am happy to report that the center has looked out for its eccentrics for as long as I have known the place and looks out for them to this very day.

A topic as abstruse as North Korean affairs is not a natural magnet for scholarly research funding. To the contrary, given the deliberately veiled nature of the economy, society, and polity in contemporary North Korea and the extremely limited corpus of "hard facts" that outside observers have to work with, supporting studies of North Korea cannot help but appear more than ordinarily risky to the conventional granting institution. I am therefore especially grateful to the organizations that had the confidence in this project to underwrite its progress and completion.

It is no exaggeration to say that this book would not have been written without the continuing support of the Korea Foundation in Seoul. This was, arguably, not the typical project for a foundation established expressly "to promote an understanding of Korea throughout the world and enhance international goodwill and friendship through . . . international exchange programs"—which makes my appreciation of the commitment all the greater. When I learned that the Korea Foundation was determined to carry on with its support for the project despite its own suddenly reduced circumstances in the wake of South Korea's December 1997 financial shock, I felt personally touched, even honored.

I would be remiss if I did not also thank the National Bureau of Asian Research of Seattle, Washington, for its support of some of the work that has taken shape, in somewhat revised form, in this volume. In particular, I should note that the bureau sponsored the original version of chapter 2 through its Project on North Korean Economic Stability. The bureau's officers and staff—its president, Kenneth B. Pyle; its executive director, Richard J. Ellings, and its indispensable office manager, Jennifer Linder—are pure delight to work with.

My progress throughout was abetted by a succession of diligent research assistants. Special credit is due Jonathan B. Tombes; tireless, dedicated, and erudite, he often seemed to know what I would need before I knew myself. I commend Gwendolyn A. Wilber and Kelly L. O'Neal for their always cheerful help. And I salute Amanda W. Schnetzer for her expert translations of the arcane documents on Soviet–North Korean relations.

Finally, every book should have a title, and I could not think of one for this volume, try as I might. It was Christopher C. DeMuth, AEI's president, who suggested *The End of North Korea*. This is not the biggest debt that I owe to Chris, nor is it likely to be the last. It is simply the latest installment in a continuing series.

The End of North Korea

1

Introduction

I n 1992, two years before his death, Kim Il Sung, the "Great Leader" of the Democratic People's Republic of Korea (also known as the DPRK, and North Korea)—to that date, the only ruler the state had ever known—began to publish a compendium of reminiscences about his life and times. Although he inhabited a society that automatically acclaimed his every utterance for its immortal wisdom, the old man could rightly believe nonetheless that he had an epic story to tell.

With the Century

This former Soviet Red Army officer, after all, had survived cataclysmic perils and had gone on to savor triumphs of historic proportion. He had launched the Korean War with the mistaken hope of quickly overrunning and absorbing South Korea (the Republic of Korea, or ROK); although his grave miscalculation in 1950 led instead to an international embroilment that devastated his country, he had managed to emerge from the disaster intact and unbowed. He battled General Douglas MacArthur, vanquisher of the mighty Japanese Imperial Army, and could claim to have concluded that contest unvanquished himself. In fact, the world's greatest power, the United States, had fought against him for three years and had been unable to defeat him.

At a young age—while still in his thirties—he had assumed control of the Soviet-type system then being established in North Korea; over the subsequent half-century, he mastered all rivals in the deadly infighting such systems naturally invite and molded the system itself so that it bestowed on him an even greater measure of direct personal command over the lives of his subjects than either Stalin or Mao had enjoyed at his zenith of power.

In contradistinction to all other communist governments (whose doctrines regarded monarchic succession as inherently counterrevolutionary), Kim had openly founded a socialist dynasty in North Korea, with his brother and then later his son designated as heir to, and vanguard of, the revolutionary tradition. And he had originated a quasi-religious philosophy, *juche*-thought. *Juche*'s 20 million avowed adherents—the entire populace of his country—had been taught that the destiny and salvation of Korean people, who had been partitioned between two separate and mutually hostile states through the settlements of World War II, would lie in an eventual reunification beneath an independent, socialist government—that is to say, Kim's own government, directed by Kim's own family.

Although Kim's memoirs ostensibly recounted events past, they were suffused with the Great Leader's confidence that he knew what lay in store for his regime—and, indeed, all Korea—in the future. The conviction that history was on the side of his North Korean project was conveyed by images throughout the book, and perhaps most significantly, by its title. Kim Il Sung chose to call his story *Segi Wa Toburo— With the Century.*[1]

As the end of Kim's century nears, very different sorts of images of North Korea are circulating internationally. Some of those were conveyed in an arresting videotape broadcast on Japanese and South Korean television in December 1998. The video, shot secretly by a North Korean refugee at the behest of a Japan-based charity, Rescue the North Korean People!, presented scenes from everyday life in several towns in the real, existing DPRK. Western journalists who watched the program described what they saw:

> [B]arefoot orphans sucking fishbones in a squalid outdoor market; women picking lice from each other's hair; men wading into a river to fish out the bodies of friends who starved to death or were shot by border guards.[2]
>
> In one scene, an emaciated boy staggers from hunger as the cameraman asks him where he lives. The child is an orphan and lives on what scraps he can find in the open air market. He is clearly close to collapse. In another harrowing scene, a small girl tries to scoop dirty water to drink from a puddle with a plastic bag. Some of the children said they had run away from state-run "relief centres" where the only food was two ladles of corn gruel a day. In some cases their parents had died or gone away to search for food and never came back.[3]

Viewers found the images shocking—heart-rending in their own right, but all the more disturbing because they were so anomalous. Desperate hunger is not supposed to strike societies that are urbanized, industrialized, and free from chaos or war. Yet urban, industrial North Korea was—and is—manifestly in the grip of a terrible food crisis. And it was not a momentary crisis. Pyongyang had formally issued an emergency appeal for international humanitarian food aid in 1995—the year after Kim Il Sung's death; international relief operations have been underway in North Korea ever since. At the end of the twentieth century, the DPRK was apparently still gaining important new capabilities—among those, the capability to build and launch multistage ballistic missiles—but the regime had lost the capability to feed its own populace.

As an epigram for the North Korean project, *With the Century* is more fitting than some readers might immediately recognize today. The twentieth century, after all, was transformed—or more precisely, disfigured—by the political philosophies of Marxism-Leninism and nationalism, and in the DPRK especially radical versions of those two fateful doctrines took life together within a single state apparatus. The twentieth century was the century of the totalitarian aspiration—and as one of the great students of Asian affairs has written, "the political system" of the DPRK looks to be "as close to totalitarianism as a humanly operated society could come."[4]

And the twentieth century witnessed the advent in international affairs of the insatiable, revisionist state: the government intent on shattering the existing international system to recast its relations with the world in a manner that would vastly extend its will. The DPRK has been a veritable model of the revisionist state. Through its implacable policies and practices, that small country has certainly made its will felt in world politics. North Korea's influence on world affairs in the second half of the twentieth century has surely been greater than would have been predicted on the basis of population and economic output alone.

Such distinctions and achievements, however, do not in the final analysis qualify the North Korean project as a success. As this bloody, brutal century comes to a close, it is apparent that the DPRK—which exemplified so many of the tragic, destructive, and ultimately unworkable political tendencies of our era—is itself a colossal failure. In fact, its failure is so pervasive, so deep, and so apparently irremediable that we may now begin to speak of, and to contemplate, the end of the North Korean project.

This book offers just such an undertaking. In the following chapters I review the history and trajectory, analyze the present dire predicaments, and examine the current options of that ambitious, dangerous, but now also dying state. I also offer an assessment of the risks that the DPRK, even in severe decline, currently poses to its neighbors and to the international community. Finally, I present a few thoughts about the ways in which concerned Western governments—in particular, the Republic of Korea, the United States, and Japan—might begin to think about the end of North Korea, and how they might prepare today to enhance stability and prosperity in Northeast Asia in a post–DPRK era.

Ending Phases

In the most obvious of senses, of course, the North Korean project is still very much with us in the year 1999. The DPRK continues to function as a state: it vigorously controls its borders (and the people within them); it conducts a foreign policy; it demands—and enjoys—all the recognitions of sovereignty. Yet at the same time, one can also say that the North Korean project, in some profound and meaningful senses, has *already* come to an end. For the North Korean project has totally failed to accomplish the missions for which it was ostensibly constructed—missions, indeed, on which the DPRK's authority and legitimacy, in large measure, have always been predicated.

Those missions were, first and foremost, the unification of the entire Korean peninsula under an "independent, socialist" regime, and, second, the implementation of a program of sustained socialist growth that would permit the state to amass steady power and allow the populace to enjoy a modicum of prosperity. The North Korean system, as we well know, has not achieved either of those objectives. More than that: from our current vantage point, it is apparent that the North Korean project, as currently constituted, is *systemically incapable* of accomplishing the very objectives that justify its existence. The failure of North Korea's unification quest and the failure of the North Korean economic formula mark the end of any positive purpose for the North Korean state.

Chapter 2 presents an interpretation of the North Korean state's relentless, bold, and yet ultimately fruitless quest for unification of the Korean peninsula on its own terms. *Interpretation* is the operative term here, as all students of North Korean affairs will appreciate. The North Korean government has, for over fifty years, enshrouded itself in deliberately fashioned mystery. By conscious and long-standing design of state, less reliable information is available about the DPRK than perhaps any other country in the modern world. To complicate matters further, "strategic deception"—that is to say, programmatic efforts to mislead potential opponents about intentions and capabilities—always seems to have figured prominently in DPRK statecraft. Pyongyang's surprise attack against South Korea in June 1950 may be the most famous of those exercises, but it is merely a single case in point. The problematic nature of that evidentiary record, it is worth noting, goes far in explaining why contemporary North Korea watchers can and often do arrive at dramatically different conclusions about the meaning and significance of given reports about, or pronouncements by, the DPRK.

Yet I would submit that from the very inception of the North Korean state, the DPRK has maintained a consistent diagnosis of the problems of divided Korea and has cleaved to a consistent prescription for remedying them. From the very beginning, Pyongyang's leadership regarded the Republic of Korea in the South as a flawed, corrupt, and illegitimate regime: as a government with little chance of surviving on its own and with no right to do so in any case. And from the very beginning, "unification," a paramount goal of state, meant to Pyongyang unification on Pyongyang's terms and Pyongyang's terms alone: preserving any vestiges of the system from the South would be inimical to that goal. Consequently, North Korea's "unification policy" from the very first was to insist on and prepare for the complete collapse of the ROK—and to hasten that "inevitable" event by every means at its disposal.

If my interpretation is correct, the surprise attack against the South on June 25, 1950, was not a deviation from North Korean "unification policy," but to the contrary a faithful representation of it.

That stab at unconditional unification, of course, did not achieve its objectives: the United States rushed to Seoul's defense; the civil war became an international war; and after bitter fighting that brought near-complete destruction to North Korea, a stalemate was ratified by the 1953 cease-fire agreement. Pyongyang's fateful thrust south, however, was by no means consigned to inevitable failure. With the benefit of hindsight, one may venture that, absent U.S. intervention, that thrust would have likely succeeded—and in early 1950, it was far from clear (even in America) that Washington considered the defense of South Korea a vital national interest.

Thus, for Pyongyang's leadership, the Korean War, far from constituting a catastrophe that impelled new thinking about the unification question, seems instead simply to have been chalked up as an under-standable miscalculation: an initial, imperfect application of a funda-mentally sound unification strategy. Over the next several decades, North Korea systematically and meticulously prepared to consummate that strategy by building its military might and waiting for the crisis in South Korea or the rupture in Washington-Seoul relations that would allow Pyongyang to make its move.

The awaited opening never arrived, however. By the 1980s, it was apparent that North Korea's unification policy—which at bottom had always been a gamble—was a lost bet. Contrary to the DPRK's carica-tures, the Republic of Korea had developed into one of the postwar world's great economic success stories. And by the late 1980s the South Korean political system, which had finally embraced the principles of constitutional democracy, was steadily gaining strength, confidence, and domestic support. The U.S.–South Korean alliance looked stronger than ever; Pyongyang's allies, by contrast, had made it clear they would not aid the DPRK if it were to provoke another international crisis in the Korean peninsula. The "correlation of forces" between the two Koreas, in Leninist terminology, had tilted unmistakably against the DPRK and seemed set only to worsen in the future. North Korea had missed its chance.

From our present vantage point, we may be tempted to conclude that North Korea's unification strategy was doomed from the start. It was not. If events had played out only somewhat differently, that strat-egy might well have succeeded. There was more than a little truth, after all, in Pyongyang's view of the ROK as a fragile and potentially un-stable system. Until the late 1980s, after all, South Korea did not effect a single peaceful transfer of presidential power; as late as 1979, a South Korean president would be assassinated by his own security chief. Pyongyang's anticipation that Washington would retreat from its com-mitment to Seoul, for its part, was not just wishful thinking: during the 1960s and much of the 1970s—as the Vietnam debacle unfolded—such a prognosis for American foreign policy would have seemed pre-scient to many independent observers.

In international press reports, North Korean leadership is often described as irrational, even mad. Such characterizations, I believe, are both inattentive and incorrect: they fail to discern the deep logic of a system whose precepts and starting premises happen to differ sharply from our own. It would be similarly misguided to dismiss North Korea's approach to unification as a crazy scheme.

Pyongyang's plan for unification-by-conquest was not a madman's dream, but rather a careful, calculating, high-risk venture. Like many other high-risk ventures, it ultimately proved to be unsuccessful. But unlike most strategists and entrepreneurs who operate successfully in high-risk environments, the Pyongyang regime evidently had no "fallback" plan. The DPRK's own chosen unification strategy, furthermore, happened to be strongly "path dependent": in doggedly pursuing it, North Korean leadership ineluctably closed off other, important options and progressively narrowed its own freedom of maneuver. With the failure of its unification strategy, North Korea was thus caught in a trap of its own design.

In response to the increasingly menacing fundamentals in its contest against the South, North Korea made a tactical decision in the 1980s to lean heavily on the Soviet Union. Far from stabilizing the "correlation of forces" for North Korea, that ill-fated move actually precipitated the DPRK's slide toward disaster. The breakup of the Soviet empire and the collapse of the Union of Soviet Socialist Republics itself between 1989 and 1991 exposed North Korea to a more perilous balance of international power (from Pyongyang's standpoint) than it had ever dealt with before. To make matters even worse, the collapse of the USSR meant the end of military aid and subsidized trade from the Soviet bloc. By the late 1980s, the North Korean system was heavily dependent on those quantities; their consequent sudden and virtually total termination sent the system into a steep downward spiral that Pyongyang has, as yet, been unable to arrest. For the DPRK, the grand vision of reuniting Korea under its socialist thrall has given way to a desperate focus on day-to-day survival.

The failure of North Korea's unification strategy, we should remember, did not presuppose North Korea's failure economically. Despite the ROK liquidity crisis in late 1997 and the subsequent repercussions thereof, South Korea has registered one of the world's fastest average rates of economic growth over the past four decades. Under those circumstances, North Korea would have lost the economic race against the South—and thus eventually, the opportunity to overpower the South—even if it had maintained a steady and fairly respectable pace of growth.

The DPRK, however, was unable even to sustain positive rates of economic growth in its long contest against the South. After apparently rapid progress in the two decades immediately following the Korean War, North Korea's economic growth seems to have slowed markedly in the 1970s.[5] By the 1980s, the North Korean economy seems to have been beset by stagnation. And in the 1990s, as we know, the DPRK entered into severe and as yet unremitting economic decline.

Although the precise dimensions of that decline are extremely difficult to estimate, the South Korean government is probably correct in asserting, as it recently did, that 1998 marked the ninth straight year of negative economic growth for the DPRK.[6] Indicative of the dimensions of that decline are North Korea's trade trends: between 1990 and 1998, according to reports by its trading partners, the DPRK's international purchases and sales of merchandise had fallen by more than half.[7] The severity of the country's economic decline is underscored by the hunger crisis that it has provoked. Again—this being the DPRK—the precise dimensions of that hunger crisis cannot as yet be quantified. But its dimensions are, at the very least, suggested by the simple fact that the North Korean call for emergency food aid from abroad is now entering its fifth year.[8] Thus, as best we can tell, even against the criterion of providing sufficient sustenance for the physical survival of the local populace—a most minimal of standards for economic performance—the North Korean economy currently qualifies as a failure.

Chapter 3 provides perspective on the failure of the North Korean economy. It cautions that communist economies are always "in crisis": that, after all, is how they are structured and how they are designed to operate. For over two decades, however, the North Korean economy has been "trading" smaller economic problems for newer and larger ones. In 1993, DPRK leadership publicly described the economy as being in "grave condition";[9] six years later, it is in still worse shape.

The DPRK economic system, I argue, is currently afflicted by "multiple severe crises." North Korea's is a command economy that has been running on something close to a full war footing for over a generation, and it is suffering the consequences of that extraordinary and extended mobilization. North Korea is also coping with an extreme and continuing "trade shock," the original cause of which was the sudden disappearance of Soviet bloc markets and aid programs almost a decade ago. And as noted, North Korea is in the midst of a food emergency from which it is apparently unable to extricate itself. Although each of those severe crises can be analyzed separately, in practice they are interlocked and mutually contingent.

North Korea's current economic dilemma appears to be historically unique in the sense that no other country has ever previously faced those three crises simultaneously. But as we demonstrate in chapter 3, the historical record—the experience of other countries, both to-day and in the past—offers insight into each of those problems. Such insights, I argue, can help us assess the prospects for North Korea's economy today.

Many other communist states have been stricken with famine. Communist systems, in fact, seem to have a predilection for famine. But to date, not a single communist state has been politically undermined by domestic starvation, even when such bouts of hunger have claimed millions of local lives. Moreover, up to now (with the single equivocal exception of Khmer Rouge Cambodia), every communist government that encountered famine also recovered from it: each managed to bring its hunger crisis to an end and to resume its own variant of "socialist development."

North Korea's hunger crisis, however, differs fundamentally from all communist famines that preceded it. In all other peacetime communist famines, the stricken society was overwhelmingly agrarian and rural; the DPRK, by contrast, had already made the transition to a predominantly urban, nonagricultural economy when its current food crisis erupted. Every previous communist famine, moreover, took place early in the tenure of the regime in question and could be traced to some particular set of newly implemented policies and practices: typically, a radical and economically destructive collectivization of the country's agricultural system. For those regimes, famine concluded when the communist authorities moderated or reversed the specific campaign that had triggered mass hunger in the first place. North Korea's hunger crisis, by contrast, did not emerge until the fifth decade of DPRK power and was not associated with any specific change in contemporaneous economic policy. Compared with previous communist famines, North Korea's current food emergency is thus far more systemic and structural in nature. Instead of signifying an early error in its economic program, North Korea's continuing food crisis may be seen as a sort of culmination of the DPRK's "development strategy."

Chapter 3 also reintroduces a point of economic history generally neglected or forgotten today: namely, that an economy can "collapse" before the regime that presides over it. That is not just a theoretical possibility: it has happened in the past. *Economic collapse,* to be sure, is an inherently ambiguous term. But one rigorous definition for it would entail a breakdown of a national food system.

The breakdown of a national food system is not synonymous with widespread hunger or even necessarily with famine. If pockets of extreme poverty exist within a country, people may starve even while the national food system itself continues to function and to service the needs of the overwhelming majority of the population. A breakdown in a national food system is a more profound disruption: it means that the ordinary rules and arrangements by which people exchange their labor for food are no longer in operation.

Such breakdowns, in fact, occurred in both Nazi Germany and Imperial Japan before the end of the Second World War. In both cases, breakdown resulted in dramatic—albeit temporary—mass exoduses from urban centers, with millions of suddenly itinerant households set on a desperate daily hunt for food. (For an industrial society, it is worth noting here, massive deurbanization is a necessary consequence of a breakdown in the national food system.) In both cases, moreover, economic collapse preceded and contributed to the downfall of existing governments—not vice versa.

To be sure, when the economies of Nazi Germany and Imperial Japan collapsed, the two countries were heading toward military defeat in a total war; at the time, their domestic economic infrastructures were under constant, withering assault from enemy air forces. By contrast, the DPRK today is neither under attack nor actively engaged in warfare. That crucial difference in circumstances should not be minimized. Yet, conversely, we may equally recognize that North Korea's economy, although ostensibly "at peace," has fared rather more poorly over the past several years than the wartime Nazi and the Imperial Japanese economies did immediately before their economic collapses.

North Korea's economic system is still cast on a downward course—a trajectory that has been shaped not by the vicissitudes of war, but instead by the chosen policies and strategies of the government. Absent major changes in direction, the DPRK is poised to progress from its current state of economic failure to an eventual condition of economic collapse.

Dead Ends

On initial consideration, it might seem puzzling that North Korean leadership should have been incapable to date of arresting its country's prolonged economic tailspin. North Korea's current dire economic condition, after all, is very largely the predictable consequence of Pyongyang's relentless enforcement of economic policies that range from the manifestly wasteful to the positively injurious (policies enumerated and detailed throughout this volume). Moderating that punitive regimen could be expected to bring an almost immediate measure of relief to the North's beleaguered economy.

The sorts of measures that might spark revitalization and sustained upswing in the North Korean economy, for their part, are hardly secret. The path to economic renewal and resumed growth runs squarely through the international economy. To the North Korean economy, like every other modern economy, international markets in goods, services, and capital offer opportunities for reducing costs, improving productivity, and promoting dynamism. In East Asia, "outward orientation" and greater integration with the world economy—expanding trade, attracting foreign investment, and encouraging technology transfer— were common to all countries that have achieved and maintained impressive rates of long-term economic growth. Significantly, those ranks today include both China and Vietnam—Asia's two other avowedly socialist states.

Why then has DPRK leadership not seized those obvious options for remedying the economic catastrophe that confronts it today? It is surely not for lack of calculation: North Korea's rulers, as already mentioned, appear to be quite rational in evaluating the alternatives before them—and, often, strikingly shrewd in seizing opportunities for gain.[10]

It is true that North Korean ruling circles at times appear to be amazingly naive about economic affairs;[11] it is quite possible, in fact, that DPRK leadership is more economically innocent than any other governing directorate in the world today. But Pyongyang's continued reticence about embarking on a more pragmatic course—and its abiding reluctance to avail its stricken populace of the benefits that would devolve from greater integration with the world economy—cannot be attributed to economic innocence alone. Rather, it would appear to be a deliberate and considered decision—one reflecting the DPRK leadership's assessment and understanding of its own North Korean system.

North Korea's leadership appears to be convinced that programs for economic revival that would be regarded as entirely unexceptional in the rest of the world would actually pose extreme—possibly mortal—peril to its own system. To those who know the North Korean system best, the seemingly "obvious" solutions to the state's economic troubles are in reality dead ends. By the same token, seemingly promising avenues for stimulating the DPRK economy through external contact are fraught with potentially lethal hazard. Ruinous as North Korea's uninterrupted economic slide has proved for what the DPRK calls "our own style of socialism," the ostensible cures for the country's economic maladies are evidently judged to be even more dangerous to the North Korean system.

Unfortunately for North Korean leadership, its assessment of its own predicament looks to be on the mark. In the struggle to escape the economic catastrophe that directly confronts North Korea's rulers, they have little room for maneuver and few viable options at their disposal. Chapters 4 and 5 offer more extended examinations of the rulers' quandary.

From Pyongyang's vantage point, as I demonstrate in chapter 4, the most compelling argument against embarking in new economic directions is that those more "practical" policies would ultimately undermine the integrity and the stability of the socialist state. From Pyongyang's perspective, the fruits of "reform communism" are indicated by the fates of the Soviet and East European governments that adopted it. Not surprisingly, North Korean authorities closely analyzed the final crisis and downfall of Soviet-bloc socialism. In their interpretation, economic pragmatism and economic reform are antithetical to socialism—and any socialist government toying with such measures is in effect experimenting with its own political defeat.

Parsing North Korean statements is typically an arduous task for those not steeped in their cadence—yet it is worth considering their content and import. Kim Jong Il's 1992 comments on the Soviet denouement, for example, would seem to offer a definitive official North Korean view of the event:

> One-step concessions and retreat from socialist principles ha[ve] resulted in ten and a hundred step concession and retreat, and, finally, invited grave consequences of ruining the working class parties themselves.[12]

The implicit corollary to that assessment, of course, is that the ordinary, unpoliced workings of economics—response to incentives and all the rest—are inherently counterrevolutionary and fundamentally subversive of the socialist project. Kim Jong Il did not shrink from those implications; instead, in 1993 he spelled them out clearly and carefully:

> [T]he basic driving force of development of a socialist society lies in . . . [the people's] ideological consciousness. . . . [In the past] there

were tendencies [in certain places] to rouse people's enthusiasm for production by means of such material levers as economic incentives. . . . In those societies which gave up education in socialist ideology and encouraged egoism, the building of the socialist economy became stagnant . . . they went so far as denying the leadership of the working-class party and state over the socialist economy.[13]

Since Kim Jong Il's formal accession as head of both party and state, North Korea's media have vociferously echoed and elaborated on that aspect of the "Dear Leader's" teachings. In September 1998—just days after the Supreme People's Assembly session that official-ly elevated Kim Jong Il to the state's "highest position"—the party's daily newspaper and its theoretical journal conjointly ran this pronounce-ment on "economic reform," "economic opening," and "economic in-tegration":

It is a foolish daydream to try to revive the economy by introducing foreign capital, not relying on one's own strength. If one wants the prosperity of the national economy, he should thoroughly reject the idea of dependence on outside forces, the idea that he cannot live without foreign capital. . . .

Ours is an independent economic structure equipped with all the economic sectors in good harmony and with its own strong heavy industry at the core. It is incomparably better than the export-oriented economic structure dependent on other countries.

We cannot allow any attempt to undermine our peculiar eco-nomic structure. . . .

We must heighten vigilance against the imperialists' moves to induce us to "reform" and "opening to the outside world." "Reform" and "opening" on their lips are a honey-coated poison. Clear is our stand toward "reform" and "opening." We now have nothing to "re-form" and "open." By "reform" and "opening" the imperialists mean to revive capitalism. The best way of blocking the wind of "reform" and "opening" of the imperialists is to defend the socialist principle in all sectors of economy. . . .

Even though anyone calls us "conservatives" we will never aban-don the principle, but will set ourselves against all the attempts to induce us to join an "integrated" world.[14]

Economic "reform" and "integration" would inevitably impel the North Korean state to relinquish its claim to absolute control over "the people's economy." But even worse, reform and opening would be vec-tors for what North Korean authorities call "ideological and cultural infiltration"—contaminants they apparently judge to be capable of destroying an established socialist system.

North Korean authorities liken "ideological and cultural infiltration" to "an invasion without the sound of gunfire."[15] As the conjoint New Year's Day 1999 editorials in North Korea's party, military, and youth newspapers warned, "[T]he imperialist ideological and cultural infiltration" is "the enemies' maneuver of seeking our internal collapse."[16] And Pyongyang has carefully described the manner in which "imperialists" manage that campaign "of interference and control":

> First, they infiltrate the bourgeois idea and culture into other countries through economic "exchanges." . . . The imperialists use these exchanges to spread their bourgeois reactionary ideology and rotten bourgeois culture and lifestyle. Technical cooperation, joint ventures, and joint management are frequently used in developing economic relations between countries. . . . Waiting for this critical moment, the imperialists have slyly placed impure elements in delegations, groups of visitors, inspecting teams, tourists entering other countries, and manipulated them in order to use them to infiltrate ideological culture. These people cunningly maneuver to create a fantasy about capitalism through contacts with the people in a given country.[17]

That depiction is precise; North Korean authorities appear to know exactly whereof they speak. Evidently, they have concluded that the ordinary workings of what others would call "the global information economy" (international communication, regular human contacts, routine technical transfers, commercial harmonization, and the like) pose direct and unacceptable political risks to the DPRK's "own style of socialism"—and therefore must be vigilantly avoided, resisted, or suppressed.

If that is indeed the case, the scope for North Korean "economic cooperation" with other countries would appear to be extremely narrow. "Linkages" and "spillover effects" are natural repercussions from economic integration, but where others welcome those properties as dynamic changes to spur economic development, North Korean leadership instead brands them as deadly political tendencies.

Cleansing international economic exchanges of potential ideological contaminants, however, will not only severely circumscribe the range and volume of activities that can be condoned; it will also strictly limit the economic stimulus that those tolerated exchanges can provide.

For precisely those reasons, as I explain in chapter 4, economic cooperation between North and South Korea remains a highly problematic proposition—one might say an especially problematic proposition, considering the special risks of "ideological and cultural infiltration" from that commerce.

The ROK is, to be sure, the DPRK's third-largest trading partner today—but that fact speaks to North Korea's astonishing economic isolation rather than to the prominence of inter-Korean commercial ties. In 1998 North-South trade turnover amounted to about $10 per capita for every inhabitant of North Korea; it has not yet reached the per capita level of $15 per year.[18] For some sense of contrast, South Korea's total trade turnover per capita amounted to almost $5,000 in 1998—that in the year of an economic slump;[19] inter-Korean trade accounted for less than $10 of that. To date, the largest part in that trickle of commerce comprises DPRK shipments of gold and other metals to the South.[20] Little chance of "ideological and cultural infiltration" there, perhaps—but also scant prospect for expanding that business, considering the condition of North Korea's mining and metallurgy industries.

My skeptical evaluation of the outlook for North-South economic cooperation might appear to be frontally challenged by a dramatic new development in inter-Korean relations: the Hyundai tourism deal. In October 1998, Hyundai conglomerate founder Chung Ju-yung and "Dear Leader" Kim Jong Il formalized a landmark North-South commercial agreement: in return for an exclusive six-year license to bring outside tourists to North Korea's historic Kumgang Mountain area, Hyundai promised to pay over $900 million to the North Korean government.[21] Between November 1998 and early April 1999 alone, some 58,000 South Korean tourists made the Kumgang visit;[22] in early 1999 Hyundai was reportedly paying the DPRK $25 million per month for that traffic.[23]

That the Mt. Kumgang venture marks a new chapter in inter-Korean economic exchanges is self-evident and incontestible. But does that also presage a new direction for North-South "economic cooperation"?

Time alone will tell. One may note, however, that the Kumgang agreement would conform nicely with any North Korean imperative for "separating business from ideological infiltration." In ferrying South Korean tourists to that scenic but remote, almost unpopulated, military region, North Korea exposes precious few of its citizens to the hazard of human contact with outsiders. The transaction also nicely averts the risks of linkages and spillover effects: the developmental implications of the project are reassuringly meager. The Hyundai deal, in other words, comes close to a certain sort of ideal: a direct funnel-through transfer payment by foreigners to the North Korean state, almost untouched by human hands—at least, in North Korea.

Whether such "clean" North-South commercial arrangements can be replicated is still an open question. And why that project should portend a surge of projects of an opposite sort—that is to say, contact-intensive inter-Korean ventures—is less clear still. Furthermore, as chapter 4 argues, such inter-Korean economic exchanges as are consummated are in themselves unlikely to alter the North Korean government's posture toward the ROK.

The ROK's current policy toward Pyongyang is predicated on the premise that enhancing economic contact between the two Koreas will modify the temperament of the Northern government and thus reduce tensions on the Korean peninsula. As Lim Dong-won, one of the policy's chief architects, recently explained, "The objective of President Kim [Dae Jung]'s 'Sunshine Policy' of engagement with North Korea is to coax the Pyongyang leadership on to the path of reform and change."[24]

North Korean authorities are well aware of that objective and—as best one can tell from their pronouncements—are thoroughly opposed to it. At almost the same moment that Lim was outlining the rationale of Seoul's "sunshine" policy, North Korean authorities rendered their own verdict on "sunshine" and inter-Korean economic relations:

> Everyone knows that the puppets came forth with the sunshine policy, the engagement policy, and reciprocity, blocking North-South economic cooperation on every occasion. . . .
> If reconciliation and cooperation are to be achieved between the North and the South, the South Korean authorities should throw away the anti-North confrontation policy and change the direction toward pro-North reconciliation policy. . . .
> It is all too clear that nonsense being carried out by the puppets regarding the issue of North-South economic cooperation is full of schemes and sophistry. The well-grounded logic of patriotism is bound to prevail over the treacherous logic.[25]

From that and many other similar official utterances, one is tempted to conclude that Pyongyang's own position is that the simple existence of the ROK qualifies as "anti-North confrontation"—and that "North-South economic cooperation" cannot be expected to promote reconciliation on the peninsula until the South Korean state disappears. Such a posture, incidentally, would not represent an eccentric aberration for DPRK diplomacy; to the contrary, it would instead conform integrally with the basic logic of the North Korean state.

If peaceable commercial intercourse between North and South Korea is, as I argue, subject to severe structural constraint, prospects for commercial relations between the DPRK and the United States are probably not much brighter. Chapter 5 lays out the reasoning behind that conclusion.

On paper, the possibilities of U.S.–North Korean trade might seem promising. The United States, after all, is the world's largest import market—but an array of American legislative and administrative sanctions has precluded commercial interaction between U.S. and DPRK concerns since the start of the Korean War. Ordinarily, one would expect that clearing away that thicket of economic sanctions (an outcome envisioned in the Washington-Pyongyang "Agreed Framework" of October 1994) would result in an upsurge of business between the two countries.

North Korea, however, is no ordinary country. For reasons already touched upon over the previous pages—reasons laid out in greater depth in chapter 5—it seems highly unlikely that the lifting of economic sanctions would lead to any appreciable volume of commercial interaction between the United States and the DPRK.

Over the past generation, North Korea has conspicuously failed to generate export revenues from trade with non-American countries in the Organization for Economic Cooperation and Development. Currently, North Korea's sales in those markets are utterly marginal—averaging less than $15 per DPRK citizen per year.[26] Amazing as it may sound in an era of burgeoning international trade, in real terms North Korea's export earnings in the non–U.S. OECD markets have been lower in the 1990s (that is, after the end of the cold war) than they were in the 1980s and were lower in the 1980s than they had been in the late 1970s.[27]

But consider what that means for any prospective economic normalization with the United States. In aggregate, those other OECD markets were and remain far larger than America's—and unlike the United States, those other markets did not then, and do not now, deny North Korea access through specially legislated barriers and restrictions. North Korea's dismal performance in those markets speaks not to some lack of access or opportunity. Instead, it attests to how poorly suited North Korea's economy is for dealing with competitive international markets and how stubbornly unwilling North Korean leadership has been to approve any adjustments that might enhance the country's trade performance.

At the risk of repetition, North Korea's extremely poor trade performance reflects a deeply embedded regime logic, not just misbegotten commercial naivete. As best we can tell from their pronouncements, DPRK authorities are convinced that the very policy changes that would enable North Korea to capitalize on opportunities in foreign markets would also directly jeopardize the state's security—and that the ultimate price of North Korean success in "capitalist" world markets would be the complete destruction of the DPRK system.

Recently, for example, a spokesman for the General Staff of the North Korean People's Army accused the United States of attempting "to destroy our socialist system" through an "'appeasement strategy' to induce us to 'reform' and 'opening'"[28]—and that was by no means an isolated official comment. If North Korean leadership truly views a more outward economic orientation as a threat to the DPRK's vital interests, the mere lifting of U.S. sanctions cannot be expected to herald the awakening of an economic relationship between the two countries.

North Korea's Endgame

To be more precise, the mere lifting of U.S. sanctions cannot be expected to herald the awakening of a *mutually beneficial* economic relationship between the two sides. As chapter 5 argues, North Korea stands to gain substantial and continuing benefits from the United States if Pyongyang can manage to formalize a *one-sided* economic relationship with Washington.

For the DPRK, the United States is potentially a source for steady flows of bilateral foreign aid—and much more. Washington, for example, could assist in securing North Korean membership in the World Bank, the Asian Development Bank, and other multilateral development institutions—organizations to which the DPRK could then apply for grants, subsidized loans, and other forms of concessional finance. Imaginably, the United States could even facilitate bilateral payments to North Korea from other countries: a settlement with Japan modeled on the 1965 Tokyo-Seoul diplomatic normalization and indexed for parity with it, for instance, could by now involve billions of dollars.

For North Korea, in short, the promise of an "economic relationship" with the United States lies not in a broadening and deepening of commercial ties, but instead in the prospect of establishing Pyongyang as a permanent recipient of government-to-government transfer payments.

At first glance it might seem that the quest for financial aid from other countries would be doctrinally inconsistent with the "self-reliance" that North Korean *juche* extols. It is not. From its very founding, the DPRK has been embarked on a perpetual hunt for subventions from abroad. During the cold war, North Korea was the constant beneficiary of aid flows from almost the entire "socialist camp": China, the USSR, and almost every country in Eastern Europe were donors. Today, North Korea is eyeing the capitalist world for aid—and the DPRK has no ideological problem with pocketing payments from that reviled source. As I suggest in chapter 5, *juche* diplomacy is a tribute-seeking diplomacy—an inversion of the traditional Korean role as tributary state in the old East Asian order—and all tribute is good tribute. Tribute not only strengthens the domestic sinews of the North Korean state but also affirms its international status, validates its international policies, and legitimizes its international authority.

Tribute is overseas aid on terms established by the recipient, not the donor. To be in a position to dictate just how foreign beneficiaries should bestow their largesse, of course, requires considerable and reliable leverage. And how to obtain that leverage? North Korean leadership apparently believes that it can achieve leverage today through a carefully managed stratagem of military extortion. By establishing itself as an ever more menacing international security threat, the North Korean state evidently means to compel its neighbors—and even better, its enemies—to propitiate the DPRK with a constant and swelling stream of financial gifts.

That is not simply surmise. North Korea's intentions have been laid out by its highest authorities. At the same September 1998 Supreme People's Assembly that elevated Kim Jong Il to the DPRK's "highest post of state,"[29] North Korea's government officially embraced a new policy objective: that of becoming a "powerful and prosperous state" *(Kangsong Taeguk)*. The precise meaning of that slogan was spelled out the following month in Pyongyang's *Minju Choson*, which declared that "defense capabilities are a military guarantee for national political independence and the self-reliant economy"; the paper further emphasized that *"the nation can become prosperous only when the gun barrel is strong"*[30] (emphasis added).

Credible military menace, in other words, is now at the heart of North Korea's economic strategy—and of its very strategy for state survival. By extracting resources from the international community through military blackmail, North Korean leadership hopes to stave off the officially dreaded specters of "reform" and "opening." That international gambit (complemented and reinforced by acute political and intellectual repression at home to bolster the domestic system) offers what Pyongyang takes as its best chance to steer its imperiled vessel of state between the Scylla of political liberalization and the Charybdis of economic collapse.

As an endgame stratagem, North Korea's is not entirely misbegotten. In fact, it may be said already to have enjoyed a measure of tactical success.

The 1994 "Agreed Framework," after all, was signed only by Washington because Pyongyang was poised to amass an arsenal of nuclear weapons. In exchange for an ostensible freeze on that program, the United States has been shipping the DPRK half a million tons a year of free oil. In addition, the United States organized an international consortium— the Korean Peninsula Energy Development Organization—to construct for North Korea two "safe" light-water nuclear reactors at an envisioned eventual cost of over $4 billion; work on that project is already underway.

North Korea has demonstrated, furthermore, that new nuclear threats can be manufactured for new, additional payments, irrespective of previous understandings.

After signing the "Agreed Framework," the DPRK began work on an enormous underground site whose observed specifications closely matched those that would have been expected from a surreptitious effort to continue a program for the development of nuclear weaponry. After detecting that suspect facility, the United States naturally demanded access to it. Subsequent high-tension negotiations in late 1998 and early 1999 resulted in an American pledge of over 500,000 tons of food aid to the DPRK—and an almost simultaneous North Korean promise to allow an American delegation to "visit" the site at Kumchang-ri.[31]

At one particularly heated moment in the Kumchang-ri inspection negotiations, a North Korean military official declared:

> "Surgical operation"–style attack and "preemptive strike" are by no means an exclusive option of the United States. . . . It must be clearly known that there is no limit to the strike of our People's Army and that on this planet there is no room for escaping the strike.[32]

He was alluding to North Korea's long-range missile capabilities, the latest advance in which was suddenly demonstrated in August 1998 by the firing—without advance warning—of a multistage ballistic rocket over the main island of Japan.[33] That missile program happens to be another instrument through which Pyongyang intends to derive concessional payments from abroad.

North Korea's leadership has signaled that explicitly. In June 1998, North Korea's state media announced that the DPRK "will continue developing, testing, and deploying missiles" as a matter of unshakable principle—but proposed that "if the United States really wants to prevent our missile exports, it should . . . make a compensation for the losses to be caused by discontinued missile exports."[34] In talks with American counterparts in early 1999, North Korean officials indicated that the "compensation" they had in mind would start out at $1 billion a year.[35]

Weapons of mass destruction are thus now the financial and political lifeline for that starving, decaying state. By the perverse logic of that design, moreover, the North Korean system's vital interests lie in *magnifying* the deadly risks it can pose to the outside world. Perfecting weaponry with ever greater reach and killing force, after all, correspondingly increases Pyongyang's scope for exacting international tribute.

Pyongyang may well look to a fearsome arsenal of weapons of mass destruction not only for sustenance but for salvation. Just as business magnates in postwar South Korea strove to balloon their concerns into hypertrophied conglomerates that would be "too big to fail," so North Korea's leaders may be gambling that they can make the DPRK "too lethal to fail."

Thinking about the End of North Korea

But that vision—if indeed it is the vision that Pyongyang's rulers today entertain—is an empty fantasy. The DPRK's extortionist diplomacy is utterly inadequate to revitalize the economic foundation on which the North Korean state rests. In a world where South Korean export revenues exceed $2 billion *a week*, the sums that North Korea schemes after are almost negligible by comparison. Under any circumstances, those sums would be insufficient to purchase a new industrial infrastructure or to prepare a work force for manning it—all the more so when extensive commercial and technical contacts with the outside world are politically unacceptable. North Korea's endgame stratagem promises only to slow the country's relative and absolute economic decline—not to reverse it. In short, as I argue in chapter 6, no prospect of "victory" for North Korea's leadership exists under any outcome from its current game plan. At the very best, that game plan will only provide more of the ghastly, deepening twilight in which the regime is already enveloped.

If I am correct that the DPRK is slated for still further decline and correct as well about the constituting logic of the North Korean system, the implications for the international community are ominous indeed.

More than any other state in the current global order, the DPRK makes its living not through the export of *goods* and *services* as those terms are commonly understood, but instead through the methodical export of strategic insecurity. Furthermore, if I am correct in my analysis of the North Korean system, the DPRK's vital interests would be grievously and irreparably injured if its government were ever to acquiesce in what the international community desires most from Pyongyang: first, a real and permanent halt to its quest for nuclear weaponry; second, a demobilization of its program for perfecting long-range missiles; and third, the establishment of genuinely peaceful relations with the ROK.

That is *not* to say that Pyongyang might not some day commit itself to one or more of those courses of action. Leadership groupings can miscalculate—and, often enough, do. But if North Korea's rulers—as they have so often stated—are totally resolved not to follow Gorbachev gently into the night, then we must only conclude that every extension of the regime's tenure will be marked by a correlative improvement in Pyongyang's ability to inflict injury and provoke instability beyond its borders.

One of the most salient and interesting aspects of the contemporary dynamic of international relations with the DPRK has been this: as North Korea fails, the international community moves to intervene with support. For Pyongyang, that is a highly satisfactory arrangement. It is less clear why that should be satisfactory to other governments around the world. Wittingly or not, the principal powers with which North Korea interacts have fallen into a de facto policy of appeasement toward Pyongyang. As a diplomatic approach, appeasement has recorded some successes at different junctures over the course of history. But those successes only occurred when the object of appeasement policy was capable of, and disposed toward, being appeased. In the DPRK, for reasons already outlined, we have strong reason to believe that the world community is dealing with an unappeasable state.

Why then today's appeasement of North Korea? If one were utterly cynical, one might say that this is easy enough to explain: weak governments have a predilection for appeasement policies, and the governments with which North Korea today contends are, in the main, weak ones. That cynical barb cannot be dismissed out of hand, for the fact of the matter is that North Korean foreign policy currently faces a most unusual international alignment. For North Korea, the governments important to its international calculations have always been (in alphabetical order) China, Japan, Russia, South Korea, and the United States. Since the end of the cold war, the character of each of those governments has changed perceptibly—in some cases, radically. By comparison with predecessors, the administrations now presiding in Washington, Seoul, Tokyo, Moscow, and Beijing are, in greater or lesser measure, less capable of mobilizing resources to project their will internationally, less oriented toward international (as opposed to domestic) priorities, or less inclined to focus attention on nonimmediate problems—or, in some cases, all of those things. This historically extraordinary conjuncture has doubtless played to North Korea's advantage.

A more charitable analysis, however, would ascribe the current appeasement of the DPRK less to a failure of nerve than to a failure of imagination. As I argue in chapter 6, conceptualizing the Korean peninsula within a two-state framework almost ineluctably draws international policymakers toward the option of protecting the North Korean system against its own decline—even though such support may ultimately worsen the security threats that international policymakers can expect to face in the future. For the stability and prosperity of Northeast Asia—but not Northeast Asia alone—it is therefore imperative for concerned governments to move from the intellectual sandtrap from which a Korean peninsula without the DPRK cannot be seen. We must begin to think carefully about the implications, problems, and opportunities inherent in a post–DPRK Korea.

As I show in chapter 6, thinking beyond the DPRK is not an impossible exercise. And if one undertakes that exercise, one can envision a distinctly less troubled Korean peninsula than the one we know today. Korean unification under a peaceable, politically free, market-oriented system—a system much like South Korea's today—could contribute consequentially to political stability and economic prosperity not only in Northeast Asia, but well beyond it.

To be sure, we should expect arduous challenges and serious obstacles to await any effort to construct a successful post–DPRK architecture for the Korean peninsula. Chapter 6 identifies a number of such potential problems. But focusing on those problems also indicates that prepared governments may have ways to mitigate them or to circumvent them altogether. If my analysis of North Korean objectives and intentions is correct, furthermore, the considerations reviewed in chapter 6 have grave and inescapable ramifications for Western policy, for they imply that the costs and difficulties attendant on establishing a successful post–DPRK order in Northeast Asia will very likely climb the longer the current North Korean regime holds power.

Some will object that my appraisal takes no account of the ROK's recently reduced economic circumstances, because many well-informed observers today hold that the South Korean financial crisis of 1997–1998 has fundamentally altered both the ROK's options for policy toward North Korea and the prospects for a Korean reunification. Yet, as I argue in chapter 6, the analysis on which that strand of currently received wisdom rests is exceedingly weak. The ROK's recent economic difficulties, I hold, have scant bearing on Pyongyang's firmly cast posture toward the South Korean system and have only the most incidental influence on the DPRK's (dismal) economic outlook. The South Korean financial crisis, I further hold, has actually had very little effect on either the optimal course for Seoul's policies toward the North or the ROK's means for pursuing them. Paradoxically, I contend, the South Korean financial crisis may have even *improved* the odds for a successful reunification on Seoul's terms. That crisis has increased pressures to implement the sort of economic reforms that could also one day expedite the economic reconstruction of the North. In addition, the crisis has changed the climate of personal expectations among South Korea's youth, who are now no longer wholly unacquainted with sudden but necessary sacrifices.

Throughout its tenure, the DPRK has demonstrated its continuing capacity to surprise. Few of those surprises, unfortunately, have been pleasant ones. In the period ahead, additional North Korean surprises doubtless await Western governments. Those surprises, however, should be distinctly less unpleasant if our citizens and our statesmen do not take the end of North Korea to be an unimaginable proposition.

2

North Korea's Unification Policy— A Long, Failed Gamble

F or over half a century, the political dynamics of the Korean peninsula have been framed by a single hasty—and fateful—decision: an August 1945 agreement between Washington and Moscow that Korea would be temporarily partitioned at the thirty-eighth parallel.[1] That almost casual act proved to be the turning point for modern Korean history. Initially envisioned as a convenient arrangement to expedite the processing of an impending Japanese surrender, that "temporary" partition of Korea relentlessly hardened into a de facto and then a de jure division of the peninsula into two mutually hostile states.

With the establishment in 1948 of a Soviet-sponsored Democratic People's Republic of Korea (DPRK) in the northern half of the peninsula and a U.S.–supported Republic of Korea (ROK) in the South, a thousand years of political and administrative unity came to an official end for the Korean nation. At the same time, the political quest for Korean reunification may be said to have formally commenced.

The Imperative of Reunification

For the DPRK government, the reunification of Korea—on the DPRK's own terms—has been an overriding policy objective since its very inception. The urgent priority accorded to the goal of unconditional unification has been fused into the fundamental documents of both party and state. The preamble to the charter of the Korean Workers' Party (KWP) declares that "[t]he present task of the [KWP] is to ensure the complete victory of socialism in the Democratic People's Republic of Korea and the accomplishment of the revolutionary goals of national liberation and the people's democracy in the entire area of the country."[2] And although the DPRK's seat of government has always been Pyongyang, the DPRK constitution from the outset stipulated that "the capital of the Democratic Republic of Korea shall be Seoul"[3]—a claim whose realization would require the prior removal of the ROK government.

From the standpoints of both power politics and ideology, the continued existence of a rival Korean state on a shared peninsula poses a threat to the legitimacy and authority, and thus to the security, of a utopian polity like the DPRK's. North Korean leading political figures have consistently extolled the ideal of a unified, independent, and socialist Korea with a quasi-religious fervor. There is no reason to doubt that in such a system of professed belief the consummation of the unification ideal would qualify as a crowning achievement—or in political terms, as the ultimate guarantor of continued state existence.

For the entire North Korean project, then, virtue and necessity appear indistinguishable where reunification is concerned. The unification of the Korean nation under direct DPRK command appears from the beginning to have ranked as an absolute imperative of state, for reasons of glory and security alike.

Pyongyang's "Unification Policy": Parameters and Evidence

North Korea has both accorded unification an extraordinarily high priority (even as compared with other states in divided nations) and approached its objective with means intuitively unfamiliar to the contemporary student of international relations. Indeed, in an era of "conflict resolution," "dialogue," and diplomatists, the North Korean government has unmistakably demonstrated its preference for the use of raw political force to achieve its objectives.

North Korea's infamous June 1950 surprise attack against South Korea,[4] after all, was nothing if not a "unification policy": as documents from the Soviet archives and interviews with high-ranking DPRK émigrés have subsequently revealed, Kim Il Sung and other top

North Korean leaders anticipated that their military offensive against the South would "unify" the entire peninsula in less than a month.[5]

As we now know all too well, that unification initiative did not work as planned. Yet judged against the limits of the knowable as of early June 1950, the North Korean military assault that launched the Korean War was hardly a madman's gamble. War is always a risky business, but as prospective campaigns go, that one seemed to offer a high likelihood of success. Indeed, stripped of its Manichaean flourishes, Kim Il Sung's bitter assessment from the summer of 1950 is probably not very far from the mark:

> Had it not been for the direct military intervention of the U.S. imperialists, we could have reunified our fatherland, and completely liberated the people in the southern half from the police state tyranny of the U.S. imperialists and the Syngman Rhee clique.[6]

In attempting to evaluate North Korean unification policy, the degree to which the plan was predicated on absolute state secrecy (what the Soviets used to call *maskirovka*)[7] is an aspect that deserves special comment. The initial success of the attack hinged largely on the fact that it took Seoul and Washington almost completely by surprise—and it took them by surprise because Pyongyang expertly concealed both its capabilities and its intentions up until the moment of truth. Less than a week before the actual invasion, for example, the DPRK was floating diversionary proposals containing new ideas for possible steps toward peaceful and voluntary unification with the South.[8] North Korea's top leadership also seems to have subjected its own administrative and military apparatuses to a corresponding measure of strategic deception as the invasion plan progressed. John Merrill notes:

> Even secret Central Committee documents that were seized by United Nations forces when they captured Pyongyang made "absolutely no mention of the forthcoming invasion." High ranking North Korean officers had "only the barest presentiment" of hostilities until the final orders were issued for the attack.[9]

So thorough and complete was the regime's devotion to strategic secrecy, in fact, that an accurate and substantive record of the proceedings leading up to the June 1950 offensive may simply not exist—even in Pyongyang.

The particulars of North Korea's approach to its "unification policy" thus pose a virtually unique analytical challenge to the conventionally trained student of foreign relations. While the past five decades offer voluminous documentation of the many proposals, counterproposals, schema, and suggestions that North Korea's leadership has advanced in its intermittent external dialogue on national reunification,[10] there is good reason to believe that the diplomatic record itself may be a highly inadequate basis for evaluating the DPRK's true aims and strategies. Given the importance that North Korean leaders may place on misleading various external actors about their strategic intentions, moreover, one must treat the formal evidentiary record of officially revealed DPRK pronouncements and actions concerning reunification as problematic. When one considers just how little reliable information of any sort is available about that preternaturally secretive state, the formidable nature of the challenges involved in accurately describing the DPRK's unification policies becomes clear.

Divining North Korea's unification policy (or policies) therefore turns out to be an epistemological puzzle, in which the questions of "what we know and how we know it" loom large and often cannot be answered conclusively. Given the gaps, limitations, and uncertainties in the evidence at hand, we must recognize that it is possible to construct dramatically different readings of the events in question and substantially divergent interpretations of the North Korean approach to national reunification from 1948 to the present.

My exposition of North Korean unification policy will attempt to apply Ockham's razor[11] to the problem of describing a central policy of a closed state that can only be perceived by outsiders through an empirical haze. Methodologically, the following narrative embraces two critical assumptions, both of which should be made explicit.

First, because the goal of reunification of the peninsula on its own terms appears to be deemed so vitally important by the North Korean government and to occupy so much of its attention and energy, the appropriate aperture for assaying North Korean state activity is one with the widest possible lens. Only a comprehensive look at the DPRK's general behavior can inform us adequately about North Korean reunification policy, precisely because pursuit of that overarching objective has required simultaneous pursuit of a fairly complex array of policies, some of which have no direct or immediate bearing on the putative object of Pyongyang's strategic attention.

Second, since "reunification" in official North Korean circles is apparently taken to mean the termination of the ROK regime and system, and the concomitant extension of the DPRK's authority over the full boundaries of traditionally Korean territory, the Marxist-Leninist paradigm of "correlation of forces" (what Soviet theorists called *sootnoshenie sil*),[12] which provides a comprehensive but class-based perspective on programmatic struggle between opposing social and political systems, may be useful—to a degree—in understanding and explaining the aims and expectations guiding North Korean strategy and behavior.

North Korea's Evolving Unification Policy

From its very first days of power, the DPRK had a clear and identifiable "national strategy" in which unification policy figured prominently.[13] The thinking behind it can be succinctly summarized.

• First, the paramount external objective of the regime is unification with southern Korea on the DPRK's terms. The Korean peninsula must be a single and national entity, organized under socialist principles and governed by the KWP.

• Second, both South Korea's regime (the ROK) and its society are weak, divided, and corrupt—inherently unstable and certainly incapable of withstanding external pressure. The ROK may collapse under its own weight, or it may require an outside push. Either way, a strong North Korean military will be needed to step in to assist with unification at just the right moment.

Such a strategy is easily read into North Korean conduct in the DPRK's earliest years. In 1948 and 1949, as the DPRK was consolidating and developing its own domestic base, Pyongyang's inter-Korean rhetoric urged the repudiation (that is, the overthrow) of "the reactionary Syngman Rhee clique." When an uprising did occur (the Yosu rebellion, 1948–1949), Pyongyang eagerly expected history to take its "natural" course. But ROK forces contained and smothered the Yosu rebellion; the "Syngman Rhee clique" did not topple. As soon as it became clear to North Korea's leadership that it could not count on a speedy implosion of the South Korean system, North Korea began careful and systematic preparations to overwhelm the ROK with superior military force. Those preparations resulted in the surprise attack against South Korea in June 1950 that launched the Korean War.[14]

For the DPRK, of course, the Korean War proved to be a disastrous miscalculation. To Pyongyang's surprise and dismay, the United States (and the United Nations) rushed to Seoul's defense. The North Korean regime, moreover, was very nearly overturned itself. Had Mao not come to Kim Il Sung's rescue in October 1950, the DPRK likely would have been doomed.

But the record of subsequent events suggests that the DPRK did not fundamentally alter its strategy or its view of unification in the wake of that calamity. On the contrary, the North Korean regime clung doggedly to its initial strategy for the succeeding decades, although that strategy was adapted to shifting circumstance and international situation.

Pyongyang's postwar "national strategy" and attendant unification policy unfolded in roughly three phases: gathering strength (1953–1962), going for broke (1962–1979), and dead end (1980 onward).

Gathering Strength, 1953–1962. Between the July 1953 armistice that suspended the Korean War and the Fifth Plenum of the Fourth KWP Congress in December 1962 at which a renewed emphasis on military buildup was formally embraced, the DPRK's formal diplomatic initiatives concerning unification with the South were episodic and for the most part desultory.[15] Practically speaking, the government's "unification policy" during those years was focused domestically—on North Korea itself.

America's dramatically renewed security commitment to the ROK and the seeming stability of the South Korean polity made reunification on Pyongyang's terms an untenable short-run option. So, instead, for the decade after the Korean War, North Korean leaders bided their time and concentrated on the reconstruction and development of the devastated domestic North Korean economy.

Even discounting inflated official claims, the growth of output between 1953 and 1962 seems to have been rapid and fairly steady. Prewar levels of production may have been reattained by 1955 or 1956; in the following six or seven years, total output may have doubled—or better.[16] Against voices in the leadership calling for greater attention to consumer needs, Kim Il Sung determined that the postwar North Korean economy would continue to favor heavily the producer goods essential to waging and winning wars.[17]

North Korea's international policy played a pivotal role in the rebuilding and augmenting of the country's economy. North Korea secured concessional aid (grants and loans) from virtually the entire socialist camp of the 1950s: China, the Union of Soviet Socialist Republics, and Warsaw Pact Europe.[18] In addition, China agreed to leave a huge troop presence in North Korea through the late 1950s, thereby both relieving Pyongyang of burdensome military expenditures and providing a pool of manpower for local construction projects.

The results of North Korea's strategy during that period were, by and large, favorable and auspicious. North Korea was apparently winning its economic race with the South.

Going for Broke, 1962–1979. In April 1960 South Korea's President Rhee was driven from office in the face of student-led riots. He was replaced by a weak, caretaker government that was itself pushed from office a year later by a military coup led by General Park Chung Hee.

During that period of obvious political vulnerability in the South, Pyongyang failed to act. According to some reports, Kim Il Sung bitterly complained about that failure after the moment of opportunity had passed and decreed that North Korea would never be caught flat-footed again.[19] That rueful resolution informed the North Korean unification policy and national strategy in the years between roughly 1962 and 1979. North Korea adopted a long-term "national strategy" that could pay off if such an opportunity arose again. In many respects, that was the period of greatest innovation and flexibility in North Korea's external policies. North Korea's distinctive approach to international relations, often alarming or exasperating to ally and opponent alike, for the most part skillfully protected and advanced international objectives and interests as defined by the county's leadership. By the end of that period, however, it had become apparent that none of the many gambles the state had wagered on its long-term unification strategy had actually worked.

Throughout the 1960s and the 1970s, North Korea established military buildup as a primary administrative objective of state policy, with awesome results. In the early 1960s, the Korean People's Army (KPA) manpower was thought to have been just over 300,000. By the late 1970s (when Washington and Seoul finally detected the buildup), North Korea's armed forces were apparently approaching the million mark, backed by a high and steadily rising share of economic output devoted to defense readiness.[20] For a country of barely 20 million people, that amounted to something like total war mobilization on a permanent basis, a state of readiness perhaps unmatched in any other contemporary economy.

The purpose of that extraordinary military effort, of course, was to put Pyongyang in a position to seize the day when that day finally arrived. As the 1960s and 1970s progressed, prospects by some measures were surely encouraging. America's ability or willingness to defend

Seoul—perforce the first consideration in any North Korean calculations about unifying the peninsula on its own terms—seemed to be eroding. The Vietnam debacle, the "Nixon Doctrine," the Carter administration's announcement that Washington would withdraw all U.S. troops from South Korea—those and other events could reasonably have been read as presaging the end of an era in the U.S.–ROK relationship. To Pyongyang's strategists, it may well have looked as if patience and vigilance would be duly rewarded.

Some elements of the DPRK's turn during the 1960s and 1970s to an aggressive pursuit of reunification on its own terms were of course visible to foreign observers.[21] But strategic deception was also an integral aspect of that new phase of reunification policy, and the effort appears to have intensified in the early 1970s. In 1971, for example, North Korea reported that it had dramatically slashed its military budget (!); in 1972, a revised DPRK constitution located Pyongyang—not Seoul—as the site of the capital; and during the years 1971–1973, for the first time in its history, the North Korean government carried out direct high-level talks with its South Korean counterparts and even signed a joint "Accord on Independent Peaceful Reunification of Korea."

In April 1975, however—immediately after Vietnam's unconditional military reunification on communist terms—Kim Il Sung, then visiting Beijing, declared:

> If a revolution takes place in South Korea we, as one and the same nation, will not just look at it with folded arms but will strongly support the South Korean people. If the enemy ignites war recklessly, we shall resolutely answer it with war and completely destroy the aggressors.[22]

To those familiar with the semiotics of North Korean official rhetoric, the Great Leader had tipped his hand.

If Kim's pronouncements in Beijing betrayed a certain impatience, one could readily understand that. For as was to become increasingly clear during the 1960s and 1970s, North Korea's unification strategy was a race against time.

North Korea's military machine might easily defeat South Korea's in a one-on-one contest, if and when the opportunity arose. But maintaining and financing the KPA was a growing burden and was undercutting North Korea's ability to engage in a long-term competition with the ROK. Just as spiraling military commitments (and the limits of stringent command planning) began to slow the pace of material advance in the North, the South (under former General Park's new government) entered into a phase of explosively rapid economic growth.

Unanticipated problems in Pyongyang's relations with its main allies, Moscow and Beijing, further complicated the "correlation of forces." The Sino-Soviet split, the Cultural Revolution, and the rise of Leonid Brezhnev (who seems to have harbored a personal loathing for Kim Il Sung)[23] meant limited political and financial support for North Korea from those traditional patrons. Soviet and Chinese leaders had also deliberately limited their security commitments to the regime: in separate secret deliberations in 1969, for example, the Nixon administration had been assured by both Moscow and Beijing that they would not come to Pyongyang's aid if it provoked another war in the Korean peninsula.[24]

North Korea's tactical response to those developments was quite imaginative. Beginning in the mid-1960s, the DPRK started to cultivate diplomatic relations with noncommunist countries: first "nonaligned states," then Western (the Organization for Economic Cooperation and Development). At the high-water mark of that diplomatic offensive, North Korea was discussing terms of cross-recognition with its perennial *bête noire,* Japan, but no deal was reached. In 1970, furthermore, North Korean foreign policy made a sharp turn toward Western markets for goods and capital. Between 1970 and 1975 North Korea contracted as much as $1.2 billion in hard currency loans, which it used for purchases of capital goods and grain from OECD countries. In 1964 over 90 percent of North Korea's trade turnover was with the Communist bloc; by 1974 North Korea's imports from OECD countries may have exceeded its imports from China, the Soviet Union, and Eastern Europe combined.[25]

Those tactical thrusts, however, could not be sustained. Almost immediately, North Korea fell into arrearage on its hard currency debts, its commerce with OECD countries subsequently collapsed, and Pyongyang's refusal to make good on the loans poisoned trade relations with the industrial democracies.[26] The overture toward noncommunist countries likewise proved to be self-limiting, as Pyongyang's new diplomatic acquaintances became familiar with North Korean distinctive official habits (for example, "self-financing" embassies supported by trafficking contraband).

Unorthodox as North Korea's approach to national unification may have been during the 1960s and 1970s, its game plan was by no means the gambit of a madman. High-risk and high-tension, to be sure: but the reading of the international scene that informed it was basically sound—

arguably even prescient. The United States *would* suffer serious foreign policy reversals in the 1960s and the 1970s; the credibility of Washington's commitment to Seoul *would* become an open question during and after the Vietnam era; the ROK *was* a politically fragile and potentially unstable polity (as was underscored in 1979 by the assassination of President Park at the hand of his own security chief).

But that strategy for national unification was at bottom a gamble, and luck does not smile on every gambler. In the mid-1970s—when the North had likely gained a decisive conventional edge over the South, and Washington's commitment to Seoul seemed to be shaky—President Park's martial law regime still looked solid. And 1979—when the DPRK probably still enjoyed a military advantage over the ROK, and the Park assassination brought turmoil to the surface in the South—just happened to be the time when the American commitment to South Korea's defense was categorically and convincingly reaffirmed by the Carter administration's decision to cancel scheduled U.S. troop withdrawals from the ROK in July 1979.[27] North Korea's strategy for national unification had missed its run, and North Korean leaders entered the 1980s grimly playing out a hand of bad cards they themselves had chosen.

Dead End, 1980 Onward. At the start of the 1980s, North Korea's "national strategy" for unification was at best a long shot. By the start of the 1990s, it sounded like a hopeless fantasy. Despite increasingly unpleasant international and domestic realities, North Korea's leadership seems to have made no substantive adjustments to its grand strategy, originally cast in the 1940s.[28] Poorly adapted as it was for the world of the 1980s and 1990s, the North Korean leadership nevertheless clung to the strategy doggedly.

As the 1980s progressed, South Korea looked ever less vulnerable to an enforced unification with the North. In their economic race, the ROK had overtaken the DPRK by the beginning of the 1980s and left it in the dust. With the first genuinely competitive presidential elections held in Seoul in 1987, the success of the 1988 Olympics, and the Reagan administration's assertive and explicitly anticommunist foreign and military policies, it was impossible to entertain the notion that the international community would regard the ROK as a problematic pariah government.

North Korea's response to those menacing changes was to continue and intensify the basic policies it had embraced in the 1960s and 1970s. Pyongyang avoided anything but reluctant and superficial diplomatic dialogue with the ROK throughout the 1980s. By contrast, North Korea's military buildup proceeded at full throttle. By 1987 some 1.25 million men or more may have been under arms.[29] By that date, in fact, the KPA may have become the world's fourth-largest armed service— behind only those of China, the Soviet Union, and the United States.

The costs of that commitment, however, were becoming too great for the DPRK's relatively small economy to bear. By the mid-1980s, according to Soviet bloc observers, the North Korean economy had entered into stagnation and was heading toward absolute decline.[30] If their particular readings were overly pessimistic, they were also probably not far from the mark. Month by month, the economic balance in the Korean peninsula was shifting against Pyongyang and was exacerbated by the burden of its military buildup.

In the USSR, analogous problems in the contest with the United States had prompted leading military figures—including Marshal Nikolai Ogarkov, at the time chief of the general staff—to call for far-reaching economic reforms to revitalize the nation's economic base in general and to advance the "scientific-technical revolution" within the war industries in particular.[31] North Korea, however, had no Marshal Ogarkov. Instead, under Marshal Kim Il Sung, North Korea in the 1980s foreswore virtually any alterations in its entrenched, cumbersome, and somewhat irrational central economic planning system.[32] Without radical economic reform, long-term competition with or confrontation against South Korea would no longer be possible. Radical economic reform, however, would necessarily weaken the North Korean leadership's political and ideological control—and might well set forces in motion that would eventually undermine the regime and the system.

Pyongyang attempted to circumvent that dilemma through a foreign policy finesse. In 1982 the death of Leonid Brezhnev opened the door to a warmer Soviet–DPRK relationship. Ominous shifts in the international "correlation of forces" had left Moscow eager for new security ties; Pyongyang, for its part, was willing to lean sharply toward Moscow in return for substantial economic and military assistance. On that basis, the two parties entered into a new arrangement highly beneficial to the DPRK.

Beginning in 1984, Moscow acquiesced in a ballooning trade imbalance with North Korea, an implicit subsidy reflecting Soviet willingness to ship progressively greater volumes of goods and military materiel to North Korea without compensating countershipments. Pricing commerce transacted in nonconvertible currencies is problematic, but at official current ruble/dollar exchange rates, Moscow's implicit subsidy to the North Korean economy would have exceeded $4 billion for the 1985–1990 period, and its military transfers to the DPRK during those years would have amounted to over $5 billion.[33] Yet despite such successful diplomacy and despite the impact that the transfers had on North Korean military potential, the day of reckoning for North Korea's unification policy could only be postponed.

"Unification Policy" in the Jaws of Disaster

The sudden, dramatic sequence of worldwide events between 1989 and 1991 associated with what is now called "the end of the cold war" represented, for Pyongyang, a catastrophe of previously unimaginable scope and proportion. In practically every particular, the elements of that great reconfiguration of global politics constituted specific, tangible setbacks to the "correlation of forces" for Pyongyang in the Korean peninsula.

A simple recap of headlines from the 1989–1991 period will convey a sense of the new and far more perilous international environment Pyongyang abruptly faced.

• In 1989 the socialist governments of Warsaw Pact Europe collapsed one after another; Nicolae Ceauşescu, the Romanian ruler with a cult of personality analogous to Kim Il Sung's own, was deposed and murdered by his successors.

• From 1989 to 1990 the Soviet Union entered into a terminal crisis: in its 1991 denouement, Soviet territory was broken into fifteen newly independent republics; the Communist Party of the Soviet Union was (briefly) declared illegal and officially suppressed; and the new government in Moscow came under the hand of a president who was avowedly procapitalist and pro-American.

• In 1990 the world's sole remaining superpower, the United States, successfully organized a multinational expeditionary force under UN auspices to confront Iraq after its invasion of Kuwait—much as Washington had in 1950, after Pyongyang's invasion of the South.

• Perhaps most portentously, the division of Germany—the other nation besides Korea partitioned by the settlements of World War II—came to an end in 1989 and 1990. The population of the former East Germany enthusiastically embraced annexation by their erstwhile ideological rivals, and in their first free outing to the polls overwhelmingly supported West Germany's governing parties.

Ominous for Pyongyang as those great changes so obviously were, their immediate ramifications for North Korea's contest against the South were, if possible, even worse. With the mortal crisis and demise of the Soviet bloc, for example, Soviet/Russian military shipments to the DPRK all but ceased; trade turnover between Moscow and Pyongyang collapsed, and the implicit economic subsidy to the North Korean economy abruptly plummeted.[34] To make matters worse, China—now no longer in competition for influence in Pyongyang—evidenced growing impatience with North Korea's economic behavior. Despite the DPRK's mounting economic difficulties, the Chinese subsidy to the DPRK was steadily and dramatically reined in.[35]

The end of the cold war brought about both economic and diplomatic dislocations on the DPRK. By early 1990, all the states of Warsaw Pact Europe (plus Mongolia) had extended diplomatic relations to Seoul. Under the banner of "new thinking," the USSR ostentatiously followed suit later that year. In August 1992, China—North Korea's last ally of any consequence—finally normalized its relations with the ROK (although by that point Beijing and Seoul already enjoyed a cordial working relationship, thanks in part to their flourishing commercial ties).

Deprived of its last elements of significant backing within the international community, North Korea was no longer able to block South Korea's entry to the United Nations. The ROK joined in 1991. But for Pyongyang, that was hardly the worst of it. North Korea's battle against the South for international legitimacy and support was suddenly far more precarious than it had ever been before. Whereas, for example, Seoul had ended up in 1992 with formal recognition from and strong ties to all four of the great powers of northern Asia (the United States, Japan, China, and Russia), Pyongyang maintained official relations with only two— and could not really claim to be on good terms with any.

The calamitous turn of international events that defined the "end of the cold war" for North Korean leadership prompted an unprecedented flurry of diplomatic activity by the DPRK. In 1990, 1991, and 1992, Pyongyang conducted a series of substantive talks with Tokyo on the topic of cross-recognition to explore the possibility that Moscow's new ties to Seoul might be countered by developing the DPRK's relations with Japan.[36] In 1991, reversing its long-standing position that Korea should only have a single, true representative accepted into the forum, the DPRK agreed to join the United Nations at the same time that the ROK was admitted to membership.

North Korea also surprised foreign governments with intriguing hints that its *Weltanschauung* might finally be changing. In September 1991 the DPRK foreign minister was quoted in an interview with *Jane's Defense Weekly* as stating that "Marxism cannot be applied to present-day realities";[37] the following year, it was revealed abroad that a newly revised DPRK constitution dropped long-standing references to Marxism-Leninism as a philosophy guiding the state.[38] But perhaps the most interesting activities were in the "inter-Korean dialogue" itself.

The years 1990–1992 witnessed a progression of state-to-state contacts that were extraordinary for the divided Korean peninsula. Those included eight official meetings at the prime ministerial level; the formalization of an agreement on "Reconciliation and Non-Aggression" and the initialing of a DPRK–ROK document on mutual nuclear inspections; and a five-day visit to the ROK by a DPRK vice premier who toured South Korean industries and discussed avenues of possible economic cooperation.

That burst of inter-Korean comity seemed to constitute a radical departure from all previous DPRK policy toward the South. Understanding the underlying motivations and intentions is therefore critical; unfortunately, those remain unclear to outsiders.

It seems unlikely that those overtures represented an effort at strategic deception, at least of the traditional variety: military unification was a less plausible option for the DPRK than ever before in the wake of the American-led Persian Gulf War in January 1991. It is possible that those contacts with the ROK betokened a reconsideration of North Korea's reunification policy at the highest levels of leadership; alternatively, it is possible that North Korean leaders were simply groping in the darkness of a new era that their ideology failed to illuminate. In any case, that episode of experimentation and seeming gestures of rapprochement came to a close at the end of 1992, when the DPRK reverted to more familiar patterns of international and inter-Korean behavior.

By 1993 North Korea's reunification policy was irrelevant, given the conditions at hand: the pressing problem was now regime survival. Pyongyang's approach to that problem was almost entirely tactical in nature and revealed a striking admixture of painful temporizing and bold maneuver. On the one hand, the North Korean leadership resolutely refused to experiment with any serious economic reforms and only dabbled in ineffectual foreign investment legislation. By late 1993 Pyongyang officially announced that its economy was in a "grave situation"[39]—but still indicated no plausible design for improving its prospects.

The reasoning behind that posture was clear enough: almost from its start, Kim Il Sung had diagnosed the crisis of Soviet bloc socialism as an affliction transmitted from "capitalism by paralyzing the people's revolutionary consciousness through ideological and cultural infiltration."[40] North Korea's leaders, correspondingly, were unwilling to expose their system casually to the grave risks of such contamination.

Kim Il Sung's death in July 1994 did not seem to alter the DPRK's stern resistance to economic experimentation. With the Great Leader's death, North Korea's leading personality became Kim Il Sung's son and heir-designate, Kim Jong Il. While little can be said categorically about the younger Kim's inclinations, his writings and pronouncements arguably evidence, if anything, even less enthusiasm for liberalized economic policies than those of his late father.

Under its current policy regime, North Korea's ability to earn hard currency is extremely limited. Sales of hard currency goods may generate roughly $1 billion a year in exports for North Korea—as compared with South Korea's total 1998 export revenues of over $130 billion.[41] Unable to purchase the foreign products its facilities require just to stay in operation, Pyongyang's ability to maintain its already diminished production levels without outside help is questionable. The emergence of an officially acknowledged food crisis in the DPRK in 1995—a crisis that Pyongyang as yet has been manifestly incapable of resolving—would seem to corroborate such suspicions. One can only infer that the prospect of economic deterioration is less unsettling to North Korean leadership than the vision of far-reaching systemic reforms.

In contrast to the continuing stasis in economic and domestic policy in the early 1990s, North Korea made a series of shrewd and daring moves in the diplomatic arena. Most of those centered on a nuclear drama, unveiled by Pyongyang in early 1993 and carried into 1994. By threatening to withdraw from the Nuclear Nonproliferation Treaty, hinting that it might already have succeeded in developing an atomic bomb, and indicating that it would soon be capable of producing half a dozen or more nuclear devices each year, Pyongyang generated a wave of international alarm. Through successive rounds of skillful, high-tension negotiations with the United States, South Korea, Japan, the UN International Atomic Energy Agency, and other parties, the DPRK finally arrived at a complex understanding with Washington (the October 1994 "Agreed Framework") whereby North Korea's program for producing fissile materials would be put on hold and eventually inspected and dismantled in return for which an American-led consortium would provide ten years of heavy oil deliveries gratis and also construct two "safe" nuclear reactors in the DPRK at an estimated cost of at least an additional $4 billion.[42]

That understanding satisfied a multiplicity of North Korean security, foreign policy, and economic goals. Perhaps most important, it heralded the possibility of a completely new and vastly improved relationship with the region's strongest power, the United States, and seemed further to promise that North Korea might be able to draw substantial long-term concessional aid from three fresh new sources: Washington, Tokyo, and Seoul. Yet even that brilliant tactical success did not rescue North Korea from the ominous fundamentals of its new position—much less restore it to one in which it could pursue its long-cherished but now inoperable unification strategy.

North Korea's leadership needed to secure steady transfers of aid from abroad both to keep its ailing economy from deteriorating further and to avoid the systemic risks posed by far-reaching liberalization. No conceivable volume of external financial assistance, though, could restore the economic balance in the peninsula to the already highly unfavorable differential of the late 1980s. Moreover, aid of any magnitude presupposed major South Korean participation. That, of course, would invite precisely the sorts of cultural and ideological contamination that Pyongyang had judged to be lethal to Soviet bloc socialism. By the same token, while North Korea urgently sought American and Japanese diplomatic recognition, any substantive deepening of relations with those two countries would in practice likely lead to contacts and pressures intrinsically subversive of *urisik sahoejuui* (the DPRK's officially proclaimed "own style of socialism").

It became clear as the late 1990s progressed that, for all the deftness of its external maneuvers, North Korea was caught in a tightening vise. In 1995, when the Korean Peninsula Energy Development Organization established through the "Agreed Framework" began its deliberations, for example, Pyongyang insisted that the promised light-water nuclear reactors not be South Korean; Seoul, which was to pay for most of the project, stated that there would be South Korean reactors or no reactors at all. Rather than jeopardize its gains from the framework, Pyongyang acquiesced in the ROK's demand. Similarly, when food shortages in 1995 prompted the DPRK to issue an unprecedented appeal for emergency food aid, South Korea donated 150,000 tons of rice. But when North Korea consumed the grain without amending its behavior toward the ROK, Seoul ceased its own grain shipments and successfully dissuaded other Western governments from extending more than token amounts of relief for that year.

Even military brinksmanship—a tried-and-true instrument in the DPRK diplomatic tool kit—seemed to be losing its former effectiveness. When in April 1996 Pyongyang escalated its campaign to replace the 1953 armistice with a peace treaty between the DPRK and the United States by sending unauthorized units of KPA troops into forbidden areas of the demilitarized zone, Washington acted as if it were unconcerned to keep Pyongyang diplomats eager to resolve the "crisis" on hold. In South Korea, those same tactics seemed to contribute to the upset victory in local elections of the ruling party and to a still less accommodationist posture toward the North on the part of its leadership. When a DPRK submarine ran aground on ROK territory in the fall of 1996, Seoul insisted on—and obtained—an unprecedented formal "statement of regret" from Pyongyang.

North Korea's leaders, of course, were past masters of extracting gains through a diplomacy of military menace. As the late 1990s progressed, Pyongyang demonstrated that it was still quite capable of utilizing those tried-and-true techniques.

In the early summer of 1998, after years of denying the fact, the DPRK suddenly acknowledged publicly that it was selling abroad the same missiles it was producing at home and warned the United States that if it "really wants to prevent missile exports it should . . . make a compensation."[43] Later that summer, without advance warning, the DPRK launched a newly perfected, multistage ballistic rocket over the main island of Japan.[44] That summer also witnessed the onset of a dispute between Pyongyang and Washington about inspection of a huge underground complex in Kumchang-ri that American officials suspected was being built to advance the country's nuclear weapons program (despite a seeming understanding under the "Agreed Framework" that all such activities in North Korea were to be suspended from October 1994 onward).[45] Over the following months, as American diplomats insisted on access to that "suspect site," Pyongyang's resistance mounted, and its rhetoric grew increasingly bellicose. At one point, there was even an official threat to "blow up the U.S. territory as a whole"[46] over that confrontation. But as North Korean leadership may well have anticipated, those manufactured crises ultimately resulted in economic rewards for the DPRK. Less than two weeks after the surprise rocket launch over Japan, American officials affirmed that the United States would commit 300,000 tons of food aid to the DPRK and declared that the rocket issue should not be allowed to derail the Korean Peninsula Energy Development Organization.[47] And just before the DPRK agreed in early 1999 to an eventual inspection of the site in question, the United States promised North Korea 600,000 tons of further food aid.[48]

That U.S.–DPRK dynamic prompted critical observers to comment that "North Korea knows the code to Uncle Sam's credit card."[49] Yet, at the end of the day, the grim fact facing Pyongyang was that its extortive stratagems were good for small charges only. The resources North Korea managed to secure through confrontational posturing amounted in 1997 and 1998 to no more than a few hundred million dollars a year. Such sums were manifestly insufficient to arrest the continuing decline of the domestic economy or to bring an end to the country's continuing hunger crisis. They were, almost certainly, not even adequate to maintain the strength of the country's conventional military forces, until then the prime instrument of North Korea's own chosen unification policy; although still imposing, that enormous apparatus had begun to age and decay, thereby steadily devaluing its utility. North Korea's tribute-oriented international policy, in short, may have been adequate to finance the bare minimum of functions essential to the operation and existence of the state, but the policy was utterly incapable of addressing the DPRK's grave and mounting systemic troubles, much less redressing the increasingly tilted "correlation of forces" between the two governments claiming sole authority over the entire Korean domain.

The December 1997 election of Kim Dae Jung as president of the Republic of Korea marked a further—and significant—setback for Pyongyang in its inter-Korean contest. Although some commentary had speculated that North Korea's leadership might favor an electoral victory by that perennial South Korean opposition candidate, the actual consequence of inaugurating Kim Dae Jung was to limit still further the DPRK's room for maneuver. Kim's very accession to the presidency demonstrated just how far political liberalization had proceeded in the South—and in fact spoke to the voting public's confidence in the strength and dynamism of the evolving ROK political system. Moreover, the elevation in the South of the longtime political prisoner and human rights activist unavoidably invited comparisons with the political process and human rights situation in the North; the automatic result was to bump North Korea's perceived international legitimacy down by yet another rung. North Korea's standard invective against South Korean leadership seemed ludicrously miscast now that a former prisoner of conscience was in charge of the country. And with Kim Dae Jung's inaugural declaration that "we do not have any intention to undermine or absorb North Korea,"[50] the officially tendered justifications for Pyongyang's stalwartly hostile posture toward Seoul became yet more remote and implausible. Indeed, the first year of the Kim Dae Jung administration offered the world the extraordinary spectacle of a South Korean government earnestly striving to engage the North in confidence-building dialogue for a reconciliation, and a North Korean government just as resolutely attempting to avoid what it apparently regarded as the peril of official bilateral contact with the South.

Whatever dreams its regime may continue to cherish about a unification of Korea on DPRK terms, the inescapable reality of the 1990s is that North Korea can no longer take even state survival for granted. The last reunification proposal offered by Kim Il Sung before his death, the "10-Point Program of Great Unity of the Whole Nation for Reunification of the Country" of April 1993, suggests as much. The tenth point in that program is particularly telling: "Those who have contributed to the great unity of the nation and to the cause of national reunification should be highly estimated."[51] Subsequent official broadcasts elaborated on the point: "What is important in appraising people is, above all, to grant special favors to those who have performed feats for the great unity of the nation and the reunification of the country, patriotic martyrs and their descendants."[52] In a departure from the form and substance of all previous utterances on reunification, the North Korean regime appeared in that instance to be urging South Korea to agree to some sort of *securité de passage* to cover North Korea's leaders—and "their descendants."

The Long Goodbye

How, on balance, do we assess North Korea's long, determined quest for national reunification? One verdict that comes to mind is Samuel Johnson's famous remark to Boswell about a certain person "[who has had] but one idea in his entire life—and that idea was wrong." Would such a judgment be too harsh for Pyongyang's reunification policy?

Possibly so, for as we have seen, the DPRK's approach to achieving unification of the peninsula on its own terms was not only feasible, but arguably promising, for some period of time. The fact that Pyongyang's approach to settling its unification problem diverges so sharply from the contemporary norms of accepted behavior in international statecraft does not by itself indicate that the DPRK's strategy has been doomed to failure.

Nevertheless, deep and fundamental flaws can be identified in that central North Korean policy. Perhaps most important, it appears to have been based on an extended, severe misreading of South Korean realities and potentialities. North Korea misjudged not only critical events within the ROK but also long-term developments. The DPRK worldview did not prepare the North Korean leadership for the possibility that the impoverished, dependent South Korean autocracy of the 1950s and early 1960s could evolve into the affluent, politically open, and popularly supported system the ROK was to enjoy by the early 1990s.

By the same token, the DPRK appears to have signally misjudged the importance of economic performance for its long-term prospects of reunifying Korea on its own terms. Marxist-Leninist "correlation of forces" analyses may be faulted for often slighting the economic element in the competition between opposing systems; North Korean strategy may be criticized on the same grounds.

Finally, like communist groups in and out of power in most of the rest of the world, North Korean leaders badly misjudged the strength and stability of the Soviet bloc. North Korea's ill-fated decision to lean toward the Soviet Union at the very moment that the Soviet system was coming undone is partly responsible for the desperate straits in which the DPRK finds itself today.

In the late 1990s, the Democratic People's Republic of Korea is a state that appears to be functioning on a sort of "life-support" basis by tactically negotiating provisional extensions for its lease on life. Given the nature of the North Korean state, those negotiations are highly circumscribed. A more extensive commercial interaction with South Korea, for example, might help resuscitate the North Korean economy, but DPRK leaders, apparently fearing that such contacts might destabilize their system, have backed away from that option. Far-reaching economic reforms have been foresworn for apparently the same reason.

Despite the often underappreciated shrewdness of its leadership, North Korea is a state with diminishing control over the events that shape its future. The cherished goal of a Korean unification may be drawing closer—but it is not likely to be a reunification on DPRK terms.

3

The DPRK under Multiple Severe Economic Stresses: What Can We Learn from Historical Experience?

Since the collapse of the Soviet bloc, North Korean leadership has repeatedly and pointedly gone out of its way to insist—both to its subjects and to the outside world—that "our own style of socialism" (*urisik sahoejuui*) is a historically unique human construct, guided by North Korea's own people-centered logic and set on its own special path of development. The immediate purpose of such demurrals is to dispute the presumption that the political and economic systems of the Democratic People's Republic of Korea (DPRK), like those of the Warsaw Pact states after which they were modeled, are destined for the trash bin of history. But the demurrals cannot distract attention from accumulating evidence that the DPRK is engulfed in severe and mounting economic problems.

One must, of course, be cautious about speaking of "crises" in communist economies. As highly centralized and politically directed planning systems, communist economies in a real sense are *always* in "crisis"; they are *designed* for "crisis"; they *respond* to "crisis." When a communist economy substitutes a smaller set of "crises" for a larger set of "crises," it is making progress and is so judged by its ruling circles. In North Korea, however, smaller economic problems are now regularly giving way to larger economic problems. They have been doing so for over a decade, but the process has visibly accelerated over the past few years.

By the mid-1980s, according to some analyses,[1] the DPRK economy had reached the limits of classical socialist "extensive" growth and had entered into stagnation or even decline. With the end of Soviet aid and subsidized trade at the start of 1991, an already faltering economy suffered a heavy blow.[2] Although North Korea remains a closed state about which reliable information is still scarce, a variety of indications pointed to a steady worsening of economic conditions. In May 1994, for example—months *before* the death of Kim Il Sung—Chinese sources were talking of "the worst food crisis in history" for the DPRK regime.[3]

A year later, Pyongyang officially launched a diplomatic appeal for emergency food aid. And in the summer of 1995—after the emergency appeal began—the DPRK suffered what by all reports was unusually heavy flood damage. Over the next several years, reports and rumors about dire hardships in the DPRK proliferated in the international media. Stories spoke of people swarming to Pyongyang in search of food;[4] of North Korean families foraging across the Chinese border for sustenance;[5] of outbreaks of cholera (a deadly disease for the severely malnourished) carrying off hundreds of people;[6] and of starvation in the industrial center of Hamhung.[7] By 1996 and 1997, both North Korean border crossers who had managed to reach China and international relief workers who had settled in Pyongyang to administer the provision of emergency food aid were talking of a "famine" in the DPRK.[8] By 1998, some of the personnel active in the international North Korean relief program were suggesting that 2 million persons— or perhaps even more—had already perished from hunger.[9] By early 1999, North Korea's highest-ranking defector was publicly estimating that the death toll in the DPRK's food crisis had come to exceed 3 million.[10] And in early 1999, South Korea's intelligence agency announced that it had obtained an internal DPRK public security ministry document purportedly demonstrating that the North Korean government itself was putting the country's death count at 3 million.[11]

Irrespective of the specific accuracy of any one of those many accounts, guesses, or reports, there can be little doubt that the DPRK is indeed under severe and rising economic stress. But in the absence of any detailed information about conditions in North Korea, how can outsiders attempt to assess the ability of the DPRK system to cope with the economic pressures that confront it?

Fortunately for outside analysts, Pyongyang's claims to uniqueness are not entirely true. "Socialism with Korean characteristics" may only be found in the northern half of the Korean peninsula, but some of the economic problems emerging from the DPRK today have been seen and studied in many places before. Historical analogy may therefore provide some insight into the problems pressing the DPRK—and into the options available to DPRK leaders for coping with the problems.

Today, we can discuss three conceptually distinct, but actually overlapping, sets of problems with respect to the DPRK economy. The first concerns the stresses faced by "war economies"—economic systems that have been subjected to a variant of central planning for the purposes of total war mobilization. The second involves severe exogenous economic shocks to centrally planned economies or economies prepared for war: historically, such shocks have been generated not only by systemwide crises, such as the collapse of the Soviet trade regimen, but also by international sanctions or wartime embargoes. The third set of problems pertains to the stresses attendant to severe food shortages under communist economies.

Modern War Economies and the Phenomenon of "Economic Collapse"

The experiences of modern industrial economies subjected to the stresses of total mobilization for purposes of national survival are perhaps most dramatically represented in World War II. Some penetrating global economic histories of that period have been written; in addition, detailed studies of particular combatant economies and specific economic sectors of given warring states have been undertaken.[12] Rather than attempt an encyclopedic summary of that literature, it may suffice to offer a few observations that relate directly to North Korean conditions and prospects.

First, at the peak of the war the combatant powers were allocating an extraordinary and perhaps historically unparalleled share of national output to their military efforts. In the United States and Japan, the war effort absorbed over 40 percent of national output in 1944; in Germany and the United Kingdom, it absorbed over 50 percent; and in the Soviet Union it may have absorbed an astonishing 60-plus percent.[13] In North Korea, by contrast, defense expenditures are estimated by the U.S. government to have accounted for about 20 to 25 percent of GNP in the early 1990s.[14] Some studies suggest that such an estimate may somewhat understate the share of national output accruing to the military in the DPRK. Even so, it would appear that North Korea is not, by those guideposts, an economy on a full-pitched war footing. To extend the analogy, by the criterion of resources allocated to military effort, the DPRK today looks like a "1943 economy," not a "1944 economy."

Second, total war mobilization during World War II was a discrete, and relatively brief, episode in the economic histories of all the combatant powers. For the United States and the Soviet Union, the period of maximal exertion lasted less than a thousand days, after which a demobilization immediately commenced. For Germany and the United Kingdom, the war lasted just under six years; the phase of full-war footing, about three years. For Japan, whose Pacific war may be said to have begun in 1937, the period of conflict was longest, but even in Japan the shift to total-war mobilization did not take place until after 1942. In contrast to those extraordinarily intense but relatively brief bursts, the DPRK's economy has been placed on something approaching full-war footing for over a generation—certainly since 1970, arguably since the mid-1960s. Whereas a full-fledged war economy has been but a historical interlude for the contemporary great powers, it is thus a continuing historical epoch in the DPRK. One might well expect qualitatively different stresses to arise on such qualitatively different time scales.

Third, several of the combatant economies during World War II apparently managed to squeeze an absolute increase in military resources out of a declining economy. That appears to have been the case, for example, in the Soviet Union between 1940 and 1942 and in Germany and Japan during portions of 1944. What is noteworthy, however, is that such arrangements were unstable and inherently unsustainable, even under the exigence of life-and-death conflict. In the USSR, those unsustainable trends were resolved by stabilization of the front, limited recovery of the domestic industrial base in areas under Soviet control, and massive "mutual aid" from America and Britain.[15] In Germany and Japan, the same inherently unsustainable trends ended with defeat and regime collapse. If North Korea today is attempting to maintain or increase what have been very substantial allocations to its military on what is now apparently a diminishing economic base, it too would appear to be embarked upon an inherently unsustainable trajectory.

Fourth, and perhaps most important, the experience of World War II attests to the fact that *economies* can indeed collapse—and not just the regimes supervising them. "Economic collapse," of course, is a somewhat ambiguous concept and has been defined in a variety of ways.[16] A certain kind of "economic collapse" is unambiguously indicated, however, when a modern industrialized economy is no longer capable of satisfying the nutritional needs of substantial portions of its population through existing mechanisms. Viewed from that vantage point, both Germany and Japan may be seen to have suffered an "economic collapse" that preceded surrender and lasted into the postwar era.

As has been documented, the national food systems of both Japan and Germany essentially broke down in the months before the end of World War II.[17] In part, those food crises reflected drops in agricultural production under circumstances inauspicious for cultivation. They also, however, spoke to pervasive disruption in the established distribution system. It was not only that the transportation system's capacities were disintegrating (although that too was surely a problem): more fundamentally, the rules by which people had previously traded foodstuffs for nonfood goods had suddenly been changed or in extremis abrogated.[18]

As a result of those micro- and macroeconomic changes, both Germany and Japan were swept by a terrifying and general hunger at the end of the war. The hunger lasted on into the peace. For most people, life became a daily quest for food. Under those new conditions, the group least equipped to manage its own nutritional security was the urban population. In consequence, both Germany and Japan underwent prolonged deurbanization (see table 3-1). In West Germany, prewar levels of urbanization were not reattained until 1950; in Japan, the 1944 urbanization ratio was not exceeded for a decade after the war. The timing of reurbanization, incidentally, seems closely related to the equalization of nutritional opportunities between city and countryside.

Table 3-1   Urban Fraction of the Total Population of Germany/Federal Republic of Germany (1939–1950) and Japan (1940–1955)

Germany/Federal Republic of Germany		Japan	
May 1939	70.5	October 1940	37.9
October 1946	68.6	February 1944	41.1
September 1950	71.1	November 1945	27.8
		April 1946	30.4
		August 1948	34.6
		October 1950	37.5
		October 1955	56.3

Source: Jack Hirshleifer, *Disaster and Recovery: A Historical Survey*, Memorandum Rm-3079-PR (Santa Monica, Calif.: RAND Corporation, April 1963).

For North Korea, the implications are straightforward: "economic collapse" can occur even in strictly managed war economies and has in the past. But are those previous cases relevant? North Korea is *not* in the midst of a cataclysmic battle; nor is it facing imminent military defeat. How then do the shocks and stresses North Korea currently confronts differ from those that led to "economic collapse" in Germany and Japan half a century ago?

Trade Shocks, Trade Sanctions, and Economic Blockades

Sudden disruptions of a country's standing patterns of trade and international finance can pose both immediate and longer-term challenges to local economic performance and the state policies designed to influence it. If output is to be maintained or increased in the face of external dislocations, far-reaching adjustments—and correlatively, the policies and mechanisms for putting them into effect—may be required. If economic contraction cannot be forestalled by policy adjustments—or if the national directorate in question is unable or unwilling to implement measures that would stabilize aggregate output—the local government and the economic agents under its authority must then cope with the stresses (including allocative conflicts and welfare losses) that necessarily accompany the restriction of production possibilities.

While major dislocations in a country's trade profile have sometimes occurred in the past as the result of deliberate design by the state's rulers (typically in tandem with a radical or revolutionary transition in domestic politics), such major shocks more often seem to be generated by great international events: systemwide economic crises, war, and coercive diplomacy (sanctions, embargoes, and the like). A considerable corpus of scholarly literature analyzes the conditions under which externally applied economic pressure is likely to achieve the political objectives desired by the states and organizations "sending" it.[19] By contrast, relatively few studies have systematically examined the political economy of adjustment to severe external economic shocks.[20] Nevertheless, examination of the historical record and reflection upon current events can cast light on the ways in which states succeed—or fail—when faced with sudden and systemic stresses on their international economic regimen.

The two world wars offer stark examples of disruption of trade and purposeful constriction of international supplies at the hand of enemy powers. In World War I, Anglo-American naval superiority permitted an embargo on the Central Powers' seaborne trade; historians judge that embargo to have become largely successful by 1915 and to have grown increasingly effective at interdicting supplies thereafter.[21] In World War II, Anglo-American naval predominance and later air superiority allowed the Allies to pursue "economic warfare" against the Axis nations by obstructing not only external trade but (through the air war) the internal availability and circulation of strategic and nonstrategic goods.[22]

It was and still is widely presumed that Anglo-American efforts to blockade enemy trade had a telling impact on the economic capabilities of the Central and Axis powers and thus ultimately on the course of the two world wars.[23] The conjunction of concerted blockade and subsequent military defeat clearly lends itself to inferences of cause and effect. But careful economic studies since those wars have suggested a more qualified and complex picture.

In the estimate of those studies, the "trade shocks" imposed on Germany in World War I and on Germany and Japan in World War II were probably not the limiting constraint on wartime production. Despite Allied success in compromising their enemies' ability to obtain or exchange resources beyond their zone of conquest, Germany in World War I proved capable of maintaining—and both Germany and Japan in World War II proved capable of steadily increasing—domestic output throughout most of the conflicts in question (in fact, until months before their final surrenders).

In Japan, for example, real GDP is estimated to have been over 20 percent higher in 1944 than it had been in 1941.[24] Even economic efficiency appeared to rise in the face of blockade and bombing: in Nazi Germany, for example, output per worker in 1944 was over 30 percent higher in consumer industries and over 60 percent higher in military industries than in 1939.[25]

How could all this be explained? Bardach's answer for the First World War applies equally to the Second: in the final analysis, "a broadly-based economic system such as that of the Central Powers bears little more than a superficial resemblance to a beleaguered fortress, compelled to surrender for lack of supplies."[26]

Although constrained to some considerable degree from economic exchange with territories not under their direct control, both Berlin and Tokyo at the height of their powers held sway over regions inhabited by hundreds of millions of people and endowed with a rich variety of natural resources. Wartime distortions notwithstanding, the economies of the Third Reich and the Japanese empire were modern and diversified;

they had already achieved relatively high levels of industrial output and had the technological, organizational, and administrative capability to expand output further—even while experiencing shortages of certain key strategic materials—through prioritized substitution of inputs and "rationalization" of production. Thanks to administrative and organizational flexibility, in fact, Nazi Germany's actual consumption of oil and oil products was higher in early 1944 than in 1940 (as was its consumption of other "strategic" goods such as chrome and rubber) despite blockade and increasingly intensive aerial bombardment by the Allies.[27] By itself, then, "economic warfare" appears to have placed surprisingly little constraint on the productive capacities of the combatant powers in the two world wars.[28]

Paradoxically, as Ellings has argued, "city-states of centuries past, lacking resources, large territories, and diversified economies, may have been more vulnerable—and more inviting of [coercive] economic measures—than many nations today."[29] The analogy extends to the Confederate economic experience in the American Civil War—arguably the earliest instance of total war in the modern era. Although economic data from the Confederacy were limited and of mixed quality, a number of studies have concluded that the North's near-total blockade of Southern trade (General Scott's "Anaconda Plan") was an important factor undermining the Confederacy's ability to continue in the war.[30]

The efficacy of the "trade shock" the Union imposed on the Confederacy derived in large part from circumstances beyond Richmond's control as of 1861. First, the South's domestic market and division of labor were limited by its rather small population—11 million, of whom 4 million were slaves. Second, the South was an overwhelmingly rural and agricultural economy—90 percent of the population and 80 percent of the labor force in the 1860 census, respectively. Third, to the extent that the Southern economy had modernized, it had strategically specialized in the production of agricultural cash crops (for example, cotton and tobacco) and was thus ill-prepared for a suddenly enforced autarky.

That being said, however, it would also appear that the unwise economic policies and practices of the Confederacy's leadership dramatically intensified stresses on the Confederacy. In the earliest period of the war, for example, before the Northern blockade was in effect, the Confederacy withheld the South's cotton crop from the world market on the mistaken belief that its cartelization of "King Cotton" would bring financial benefits or foreign intervention, or both; as it happened, overseas textile manufacturers developed substitutes for Southern cotton, and the South lost a major opportunity to finance part of its war effort. Southern policy also prohibited trade with the Union across the land border that the two sides shared, even though such trade was evidently much more beneficial to the Southern monoculture economy than to the more diversified Northern economy.[31] The Confederate states resorted to highly inflationary fiscal and monetary policies to finance their war effort; the resulting hyperinflation (price increases averaged roughly 10 percent per month over the course of the war) surely exerted an independent effect on commerce and production. Episodic "impressment" (unremunerated requisition) of marketed farm goods and promulgation of price controls contributed to a breakdown of *domestic* trade and a retreat to subsistence enclaves within the economy. Finally, a conspicuous lack of coordination of economic policies among the Confederate states themselves increased the risks, costs of information, and "transaction costs" facing all economic agents in the wartime South.

To be sure, none of that is to argue that the South could have won the war—or vastly prolonged the war—with more auspicious economic policies. As Hirshleifer intimated, the South's defeat at the hands of the North seems to have been seriously "overdetermined."[32] Nevertheless, the strikingly untoward nature of the South's adjustment policies to the "trade shocks" that buffeted it should remind us that official responses to external economic dislocations can magnify the economic stresses in the domestic economy—and not only in theory.[33]

In more recent times, numerous states have been forced to cope with significant dislocations in their external economies owing to systemwide global crisis or coercive economic diplomacy.[34] For our purposes, a brief review of four cases from the developing areas may be most informative: the Republic of South Africa, Vietnam, Cuba, and Iraq.

Of the four countries, South Africa experienced the mildest external economic shocks—precipitated, in this instance, by an international campaign for antiapartheid trade and investment sanctions after 1985. Because South African exports were in the main homogeneous and highly marketable primary products, South Africa did not suffer any significant contraction in trade volume as a result of the sanctions campaign. Between 1985 and 1990, for example, the volume of imports and exports increased by about 10 percent, and the country continued to run a current-account surplus (albeit a declining one). Sanctions did, however, affect international business confidence: more than half the multinational corporations with investments in South Africa sold their holdings; new direct foreign investment essentially ceased; and money center banks became extremely wary about extending credit to either the South African public or the private sector.[35] South Africa's estimated GDP grew sluggishly after the onset of international sanctions, and estimated per capita GDP actually declined slightly (by about 4 percent) between 1985 and 1990.[36]

How much sanctions had to do with that stagnation, however, is unclear; for a variety of reasons—including expensive *dirigiste* policies—economic growth in South Africa had been steadily slowing down for a generation beforehand.[37] Be that as it may, the perceived pressure of those sanctions proved to be instrumental in bringing the apartheid regime to an end. That relinquishing of state control under relatively limited external economic pressure can be explained diversely; one important factor, however, may relate to solidarity and regime legitimacy. A willingness among South Africa's "races" to share sacrifice in the face of perceived economic loss was simply not an option with antiapartheid sanctions. Even within the "white" population, antiapartheid sanctions exposed deep fissures (between an English-language community principally employed in the private economy and an Afrikaans-speaking population largely employed by the public sector). Furthermore, apartheid had already lost substantial credibility among its ostensible prime beneficiaries: in 1986, for example, South Africa's Dutch Reformed Church (the faith in which the overwhelming majority of Afrikaaners confessed) reversed its earlier teachings and declared that apartheid had no scriptural basis or justification.

Vietnam offers the example of a planned economy directed by a Marxist-Leninist party that adjusted successfully to serious external economic shocks. With the final crisis of the Soviet Union and the dissolution of the Council for Mutual Economic Assistance (CMEA) in June 1991, the framework through which Vietnam heretofore had conducted the great bulk of its international commerce suddenly evaporated. Trade turnover with the former CMEA states, under a new regimen of unsubsidized market prices, completely collapsed: in nominal dollars and at official exchange rates, both imports and exports with the former Soviet bloc fell by about 90 percent between 1990 and 1991. That drop amounted to well over 50 percent of Vietnam's total trade turnover for 1990 (once again measured in nominal dollars and at official exchange rates).

Vietnam's economy, however, did not contract under that shock: instead, real GDP is officially estimated to have risen by 6 percent in

1991.[38] In that same year, aggregate trade volume is officially reported actually to have expanded. Thereafter, Vietnam's trade turnover grew even more briskly. Between the beginning of 1990 and the end of 1997, Vietnam's export growth averaged a reported 27 percent per year, its import growth averaged an official 26 percent per year, and real GDP growth averaged an official 7.7 percent a year.

While all those figures may somewhat overstate Vietnam's performance, there is no doubt that the Vietnamese economy fared very well despite a severe interruption of its standing trade patterns. How did it manage that feat?

Intangible factors—including good luck—may have played a role. But the most obvious factor in that successful adjustment was the policy regimen that the Vietnamese leadership embraced. From 1986 on, Vietnam's rulers had embarked upon *doi moi* ("a new way") economically. Their program—a tightly politically controlled economic liberalization buffered by stabilization measures—had been in place for several years when the Soviet trade crisis began to loom. In response to the impending crisis, Vietnamese economic policy grasped for export-led growth with stabilization. A series of devaluations made Vietnamese products (primary or labor-intensive goods) attractive in the international marketplace; interest rates at savings institutions were indexed against inflation; and the budget deficit (8 percent of GDP in 1990) was ruthlessly slashed (down to 2.5 percent of GDP in 1991).[39] Vietnam's macroeconomic policy adjustments in the early 1990s are in some ways reminiscent of South Korea's shifts in economic policies in the 1962–1965 period, the years that set the stage for South Korea's transition to export-led growth. Perhaps that should come as no surprise, insofar as South Korea's entry into an outward-oriented economic regimen was similarly propelled by policies anticipating an external economic shock (in Seoul's case, an anticipated termination of American economic assistance).

In contrast to Vietnam, Cuba's economy to date has not adjusted successfully to the termination of Soviet-bloc aid and trade. Official U.S. estimates suggest that the nominal dollar value of Cuba's total imports and exports both had fallen by over 70 percent between 1989–1990 and 1994–1995.[40] Although GDP estimates for the Cuban economy are problematic, it is apparent that the system has suffered a severe downturn. According to some assessments, Cuba's GDP in 1993 was only half as large as it had been in 1989;[41] in 1994 and 1995, according to others, per capita GDP growth may also have been marginally negative.[42] Cuba's aggregate economic performance may have improved somewhat in the mid- to late 1990s. For the 1995–1998 period, official trade data point to an upturn in both imports and exports, and official national accounts data register consistently positive GDP growth for the 1995–1998 period. International students of the Cuban economy, however, have questioned the reliability of Cuba's new GDP numbers.[43] And while outside analysts believe that Cuban trade performance has improved since the *annus horribilis* of 1993, that recovery should not be exaggerated. According to U.S. intelligence estimates, for example, Cuba's trade turnover for 1997 was only just over two-fifths as high as it had been in 1990.[44]

For a cash-crop export economy with a relatively small population (11 million), unrealistically advantageous terms of trade with its erstwhile CMEA partners, and a fairly high ratio of CMEA trade to domestic output, the short-term problems posed by the abrupt disappearance of the Soviet trade bloc would be formidable under any circumstances. Havana's policies, however, appear to have intensified rather than relieved the structural pressures on the Cuban economy. In the memorable (if not completely accurate) description of one Cuba specialist, the Cuban approach to its trade shock problems has been "a unique case of anti-market reform."[45] For several years after the trade shock, the Castro government embraced a somewhat contradictory strategy that included more stringent rationing, tighter trade controls, stimulation of domestic socialist "infant industries," deficit financing, and development of hard-currency enclaves (most notably tourism).

To date the strategy has failed to spark recovery for self-evident reasons. Under Cuba's socialist institutional structure, "supply-side" responses are difficult to elicit; the turn against market mechanisms after 1989 only reduced the elasticity of supply further. On the demand side, the lurch toward deficit finance created even greater disequilibrium in the peso sector of the economy (for example, the official economy); in tandem with stricter trade controls, the effect was to forestall employment of underutilized factors of production, to complicate the purchase of needed intermediate goods, and to hinder the reallocation of resources.

Unlike the American Confederacy's unfortunate commercial and financial strategy, Cuba's adjustment program may not be a matter simply of economic naiveté. Political and ideological calculations likely frame Castro's vision of adjustment policies; it seems quite possible that prolonged depression and economic decline could be viewed by the leadership as preferable to potentially destabilizing recovery. In any event, to date the Castro regime has demonstrated that it can deal to its own satisfaction with the political consequences of its continuing economic slump. The efficacy of Cuba's extensive internal security services is crucial to that strategy.[46] Also important has been the regime's acquiescence after 1993 in a creeping "dollarization" of a still formally illegal private-service economy. "Dollarization" has permitted the regime implicitly to renegotiate its social contract with the citizenry by lowering state guarantees while still holding out the possibilities that basic needs might be met through other (extralegal) channels and activities. Irrespective of its economic merit or its long-term ideological viability, that has proved to be a shrewd political tactic for defusing some of the stresses Cuba's more overarching economic strategy seems to have created.

Iraq, finally, presents the example of a militarized economy that has been under strict and fairly watertight international trade sanctions. Since August 1990, when its forces invaded Kuwait, Iraq has been subject to United Nations' sanctions that severely limit its ability to generate export earnings through oil sales (which accounted for perhaps 90 percent or more of Baghdad's revenues in the 1980s). According to official U.S. estimates, Iraqi oil exports, which averaged 1.6 million barrels a day in 1990, averaged only 100,000 barrels per day from 1992 to 1994.[47] Oil revenues, which had averaged over $11 billion a year between 1985 and 1990, fell to an estimated $1 billion a year or less between 1992 and 1994. Estimates of Iraq's total economic decline vary, but many informed observers guess that per capita output fell by more than half between 1990 and 1995. In addition to those economic setbacks, Iraq also suffered an economically and politically costly destruction of much of its military force during its 1991 defeat in the Gulf War.

As long as the economic sanctions against Iraq are effectively implemented, it has little alternative but to endure a pronounced economic slump. Iraq's fundamentals are not auspicious for counteracting the economic impact of tightly enforced restrictions on its international trade. Iraq's was a relatively undiversified economy, highly dependent on oil exports for its international earnings, characterized by a fairly high ratio of trade to domestic output. Its national population is neither large (about 20 million) nor particularly well educated (over 40 percent adult illiteracy, according to the World Bank);[48] those particulars place distinct limits on both the potentialities of the domestic market and on the capabilities of economic agents and organizations to respond to exogenous economic shocks.[49]

Just as with Cuba, however, years of steep economic decline do not yet seem to have brought Iraq's ruling powers to the point of political crisis. And, as with Cuba, much of the regime's success to date in quelling potentially destabilizing pressures can be credited to the system's carefully developed capabilities for social control and to the political skills of the top leadership.[50] The internal security apparats operated by the Iraqi state and by the Baath Party appear to be fearsomely efficient—possibly the "best" ever in the Arab-speaking world. Saddam Hussein's personal role in keeping a complex and potentially highly volatile situation under control, moreover, should not be minimized. Leadership matters, and whatever else may be said of him, it would appear that Saddam understands Iraqi politics better than any of his domestic or international opponents.[51] Centralizing control around a core group of trusted family members, relying heavily upon the loyalty of his own clan (the Takriti), and playing to the powerful strain of stubborn and defiant nationalist sentiment for the many groups with which he would otherwise have little affinity have proved so far to be a winning formula for Saddam Hussein.

From the standpoint of economic management, while it is incontestable that international sanctions have dramatically reduced Iraq's production possibilities, it also seems to be the case, as Patrick Clawson has argued, that "Iraq has adjusted to sanctions to a degree not anticipated by people who placed high hopes in sanctions when they were first adopted."[52] Strict and austere rationing (enacted the month of the UN sanctions) has afforded the population under Saddam's control a guarantee of (bare) caloric adequacy. In contrast to the populist package of responses to economic difficulties so often proffered in modern Middle Eastern politics, Baghdad ruthlessly cut back public-sector employment (including military personnel) after sanctions and battlefield defeat; at the same time, Baghdad attempted to stimulate the growth of the private service sector by relaxing previous restrictions on it. Demonstrated indifference to the prospects of Iraq's "middle class" (educated workers lacking direct access to hard currency or tradable goods) permitted a strategy in which the burdens of adjustment fell disproportionately on that group. Ingenious efforts to circumvent sanctions—through border smuggling, illegal sale of booty from Kuwait, drawdown of gold stocks, expenditures from unidentified (thus unfrozen) foreign bank accounts, and other devices—have enhanced the regime's capabilities to procure imports from abroad. Although such magnitudes are conjectural, some observers guess that Iraq has managed to import about $3 billion in goods and services a year—far less than before Baghdad's Kuwait adventure, but roughly twice what the UN sanction regimen originally envisioned. What Clawson observed about the advent of the sanctions regime seems to obtain, at least to some degree: "Outside analysts . . . had only the vaguest idea of what Iraq had in the way of stocks and adjustment capacity when the sanctions started."[53]

And what of North Korea? As Pyongyang's leadership has repeatedly emphasized,[54] the unexpected loss of Soviet aid and trade in 1990 and 1991 constituted a serious setback to the national economy. If so, it was a setback from which DPRK trade performance has yet to recover: the absolute volume of North Korean trade turnover (calculated in current dollars and at official exchange rates) is believed to have declined almost continuously between 1990 and 1994[55] and appears to have fallen still further since then. On the one hand, North Korea's trade fall-off does not seem to have been so precipitous as Cuba's or perhaps Iraq's. On the other hand, in absolute terms DPRK imports per capita—perhaps $50 a year—are far lower than Cuba's (about $180) or Iraq's (perhaps $150), and North Korea's current ratio of imports to domestic output is also probably far lower.

Unlike wartime Germany and Japan, North Korea has only a medium-sized domestic population (20-some million people) and only a moderate endowment of the natural resources its economy requires to continue functioning (energy products being perhaps the most critical constraint). Without securing access to such resources through imports, the DPRK's socialist economy, as currently structured, can be expected to undergo continuing stagnation and decline.[56] To date, however, no turnaround in DPRK trade performance is evident.

In that respect, North Korea's response to its Soviet trade shock differs diametrically from Vietnam's, where external economic pressures were met by output- and productivity-augmenting macroeconomic policy shifts. North Korea's circumstances also differ from Iraq's, where formally applied international trade pressures cannot be relieved without the nation's first explicitly conceding to foreign diplomatic and military demands. The North Korean case is most analogous to the Cuban, where the regime also theoretically has the option of revitalizing trade through economic liberalization but declines to do so.[57]

In both Cuba and North Korea, Communist Party leadership appears to have calculated that it is preferable to deal with the economic stresses created by the nations' respective trade shocks than to attempt seriously to alleviate them. Like Iraq's, both Cuba's and North Korea's state systems and official ideologies seem well suited to handling the political turbulence that might ordinarily accompany economic decline. Both Havana and Pyongyang can rely on world-class internal security forces; in North Korea, moreover, the degree of social control may be even more complete than in Cuba. Both national directorates (in contradistinction to apartheid South Africa's) have striven to inculcate the sentiment of solidarity in the face of common sacrifice—a theme that may resonate especially in countries with a tradition of nationalist resistance to foreign pressure. More subtly, both regimes can play upon popular anxieties about what the future may hold if their political systems should fail: upon what "unification" will mean if it comes on terms established by hostile and unforgiving compatriots.[58]

In meeting the common challenge of managing the stresses attendant on inadequate adjustments to exogenous economic shock, the Cuban and North Korean regimes appear to have some contrasting assets and liabilities. On the one hand, it would appear to be to North Korea's advantage that its population was larger, that its socialist economy was more diversified, and that its dependence on foreign trade was lower at the onset of its trade shocks. It would also seem to be to North Korea's distinct advantage that communication with the outside world—a factor that may bear on public perceptions of regime legitimacy—has been so much more restricted. On the other hand, North Korea's defense effort appears to be far more costly to the national economy than does Cuba's; all other things being equal, Pyongyang's military commitments mean that the DPRK economy would have to cope with the greater stresses under exogenous external shocks. By the same token, while the North Korean socialist economy may be more diversified than the Cuban, it also appears to be even more severely distorted;[59] with other things equal, that suggests that supply-side responses to exogenous shocks would be more inadequate. Finally, and perhaps most important, diverse indications suggest that North Korea is far nearer the margin of nutritional subsistence today than is Cuba. Qualitatively, ideologically, and politically, coping with a shortage of consumer goods is fundamentally different from coping with the specter of hunger.

Food Shortages and Hunger Problems
under Command Planning

North Korea is certainly not the first centrally planned economy to confront domestic food shortages. Episodic but severe food shortages are in fact a characteristic and arguably predictable consequence of the twentieth-century Marxist-Leninist state's approach to economic management and economic development. Indeed, until recently the DPRK seemed to be something of an exception to regional rules. Up until the early 1990s, North Korea was the only communist state in Asia that had *not* suffered from a severe food problem, a bout of mass hunger, or a famine.

Mongolia and North Vietnam, for example, both experienced serious food shortages within the first decade of communist rule (for Mongolia, in the early 1930s; for North Vietnam, in 1955 and 1956).[60] Outright famine erupted in the Soviet Union on several occasions, perhaps the most devastating being in 1933;[61] it gripped China in the years 1959 to 1961,[62] and it engulfed Cambodia from 1977 to 1979.[63]

The operative and defining feature of virtually all previous food crises under communist states is that they were policy-induced—or at the very least, policy-intensified. The single obvious exception to that generalization involved the nutritional shocks that befell the Soviet Union in war time from 1941 to 1945.[64] Government policy and practices either directly caused or severely exacerbated each of the aforementioned famines. And in virtually every previous serious food problem experienced under communist rule, extreme food shortages have been the direct result of a new regimen of far-reaching state interventions into agriculture.

In almost every case, moreover, the afflicting state interventions have been almost identical. The three overlapping policies typically to come into force immediately before a severe communist food shortage have been: a sudden decreed change in property rights or ownership structure on the farm; significantly increased state taxes or procurement quotas for agricultural produce; and a promulgated shift (that is, deterioration) in the established terms of trade between food and nonfood goods.

Owing to the nature of those interventions and the incidence of their costs, severe food shortages under communism have typically been a rural—not an urban—problem. And generally speaking, the severity of the food shortage has varied in proportion to the intensity of the state's adverse policy interventions. The 1933 Soviet famine in Ukraine, for example, appears to have been largely brought on by sharp increases in stipulated procurement quotas in 1932; the great Chinese famine followed the communization of farms, the widespread institution of communal "mess hall" dining, and a drastic increase in procurement, all in 1958 and 1959; the Cambodian famine was triggered by an indigenous and perhaps even more radical application of the same "Great Leap Forward" techniques.[65]

Note that the major loss of life exacted by famine in each of those instances required active and severe indifference on the part of state authorities to the plight of their rural subjects. The Soviet Union's 1933 famine ("excess mortality" of approximately 7 million)[66] was essentially delimited to the borders of the Ukrainian SSR, and not by accident; the Stalin government had chosen to use hunger as an instrument of terror in its quest to achieve complete mastery over a still largely unwilling nationality. Indeed, during the depths of the Ukrainian famine, Soviet troops were actually emplaced at border points to prevent travelers from smuggling food into the desperate region. In Cambodia ("excess mortality" of approximately 1 million),[67] hunger was selectively inflicted on the "new people" who had inhabited areas not controlled by the Khmer Rouge in the early 1970s; the official attitude toward the suspect "new people" was epitomized in the Khmer Rouge aphorism, "To save you is no gain—to destroy you is no loss." In China ("excess mortality" of approximately 30 million)[68] famine was not used purposefully as a tool of social control; instead, deadly hunger spread and worsened as the Maoist government stubbornly pressed on with its Great Leap Forward program, in apparent disbelief of all reports of the dire hardships it was causing in the countryside.[69]

Because severe food shortages under communist governments were typically policy-induced, the states in question were commonly able to "solve" their food crises simply by relaxing or moderating harsh and destructive innovations. After a terrible fall-off in the country's livestock population, for example, the Mongolian People's Republic in 1933 relented on its collectivization of animal husbandry and postponed that objective until after World War II.[70] North Vietnam's "food crisis" subsided with a drop in procurement quotas and an improvement in agriculture's terms of trade.[71] Ukraine's famine ended when the Soviet government reduced the procurement quota for the republic and lifted the de facto embargo against food shipments into the region. In China, policy changed course when food shortages began to affect the urban centers; at that point, the government reduced procurement quotas, improved the terms of trade for foodstuffs, switched from being a net exporter to a net importer of food grains, and acquiesced in a headlong retreat from communal farming, even to the point of temporarily permitting tenancy-style individual farming throughout much of the country.[72]

One may observe that those aforementioned food crises, though triggered by predictably injurious state policies and thus at least theoretically corrosive of state legitimacy, did not typically result in regime crisis, political destabilization, or state collapse. The only instance to date of a communist state's downfall at a time of severe and mounting hunger is that of Democratic Kampuchea in 1978—and the precipitating factor in that case of state collapse was not the hunger of the local population, but instead the invasion and occupation of the country by military forces from neighboring Vietnam after several years of steady and escalating diplomatic friction between Phnom Penh and Hanoi.

Severe food shortages, furthermore, seem to have placed no obvious or general constraints on the conduct of foreign policy for the communist states affected by them, at least in the past. During the Ukrainian famine, Soviet foreign policy was not hindered or disrupted in any visible manner; in fact, one of Moscow's key diplomatic objectives of the day—normalizing relations with Washington—was achieved in 1933. The existence of severe domestic famine, likewise, has not historically served as a moderating influence on the international policies of the stricken communist state. Recall the example of China: from 1959 to 1961, Beijing not only adhered to an increasingly confrontational posture toward Moscow and escalated its "Three Worlds" rhetoric for international anti-imperial revolution, but also engaged in border disputes and border clashes with India.[73]

How did communist states in the past maintain social and political control during periods of severe food problems? Despite variations from one case to the next, the basic patterns seem to have been the same: the governments in question maintained a ruthless monopoly of force in the countryside and imposed relentless censorship over all media of communications. In practice, the monopoly of force, applied through both internal security organs and local party structures, preempted organized discontent in the countryside. Terror and official violence figured in all of those efforts to cow local peasants, but the prevalence and intensity of such direct physical threats seems to have varied widely both between and within the countries under consideration. No less important, the monopoly of force was used to prevent peasants from moving from stricken areas and to preclude unauthorized migration more generally.[74] Despite strict controls on travel, over 20 million Chinese peasants made their way to cities between 1958 and 1960.[75] That was a critical factor in the mounting pressure on urban food supplies and thus ultimately in reversing the "Great Leap" policies. Thoroughgoing censorship—including stringent penalties against individuals for breaking censorship discipline—was required and enforced to suppress information about unfolding local food crises. Suppressing such information served a multiplicity of purposes: it left victims of the food crises atomized and isolated from other potential grievants; it protected the image of infallibility, competence, and success that every vanguard party strove to create and, arguably, required to function effectively; and it deceived adversaries, both at home and overseas, who might capitalize on any signs of weakness in the country in question. China's amazing success in controlling information about the Great Leap famine is indicated by the fact that foreign researchers generally did not begin to suspect the true magnitude of the 1959–1961 losses until fully two decades after the event.

What does the historical experience of severe food shortages under communist regimes suggest about the current North Korean situation? At the moment, it is difficult to assess the actual extent and incidence of severe hunger in the DPRK—much as one would expect, historically speaking, from a well-functioning communist regime. Such details matter greatly. Lacking them, one may begin by observing that communist regimes in the past have managed to cope politically with deadly hungers that have ravaged broad portions of their population, even for several successive years—and have furthermore sometimes emerged from those food crises to enter or resume a period of brisk industrial growth.

At the same time, a number of obvious and important differences between the current North Korean food problem and earlier communist food crises can be identified. For one thing, all previous severe food shortages in communist economies took place in countries that were overwhelmingly rural and agrarian. Mongolia, North Vietnam, Ukraine, China, and Cambodia were all 80-plus percent rural at the time. North Korea, by contrast, had a predominantly nonagricultural and urbanized economy by the late 1980s.[76] North Korea's food problem differs from previous food crises under communism in that it apparently affects an economy with distinctly higher per capita production capabilities (including a relatively high-productivity, high-input agricultural sector). That means, among other things, that achieving household-level "food self-sufficiency" is simply not an option for most of the North Korean population; in the past, that always was an option for communist populations under extreme nutritional stress.

Second, the timing of the current North Korean food problem differs dramatically from that in previous communist food crises. In virtually all previous communist food crises, the big food problems occurred within a decade of the establishment of the regime. Those crises may be seen as part of the process of system consolidation. One could even argue that they were part of a grim "learning curve" about food security for those earlier communist regimes. In North Korea, by contrast, the food crisis of the mid- to late 1990s has emerged in a fully mature Marxist-Leninist polity, in which a vanguard party has held power for fully half a century.

Third, in previous communist food crises, the offending policy interventions contributing to nutritional distress were both newly introduced and self-evident, thus lending themselves to a relief through policy reversal. It is not clear that North Korea follows that pattern.

Surprisingly little seems to be known about North Korea's contemporary agrarian policies or their actual implementation in practice. DPRK media extolled the virtues of a "transition to all-people's ownership in agriculture" in 1994 and early 1995[77] but went silent about that after the official appeal for international food aid and the official announcement of massive damage from flooding later in 1995. Does one infer that a change in property relations on the cooperatives was attempted but shelved after disastrous results? Alternatively, does one infer that, in attempting to transform the farmers into state employees, the campaign was an abortive effort to extract greater surplus from them— and signified official recognition that North Korea's food situation was already ominous in the *early* 1990s? Without additional information, it is difficult to say.

If we could trace North Korea's current food difficulties to an ill-advised lurch in agricultural policy, we would expect the problem to be intrinsically remediable through a relaxation and liberalization of the economic regimen. (Whether such a direction would be politically acceptable to DPRK authorities, of course, is another question.) If, on the other hand, we cannot link the current food shortages to obvious and untoward recent policy changes, that would suggest that the problem is more deeply systemic in nature and therefore ultimately perhaps much more intractable.[78] Whichever the case may be, it is apparent that the North Korean economy is organizationally more complex than were the communist economies beset by severe food shortages in the past. Although those complex linkages are conducive to enhanced productivity, they may also paradoxically make the food problem more difficult to solve if economic planners insist on cleaving to what they view as a "low-risk" economic strategy.

A final difference between the current North Korean food problem and earlier communist food problems concerns the role of information and communications. It is not possible, in this era of "information revolutions," for the DPRK to suppress information about its food problem completely. Nor, for that matter, is it clear that the regime wishes to do so: witness the appeals for international emergency food aid in 1995 and subsequent years.[79] It seems quite possible that more information about the nation's hunger troubles might circulate domestically in North Korea today than in any previous communist food crisis, North Korea's formidable monopoly of local media notwithstanding. How such a difference might bear on systemic stresses is impossible to quantify but is worth keeping in mind.

Given some of the basic differences between the forensics of the current North Korean food problem and previous food crises under communism, it may be worthwhile to speculate about the arithmetic of food shortage in the DPRK—that is, about the magnitude and regional distribution of production shortfalls—in conjunction with the geography of food demand within the DPRK. If the rudimentary "food balance sheets" constructed by outside observers are correct, North Korea is currently experiencing an annual "deficit" of roughly 2 million tons of cereal.[80] Assuming those estimates to be correct and assuming further that neither reserve stocks nor external humanitarian aid fully make up the loss, how would the DPRK's political economy cope with an absolute drop in grain supplies of, say, 1 million tons?

Three hypotheses come immediately to mind. First, in the face of a shortfall of that order of magnitude, the socialist distributional mechanisms in the DPRK economy would be placed under extraordinary pressure—unprecedented pressure, in fact, in the annals of the centrally planned economy. That would be so, quite simply, because a much greater proportion of the total population does not produce its own food in the DPRK today than was the case in any of the communist systems that experienced severe food shortages in the past. From the standpoint of state security, of course, avoiding a breakdown in the state food distribution system would be a matter of the highest urgency—but it would also be a formidable challenge.

Second, with a hypothetical grain shortfall of that magnitude, it would be impossible to spare the urban population and the nonagricultural workforce from significant nutritional reversal. That is so, quite simply, because the DPRK's labor force has too few farmers to permit a policy of "squeezing the countryside" any realistic chance of success. If roughly one-fourth of the civilian labor force toils in agriculture, as official statistics suggested it did in the late 1980s,[81] forcing the entire production shortfall onto the farm population would require a *zero* calorie diet of them. If farmers are to be sturdy enough to harvest their next crop, neither that nor many other "solutions" predicated on extreme deprivation for the farm population can be feasible. Urban areas, which house the majority of the DPRK's population, must also assume the brunt of adjusting to cereal shortfalls of the magnitude hypothesized here.

But we would not expect the pain to be shared entirely equally by the DPRK's nonagricultural population, which brings us to the third hypothesis. In the DPRK's official distribution system, some claimants are more equal than others: among the groups treated with special consideration are the military, inhabitants of Pyongyang (and perhaps a few other major cities), and the families of workers employed in priority enterprises. Those groups, however, happen to encompass a fairly large proportion of North Korea's nonagricultural population: perhaps as many as 6 million of a nonagricultural population of perhaps 18 million. In a zero-sum game in which the objective is to protect one's own nutritional status, the ratio of more privileged to less privileged claimants could matter greatly to specific outcomes. We might therefore speculate that groups expected to suffer special nutritional stresses from a food shortfall of the magnitude hypothesized here would include the rural nonagricultural civilian population and the inhabitants of second- or third-tier urban centers without access to such priority professions as military industries or those that generate hard currency.

Under such circumstances, one would expect intense pressures among those groups to "solve their own food problem." Among the constellation of personal solutions imaginable would be reverse migration (from cities to food-producing agricultural cooperatives) and extra-legal barter with food-producing areas. While relieving nutritional distress for less privileged segments of the nonagricultural population, however, all those adjustments would tend to undermine or compromise the functioning of the DPRK official economic system as it is currently constituted.[82]

Concluding Observations

This chapter can conclude with five summary points. First, the economic pressures and problems confronting the DPRK's socialist system
today appear to have no precise analogy in recent historical experience.
Some countries have coped—or failed to cope—with the great challenges entailed in mobilization for total war. None, however, appears to
have been set so close to a total war footing for so long a period of
time—certainly no country at the DPRK's rough level of per capita output. Other communist states have experienced severe food shortages,
but in none of them did food crises emerge after "socialist transformation" was long completed and "socialist construction" had been in
progress for decades. The exogenous external shock to North Korea's
trade regimen over the past several years is analogous, in magnitude
and timing, to those in Cuba and Iraq—but the DPRK economy faces
additional stresses that the latter two systems do not.

Second, although the pressures on North Korea's political economy
today are acute and still mounting, the DPRK's polity would also appear to be exceptionally well suited to dealing with the economic stresses
it now endures. The DPRK enforces an exceptional degree of social
control over its subjects and reinforces that control by a to-date singularly successful policy of obstructing communication and contact with
the outside world. All that appears to make the "rules of the game" for
managing economic decline rather different from those in societies and
polities with which outside observers are more familiar.

Third, regardless of the DPRK's success to date in managing the
stresses that have accompanied its economic decline, it is well to remember that economies under severe stress can in fact collapse—and
in fact have done so in the relatively recent past. Although economic
collapse is a somewhat ambiguous concept—a term whose meaning is
made no clearer by promiscuous use in political rhetoric—one incontestible indication of *economic collapse* is a hunger crisis precipitated
by a breakdown of the national food system (construing that system
broadly). An industrial economy that can no longer arrange to feed its
people is an economy in collapse. It is also worth recalling that in Germany and Japan—the two clearest cases of economic collapse in our
century—economic collapse *preceded* regime collapse, not vice versa.

Fourth, while the cataclysmic conditions that led to economic collapse in Germany and Japan were fundamentally different from the constellation of economic problems currently plaguing the DPRK, the quali-

tative difference in the economic stresses in question does not in itself indemnify the DPRK against the risk of a similar qualitative outcome. If the DPRK system has singular capabilities in certain areas, it may also have weaknesses and limitations that are not well understood by outsiders (or perhaps even by top leadership). To understand the nature of the interplay between economic stress and regime capability in the DPRK, then, it is not enough to focus on current economic trends. To the contrary, it would seem absolutely essential to start with a better understanding of the performance and limitations of the DPRK economy before it entered into the present period of mounting economic stresses. Only in that way could it be possible systematically to assess the ability of the DPRK political economy to surmount or endure its current economic challenges.

Finally, it is worth asking about the sorts of externally observable signals of impending systemic dysfunction that students of North Korea should watch for. We must presume that much of the information we would want will continue to be unavailable (specific economic policy directives and the manner in which they are actually implemented, for example). One possible indication of unmanageable economic stresses, however, could come from demographic data. Migration data, for example, could indicate whether "deurbanization"—a necessary consequence of breakdowns in a national food system—has begun or is accelerating in the country as a whole or in particular regions. As already mentioned, my hypothesis is that deurbanization would first occur in the second- or third-tier cities—not in the privileged, "imperial" capital of Pyongyang. Vital statistics—birth rates and death rates—could similarly indicate whether the local population is undergoing severe social and economic stresses and whether the DPRK polity can still protect against the social upheavals that are registered in "demographic shocks."[83] Like all other sorts of DPRK data, demographic data are hard to come by. But because they stand to provide singularly unambiguous representations of the systemic stresses we have discussed, they are well worth continuing to seek.

4

★

Inter-Korean Economic Cooperation: Rapprochement through Trade?

With the fundamentally menacing security situation of the Korean peninsula in the background—and hopes episodically buoyed by such events as the 1994 Washington-Pyongyang "Agreed Framework" or the 1998 inauguration of the incoming Kim Dae Jung administration's "sunshine policy" in the foreground—analysts and policymakers both in Korea and beyond are today anxiously examining and evaluating the nonmilitary instruments of diplomacy at their disposal in their quest to preserve the region's fragile peace.[1] Among those diverse alternatives to force, perhaps none is accorded such promise as a purposeful intensification of inter-Korean economic activity. Over the past decade—and in striking contrast to the first four decades of their existence—Korea's two states have agreed in principle to trade with one another. In practice, that commerce has at least arguably become consequential. It is widely believed, for example, that South Korea is now North Korea's third-largest trading partner and that it has held that status for most of the 1990s.[2] Cumulatively, the volume of North-South trade, in Seoul's official estimate, is fast approaching $2 billion[3]—not a small sum, some would say, for countries formally locked in a state of war. With major inter-Korean projects both public[4] and private[5] already contracted and underway, North-South commerce would seem poised not only to continue, but perhaps to expand significantly, in the years ahead.

By broadening and deepening North-South commercial contacts—through trade, joint ventures, technology transfer arrangements, infrastructure development projects, and perhaps other initiatives—many observers believe that it will be possible to lessen tensions in the Korean peninsula and thus create a community of mutual financial interests to weigh against and counterbalance confrontational tendencies. In addition, many Western and South Korean proponents of increased North-South economic cooperation expect that the process of forming commercial ties with North Korea may have a beneficial effect on Pyongyang's internal decisionmaking—as the regime (by that thinking) liberalizes or at least relaxes through exposure to the outside world. The theory behind that viewpoint may be described as "rapprochement through trade"—*Annäherung durch Handel,* so to speak—a distinct but nonetheless familiar variation of the formula pursued by the Federal Republic of Germany over the generation before its ultimate peaceful reunification.[6]

Arguments for Rapprochement through Trade

Proponents of such an approach to reducing tensions in the Korean peninsula can make four independent, but interrelated, arguments for their case. The first, quite simply, is that the North Korean system is objectively in need—perhaps in desperate need—of precisely those quantities that intensified inter-Korean economic cooperation could provide. The North Korean economy, after all, is under intense pressure, and its performance appears to have deteriorated sharply in recent years. Despite the famous scarcity of official statistics from the Democratic People's Republic of Korea (DPRK), students of the North Korean economy from South Korea, the West, and even from Russia generally agree that its condition has devolved from "stagnation of the Eighties" to "decline of the Nineties."[7] Moreover, scholars widely agree that a major factor contributing to North Korea's current economic woes was the trade shocks it suffered in the aftermath of the "revolutions of 1989." In the 1980s, according to Western estimates, something like three-fifths of North Korea's total trade turnover was transacted with the Warsaw Pact states.[8] Between 1989 and 1991, with the advent of hard currency terms of customs settlement in that region, the DPRK's trade with that grouping plummeted by two-thirds or more—so sharply, in fact, that the total volume of North Korean trade contracted by over a third, perhaps even by as much as a half.[9] The end of aid and trade from the Council for Mutual Economic Assistance bloc may have been an even more serious blow to the North Korean economy than those rough totals would suggest, insofar as CMEA states had been directly involved in designing, constructing, and maintaining so much of North Korea's industrial infrastructure.[10] In short, if North Korea is to recover even to its hardly enviable economic status circa 1988—much less progress beyond status quo ante—it is essential that international economic bonds be formed to replace the ones severed by the end of the cold war.

A second argument is that North Korea's leadership is well aware of the country's deep economic difficulties and of the urgency with which trade opportunities and other international economic contacts must now be pursued. Note that this second point is quite different from the first; in the past North Korean planners have not always cared, and may not even have understood, when their policies were imposing distortions and costly inefficiencies on the national economy.[11] In December 1993—for the first time in the regime's history—the end of a multiyear economic plan was heralded by the announcement that its key objectives and targets had not been achieved; the official communiqué, moreover, specifically attributed the plan's failure to the collapse and disappearance of "world socialist markets."[12] A few weeks later, in Kim Il Sung's annual New Year's Day address, promotion of foreign trade was explicitly accorded a "top priority" in economic policy for the coming year.[13] Kim's pronouncement, however, followed rather than preceded policy movement consistent with an economic opening by Pyongyang. Over the previous three and a half years, in fact, the North Korean Supreme People's Assembly had been the scene of a comparative flurry of legislative activity, having passed and enacted perhaps a dozen laws intended to encourage foreign business to participate in North Korea's economic development and having even amended the DPRK constitution to countenance certain kinds of private property relations within its administrative jurisdiction.[14] After Kim Il Sung's July 1994 death, all sessions of the DPRK Supreme People's Assembly were suspended for more than four years; from a formal standpoint, no new legislation of any sort could be issued during that hiatus. With the assembly's September 1998 convocation that ratified Kim Jong Il's accession to the state's "top position," however, a revised DPRK Constitution was also issued. That document contained three articles pertaining to foreign trade, including one (Article 37) specifically stipulating that the "State shall encourage . . . joint venture enterprises with corporations or individuals of foreign countries."[15] Thus, while North Korea's decisionmaking structure remains mysterious to the outside world, the regime can be seen as sending out continuing signals of a top-level commitment to effecting an improved trade situation.

The third argument is that an economic opening in North Korea would be in South Korea's own financial interest, rather than simply an exercise in checkbook diplomacy. With its rapid economic development and concomitant increase in wages, South Korea has, over the past decades, moved far along the "product cycle"; whereas South Korean management retains considerable expertise in producing lower-wage goods, it lacks the lower-wage labor force necessary for them. Instead of moving operations out of the Korean peninsula or closing them down altogether, integration with North Korea would offer South Korean *chaebol* local opportunities for expanding production and profits.[16] To the extent that increased economic ties could foster development and modernization in North Korea, moreover, such ties would (by that thinking) ultimately reduce the cost of unification that South Korean taxpayers and businesses would be forced to bear. As they have contemplated the example of Germany, analysts and policymakers in South Korea have been stricken with a variant of "sticker shock"; from the initial post-*Einheit* calculations by the Korea Development Institute of under $250 billion[17] to the 1994 announcement by the Twenty-first Century Commission of a $1.2 trillion price tag for the venture[18] to the 1997 estimate by American economists of a $1.7 billion capital requirement for North Korea to raise its per capita income to 60 percent of the level in the South,[19] the estimated costs of Korea's reunification seem to have risen inexorably.[20] Containing those costs, proponents of inter-Korean trade argue, can only be in the Korean national interest.[21]

Fourth, South Korea has a record of demonstrated success in bringing formerly hostile communist states to the point of rapprochement and beyond, through economic diplomacy.[22] The Republic of Korea's *Nordpolitik*, launched in July 1988, resulted in an almost immediate improvement in relations with several East European states—improvements, one should note, that predated their internal crises the following year. *Nordpolitik* similarly brought ROK–USSR relations to a state of positive civility, if not outright good-neighborliness, in the period before the eventual dissolution of the Soviet Union. With China, where communist rule has been maintained, the ROK enjoys a large and seemingly ever-growing commerce, and the two states have moved beyond the formality of mutual recognition into a substantive diplomatic relationship. The latest success for South Korean economic diplomacy is the Socialist Republic of Vietnam. One should remember that *Nordpolitik* has, in several instances, overcome bitter memories and tangled historical legacies: the USSR, after all, was responsible for the horrifying KAL 007 incident, and South Korean forces fought in major if undeclared wars against both Chinese and Vietnamese troops.

Taken together, those arguments may seem to speak convincingly to the possibility of an inter-Korean rapprochement based on trade. In this chapter, however, I attempt to demonstrate that they do not. Under current conditions, I argue, the chances that an expansion of economic contacts between North Korea and South Korea could lead to a reduction of tensions in the peninsula, much less pave the way for a genuine rapprochement between those two embattled states, must be judged as remote.

Attention to the particulars of the situation will demonstrate that the actual scope for *mutually* beneficial economic contacts between North and South is much more limited than is often supposed, owing to stark but sometimes overlooked constraints. A review of the experiences of other communist regimes furthermore indicates that trade with—and even subsidies from—capitalist countries did little to moderate the policies, much less alter the viewpoint, of top leadership on matters relating to national security. Finally, a closer examination of the situation in contemporary North Korea seems to suggest that its disposition of policy—legislative activity and official pronouncements notwithstanding, Kim Il Sung's death notwithstanding, and even the "Agreed Framework" and the "sunshine policy" notwithstanding—remains overwhelmingly hostile to anything more than a limited, tightly policed, tactical commercial opening to the South.

This is not to say that Pyongyang might not accept financial assistance, even outright bequests, if Seoul offers them. It is instead to argue that such transfers, under current conditions, would be exceedingly unlikely to promote the cause of rapprochement—and might actually increase security dangers in the peninsula. Unless and until there is evidence of dramatic change in the external strategy (or internal political structure) of the DPRK, it will be unrealistic and unreasonable to expect commerce to serve as a diplomatic vehicle for improving relations between the two Koreas.

Mutually Beneficial Economic Contacts:
Complicating Factors

At first glance, it might seem as if the scope for trade and economic cooperation with North Korea should be vast. After all, the DPRK's economic situation seems dire; its consumers' shelves are all but empty; its factories are by and large outmoded; its technological level is poor; its infrastructure in communications and transportation is underdeveloped; its hunger for imports is intense. Yet it does not follow from those particulars that prospects for inter-Korean economic cooperation are necessarily bright.

It is important to remember that the very regime and many of the very policymakers that have led North Korea to its current economic circumstances will also be presiding over any new initiatives undertaken in international economic relations. The criteria by which those leaders will weigh alternative possibilities for participating in the world economy are exceedingly complex. Suffice it to say that theirs is not the neat framework favored by students of neoclassical welfare economics.

One may object, of course, that this elusive neoclassical schema is never actually observed in the wild—that international trade policy almost always deviates from neoclassical economic doctrine's strictest conditions. In South Korea, it has been widely argued, government policy for several decades made a practice of "getting prices wrong," even as the country prospered through export-led growth.[23] But such deviations from that doctrine do not prima facie invalidate the principles, or the analytics, behind it. To the contrary, a growing corpus of studies indicates that South Korea's economic success over the past generation may have been achieved despite, rather than because of, the government's far-reaching attempts to recast "comparative advantage" in the national economy.[24] Those studies have long found an echo (if not a validation) in policy circles in Seoul, where industrial policy and other *dirigiste* interventions were increasingly described as expensive luxuries the nation cannot afford if it is to make a final advance into the rank of affluent Western societies—all well before the financial crisis of 1997.[25]

The point here is that South Korea, during its economic ascent, may have chosen to "get prices wrong," but it can also get them right when it so wishes—both domestically and in relation to the international economy. North Korea, by contrast, cannot. Not being able to do so, it correspondingly has no rational basis for assessing the economic merit of alternative proposals in the areas of import, export, joint venture, or infrastructure development.

North Korea's dilemma is hardly unique. Quite the contrary, it is completely characteristic of what Janos Kornai describes as the "classical socialist system."[26] Kornai's exposition of the workings of that system deserves and rewards careful reading. For the sake of brevity, a single selection may do:

> The segregation of domestic prices from import and export prices paid and received on the foreign market relates closely to the absence of a uniform rate of exchange between the domestic currency and each foreign currency. Nominally, an official rate is set . . . but in reality, this exchange rate is modified by various multipliers. . . . A tangle of taxes, tariffs, tax and tariff concessions, and temporary and permanent subsidies intervenes between the price paid or received on a foreign market and the price at home. Ultimately, there is no way of telling what a ruble is worth in dollars.[27]

What obtains for dollars and rubles holds as well for the two Korean *won.*

The consequences of such a priceless approach to international economic exchange are diverse. One of those is the classical socialist trade strategy, vividly depicted in Jan Winiecki's memorable phrase: "How to specialize with knowing one's comparative advantages."[28] In the context of a permanent "import hunger," "export aversion," and "propensity to indebtedness," however, the absence of reliable information about scarcity costs and opportunity costs has very real administrative implications. As Kornai explains:

> It is in the interest of everyone except those at the peak of the pyramid for capitalist imports to be as large as possible; there is no internal inducement to limit the demand voluntarily. The situation makes direct control of imports inevitable. . . . [Conversely,] the practice of forcing exports develops. Fulfillment of export assignments becomes one of the compulsory requirements of the plan.[29]

Lacking firm economic criteria for international commercial decisionmaking, classical socialist systems—like North Korea's—necessarily determine the volume and mix of imports and exports, the hierarchy of joint ventures, and the priority of investment projects by a political calculus. Within that calculus many noncommercial considerations intrude. We need mention only two of those to appreciate just how firm the constraints against a progressive expansion of North-South commerce presently are.

For the current leadership of the DPRK, the paramount objective today, as in the past, is the preservation and expansion of Korean socialism's power. Any developments that might destabilize or undermine "our Korean way of socialism" would be viewed as grave threats to national security and handled accordingly. One has good reason to think that North Korean authorities regard contact with individuals and information from the outside world as precisely such a destabilizing factor for their society.

One official post-mortem for socialism in Eastern Europe and the USSR, for example, attributed the collapse of those regimes to "imperialist" efforts at "infiltrating corrupt bourgeois ideology and culture into socialist countries in a bid to inoculate them with the wind of liberalization."[30] Yet to an inescapable degree, an increase of imports from capitalist countries—and even more so, the establishment in North Korea of joint ventures and foreign direct investment projects—run the risk of exposing the local populace to exactly the aforementioned corrupting winds. Those risks, from the standpoint of Pyongyang, may seem to be especially perilous if the agents of "corrupt bourgeois ideology and culture" were none other than Koreans from *"Nam-Choson."* For that reason alone, a general and unrestricted expansion of trade and commerce with South Korea, under current conditions, must be seen as out of the question; any arrangements agreed to would presumably be sanctioned because they were judged to make a minimal impression on the populace and to exert no significant impact on existing political arrangements.

That does not mean, however, that "noninoculating" economic contacts would necessarily meet with official approval. Like other Marxist-Leninist states, North Korea's leadership analyzes the struggle between "imperialist" and "socialist" camps in terms of the "correlation of forces." Such a concept is similar to, but arguably more subtle than, the familiar Western notion of "balance of power."[31] For Marxist-Leninist policymakers, it is axiomatic that one would never voluntarily encourage an unfavorable shift in the "correlation of forces" against the "main enemy." Yet it is easy to imagine a variety of ways in which expanded economic contact with South Korea might be construed to constitute just such an adverse shift. Substantial increases in North-South trade, joint ventures, and investment projects, for example, could easily be seen as increasing the DPRK's dependence upon the Republic of Korea. Such fears would not be irrational. Extensive literature documents the leverage that large trading partners may exert over smaller countries.[32] As "front rankers" in the struggle against imperialism would also surely know, "fascist" powers have a particular proclivity to use their international economic influence to affect the policies of smaller, neighboring countries.[33] Projects and possibilities that would expose North Korea to such pressures from the South would tend to arouse the utmost of suspicion.

Thus, the paradox. As presently organized, the North Korean economy may have something like an unquenchable demand for imports and overseas capital. As constituted, however, that same system has no economic basis for discriminating among projects and must do so instead on political grounds. For political reasons, the regime as presently constituted, for reasons of self-interest, may be expected to lean against regularized economic ties with South Korea—and to lean most strongly against initiatives that might carry the danger of encouraging what those in South Korea and the West would think of as "rapprochement."

Trade and Rapprochement under Other Communist Regimes

Let us now turn to the experiences of three other communist states: East Germany, the Soviet Union, and China. What guidelines and lessons emerge from those cases?

The German Democratic Republic (GDR). After a generation of *Ostpolitik*, a complete political rapprochement between West and East Germany was consummated by the accession of the territories of the former GDR into the Federal Republic. Having occurred essentially without violence, that was as happy a conclusion to the conflict between those two states as any observers would have dared imagine.

Does the successful result justify the FRG's inter-German policy—with its heavy emphasis on expanding trade with, and offering economic assistance to, the GDR?[34] In the view of Timothy Garton Ash, one of the most incisive chroniclers of that reconciliation, it does not. In his words:

> What is clearly wrong . . . is to judge the policy only by its final ending—revolution and unification. This may be good enough for politicians, but it is not good enough for historians. That outcome was very far from inevitable, and we must look at the interim as well as the final balance sheet.[35]

The reality as Garton Ash depicts it was more troubling. In his estimate, whereas a succession of governments in Bonn sought to effect a "liberalization through stabilization" of East German polity, the actual contribution of those efforts was "stabilization without liberalization" of the regime. In his view:

> [The GDR devised] a fairly shrewd strategy for political survival. . . . [T]he economic growth to underpin this welfare and consumer provision was not to be achieved by further market-oriented economic reforms . . . [but] by making the existing system (and people) work as hard and efficiently as possible; second, by technological innovation . . . and, last but not least, by opening to the West.
>
> One might describe this strategy as one of reform substitution. Social benefits and consumer goods were offered to the people not as complements to a reform, but as substitutes, and one of the main substitutes for reform was—imports. Imports of Western technology, whether obtained legally or illegally, . . . [i]mports of goods . . . [i]mports of DM. . . .
>
> Honecker was able to sustain this strategy virtually unchanged into the second half of the 1980s, thanks partly to (East) German good housekeeping . . . but also crucially, and increasingly, to the financial and economic advantages of the relationship with West Germany. . . .
>
> From the outset. . . the opening to the West was accompanied by redoubled efforts to maintain the Party's political control and ideological rigor. [*Stasi* chief Erich] Mielke would instruct his subordinates in the Ministry for State Security that for them peaceful coexistence meant "above all struggle." . . . [T]here was also an ideological escalation of what was officially called *Abgrenzung* (with connotations of "drawing the line" and "fencing off").[36]

In the period since German reunification, another aspect of the contradictions in *Ostpolitik* has come to light—one not mentioned in Garton Ash's evaluations. With the transfer of the archives of the GDR *Volksarmee* to the *Bundeswehr*, researchers and analysts have been able to glean a more accurate impression of East Germany's military posture toward West Germany during the era of detente. According to a recent study, whose results were deemed sufficiently significant to merit announcement by the German minister of defense,[37] the *Volksarmee*'s disposition against West Germany was more menacing and hostile than NATO planners had appreciated during the cold war.[38] Military preparations were for aggressive and unforewarned in-depth assault; munitions and equipment reserves for war fighting were much greater than had been supposed; and troops were kept, during the final years of East German socialism, on a state of virtual round-the-clock readiness for the command to begin the offensive.[39] Far from ushering in a relaxation of tensions, it appears as if *Ostpolitik* coincided with an increase in confrontational tendencies.

The East German regime, of course, could not launch an offensive of its own accord. The GDR was not an independent actor in the international arena. Its very lack of independence, in the final analysis, proved to be the decisive factor in German-German rapprochement. The Honecker regime collapsed after the Gorbachev Politburo indicated that Moscow would no longer support the GDR against internal challenges.[40] West German policy may ultimately have helped to undermine the GDR by contributing to a false sense of security on the part of the Socialist Unity Party's leadership—or as Garton Ash puts it, "[T]hey got it right because they got it wrong!" But as he also observes:

> It does not, of course, follow that getting it wrong is an advisable course in future dealings with other dictatorships. . . . The *salto morale* from stabilization without liberalization to liberation by destabilization only succeeded due to overriding external factors, above all the changes in Soviet policy and Eastern European politics, plus a generous slice of luck.[41]

The USSR and the Politics of Trade. Did economic cooperation with Western countries contribute to the Soviet Union's eventual effort at rapprochement with its erstwhile "imperialist" enemies? Observers who hold opinions on that question tend to hold them firmly; it is not obvious that proponents can be convinced or converted by reading a few short paragraphs.

Nevertheless, several comments on the Soviet experience seem in order. First, purposeful and dramatic expansion of economic contacts with capitalist countries took place in the Soviet Union under the Brezhnev Politburo. That period is now recalled in Russia as the "era of stagnation"—a time of neither political liberalization nor economic reform. Significant Soviet increases in commercial ties with Western countries in the early 1970s, moreover, were followed by a turn toward adventurism and confrontation in Soviet foreign policy in the late 1970s and early 1980s.[42]

Second, the changes in economic, political, and international policies that were inaugurated under Mikhail Gorbachev were adjustments in response to severe pressure. Note that this is not to suggest that Gorbachev's specific menu of adjustments was somehow "inevitable." Gorbachev inherited an "impoverished superpower," to borrow a phrase from Henry Rowen and Charles Wolf,[43] and struggled desperately—ultimately, unsuccessfully—to chart a course for it toward a viable modus operandi. It is worth recalling, however, that reform of the foreign trade sector—what we might call trade liberalization—never really made it off the table during the Gorbachev years. Joint ventures, programs for technology transfer, foreign direct investment, and the like were eagerly described and discussed by newspaper commentators, Soviet reform economists, and even by some within the Gorbachev circle, but those words never translated into action.[44] Gorbachev's was a rapprochement *without* economic cooperation—apart from the "cooperation" of accepting aid bequests from the West.

Third, it now appears that the Soviet Union's military buildup after the early 1960s and its expanded commerce with Western countries over that same period were not entirely unrelated phenomena. Igor Birman has made a strong case for the proposition that the Soviet military buildup was financed in part by "off-budget" subsidies and allocations.[45] The "profit" used to plug that hole in the Soviet state budget appears to have come in part from the arbitraging of "hard currency rubles" against domestic rubles. Thus, in at least that administrative sense, economic cooperation with Western countries directly underwrote the confrontational tendencies that, it was hoped, trade expansion might help to mitigate.

Trade Liberalization in China, 1978–1998. It is perhaps the instance of Chinese trade liberalization that offers proponents of an economic opening in North Korea their fondest model. The story of that dramatic succession of initiatives and reforms has been well recounted already[46] and does not require repetition here. What may be more pertinent is a reminder of some of the key differences between China's recent experiences and the current outlook for North Korea.

First and foremost, China's economic opening followed a change in the country's supreme leadership. It was only with the consolidation of power by Deng Xiaoping that the move toward world markets commenced. Deng Xiaoping, for his part, was not a sudden convert to the proposition that increased participation in international markets would redound to China's national interest. He had held, and expressed, variants of that position for decades—a fact that helped to account for his political travails during the Maoist era. The contrast in Pyongyang today is self-evident—Kim Il Sung's death notwithstanding.[47]

Second, Beijing's leadership has indicated its confidence not only in the permanence of its new approach to trade but also in its ability to withstand the destabilizing turbulence unleashed by increased contacts with citizens from the state with which it is locked in a battle for legitimacy. As early as 1990, over 21 million letters a year were crossing the Taiwan Strait; by 1992, over 1.5 million Taiwanese were visiting the mainland annually.[48] By 1998, according to official Chinese sources, Taiwanese entrepreneurs had established over 40,000 projects throughout China;[49] fully one-seventh of the entire population of Taiwan, moreover, was said to have already visited the Chinese mainland.[50] To ask the question whether Pyongyang would countenance such a traffic today is to answer it.

Third, China's rulers embarked upon a relaxation of direct administrative controls over interactions with the international economy almost at the outset of the process of economic opening. By the early 1990s, over 3,600 foreign trade corporations in China were authorized to conduct export business;[51] even in the mid-1980s, over 800 such firms were registered in operation.[52] In Guangdong province by itself, reportedly nearly 900 foreign trade corporations were doing business by the end of 1987.[53] By contrast, North Korea was said to have a total of 128 authorized foreign trade corporations as of late 1992.[54] In 1998, moreover, the total number of North Korean trading companies had reportedly been reduced to "around 100."[55] North Korea, of course, is far smaller than China; its population may amount to barely one-third of Guangdong's. But the point here is not foreign trade organizations per capita, but rather their absolute number. As an administrative and cybernetic matter, it may be possible to coordinate and tightly control the activities for 100 separate foreign trade organizations; it is hard to imagine doing so for 1,000 of them. North Korea has to date given no indication that it wishes to relinquish direct administrative control over any activities occurring in the sphere of external economic relations.

North Korea's Approach to Economic Cooperation

An extended discussion of current practices and policies in North Korea could detail the impediments that were emplaced against an inter-Korean rapprochement through trade during Kim Young Sam's presidency. Some of those would include: statist measures that have increased the distance between the DPRK's domestic markets and foreign markets;[56] demotion in 1993 of the political personalities most closely associated with the arguments for gradual economic opening;[57] continuing intransigence in redeeming outstanding debts to foreign creditors;[58]

continued military buildup; an emphasis on utilizing trade leverage to influence the foreign policy of its major capitalist trading partners;[59] and reports that the government's approach to the announced special economic zones around Najin and Sonbong is to "force residents in the region . . . to move out and [to] replace some of them"—an approach described in one report as a "region-lockout opening policy" *(kukchi pyeswoehyong kaebangchaek).*[60] One might further point to some of the inauspicious indications about North Korean policy that have to date emerged during Kim Dae Jung's presidency: the reported arrest of the North Korean official responsible for the development of the Najin-Sonbong "Free Economic and Trade Zone";[61] the reported autumn 1998 official renaming of that zone to remove the word *Free* from its title;[62] the apparent demotion of North Korea's bureau for economic cooperation with the South (the DPRK Administrative Council External Economic Affairs Commission), which reportedly is now a subsidiary branch of the North Korean trade ministry;[63] and the explicit delimitation, in the new September 1998 DPRK Constitution, of North Korean joint ventures with outsiders to *"a special economic zone"* (emphasis added)[64]—a step backwards, one might think, from the 1992 constitution, which placed no geographic strictures on the areas within which joint ventures were to be encouraged. But perhaps the most significant impediments are evidenced in the pronouncements of the regime's top leaders.

Kim Jong Il's declarations are of particular interest in this regard. Not only had he (according to his father's public statements) taken over the day-to-day management of the country's domestic and foreign policy in the last years of the Great Leader's life, but he has now, after a delay of several years, formally acceded to North Korea's top positions in both party and state. Kim Jong Il's words should thus provide insight into the outlook that informs official North Korean policy today and perhaps tomorrow.

A few statements by Kim Jong Il in recent years deserve special attention. Early in 1992 he issued this assessment of the reasons for the collapse of the Soviet bloc:

> One-step concessions and retreat from the socialist principles ha[ve] resulted in ten and a hundred step concessions and retreat, and, finally, invited grave consequences of ruining the working class parties themselves.

Some months later, surveying the prospects for that same region, he stated:

The resurgence of socialism is the only way out of the political, economic, ideological and moral confusion and crisis in the countries where capitalism has revived.[65]

In March 1993—days before North Korea announced its withdrawal from the Nonproliferation Treaty, the event that triggered the "North Korean nuclear crisis" of 1993 and 1994—he offered the following assessement of the domestic challenges at hand:

In the past . . . the remoulding of people's ideological consciousness was neglected in the practice of socialism because of the failure of the understanding that the basic driving force of the development of a socialist society lies in . . . their ideological consciousness. In particular, there were tendencies to rouse people's enthusiasm for production by means of such material levers as economic incentives. . . . If . . . emphasis is put merely on material incentives, this will reduce people to egoists. . . . In those societies which gave up education in socialist ideology and encouraged egoism, the building of socialist economy became stagnant. . . . [T]hey went so far as denying the leadership of the working-class party and state over the socialist economy.[66]

In August 1996, just days after the first joint venture between the DPRK and a South Korean company started operations in the North Korean port city of Nampo,[67] he issued this instruction to his country's youth:

Young people must . . . smash every attempt of the imperialists and reactionaries to disintegrate our socialism. They must sharpen their vigilance against the infiltration of all manner of antisocialist ideas and bourgeois mode of life, reject them categorically and staunchly defend the socialist ideology and our socialist system from the abuses, slanders and subversive moves by the enemies of socialism.[68]

In 1997, a few months before his acclamation as general secretary of the DPRK Korean Workers' Party, he provided this assessment of "capitalists"—whose same capital, presumably, would be utilized in the joint ventures that the North Korean government sanctioned:

The exploiting class which owns all the means of production and wealth in the capitalist society is interested only in making money. . . . Under capitalism there can be neither national equality nor free development of nations. . . . As the reality shows, in the countries which introduced the imperialists' "prescription," social problems and economic difficulties have become more serious and national dispute become aggravated.[69]

And in 1998—before his formal elevation to the DPRK's highest state office and after Kim Dae Jung had unveiled the principles of his administration's new "sunshine policy"—Kim Jong Il warned that:

> The south Korean authorities' anti-north confrontation policy is the root that gives rise to misunderstanding and distrust between the north and the south. . . . If the south Korean authorities continue to pursue the hostile anti-north confrontation policy, it will be impossible to create an atmosphere of trust and reconciliation between the north and the south. It will only increase tension and bring about an inevitable result.[70]

Many North Korean pronouncements admittedly have a certain delphic quality, and it is not always obvious that Western observers can correctly parse statements that their North Korean interlocutors feel to be crystal-clear. Taken together, however, those statements may be interpreted as offering a particular worldview. It is a worldview in which the setbacks to Soviet socialism are presumed to be merely temporary. By extension, the setbacks for North Korea in the international arena would also be seen as temporary. It is a worldview in which "concessions" in policy—what are perhaps regarded in the West as "reforms"—are considered not only inappropriate but absolutely fatal; in which any "capitalist" permeations threaten "our socialism" and must be "smashed"; and in which South Korea's implacable hostility to the North Korean system is not only taken as a given, but viewed as leading to "an inevitable result."

Proponents of rapprochement through trade would do well to reflect upon the Dear Leader's words. For in the final analysis, both the oscillating tensions in the peninsula and the impediments to expanded inter-Korean economic cooperation have less to do with technical issues than with the intentions of governments—and there is little evidence of any fundamental alterations of the latter in Pyongyang today.

5

Prospects for U.S.–
DPRK Economic Relations

For most of the history of the always troubled relationship between the governments of Pyongyang and Washington, the nature of the economic linkages between the Democratic People's Republic of Korea and the United States could be described in a single phrase: essentially nonexistent. Three days after the outbreak of the Korean War on June 25, 1950, the U.S. Congress approved legislation to ban all American exports to North Korea. Over the next four decades, the scope and specificity of U.S. legal sanctions against commercial and financial transactions steadily expanded. By the early 1990s, possibilities for any economic contact between the two countries were proscribed by at least ten separate American laws.[1] (See table 5-1.) Discretionary regulatory strictures, enforced by presidential authority but enjoying broad bipartisan support within Congress, further limited any remaining opportunities for commercial engagement between the two countries.

In the mid-1990s, however, America's posture toward economic contact with North Korea changed suddenly and substantially. With the signing of the U.S.–DPRK "Agreed Framework" on October 21, 1994 (a document through which American and North Korean negotiators jointly outlined a peaceful resolution to the North Korean nuclear confrontation of 1993–1994), America formally embraced a new approach toward economic relations with the DPRK: an approach that envisioned not only a progressive expansion of bilateral trade but also a de facto

Table 5-1 U.S. Sanctions against North Korea

Date	Related Laws	Sanctions
1/28/50	Export Control Act	Ban on exports to North Korea
12/17/50	Trading with the Enemy Act	Freeze on North Korean assets in United States; announcement of the Overseas Assets Control Regulations, which virtually placed a total ban on trade and monetary transactions with North Korea
9/1/51	Trade Agreement Extension Act	Prohibition from giving most-favored-nation status to North Korea
8/1/62	Foreign Assistance Act	Ban on grant of aid to North Korea
1/3/75	Trade Act of 1974	Prohibition from giving Generalized System of Preferences benefits to North Korea
5/16/75	Export Control Act	Application of a comprehensive embargo on North Korea by the U.S. Ex-Im Bank
10/5/86	Act on Ex-Im Bank	Prohibition from giving credits to North Korea by the U.S. Ex-Im Bank
1/20/88	Export Control Act	Listed as a terrorism-supporting country, North Korea was subjected to bans on trades, grants by the Generalized System of Preferences, the sale of articles listed among the munitions control items, and aid and credits from the Ex-Im Bank; U.S. instructions to vote against any international monetary institution's decision to grant aid to North Korea
4/4/88	International Arms Trading Regulations (revised)	Ban on sales of defense industry materials and services as well as imports and exports with North Korea
3/6/92	Munitions Control Items	Confirming North Korea was involved in giving missile technology to Iran and Syria, the United States banned the export of articles listed among the munitions control items and the government's contract with North Korea for two years; application of those bans on all activities of North Korea related to the manufacture of missiles, electronics, space aviation, and military aircraft

Source: Zachary S. Davis et al., *Korea: Procedural and Jurisdictional Questions Regarding Possible Normalization of Relations with North Korea,* Congressional Research Service Report for Congress (Washington, D.C.: Government Printing Office, November 29, 1994).

commitment to a long-term program of direct official aid from Washington to Pyongyang. Under the parameters of the "Framework Agreement," the U.S. government would provide (and the American public would pay for) up to half a million tons of heavy oil for North Korea per year until the "safe" Western-style nuclear reactors that were to be constructed in the DPRK by, and financed through, the new Korean Peninsula Energy Development Organization became operational. Commercial relations between the United States and the DPRK, for their part, were to be normalized as progress in other areas of contention was achieved.

America's embryonic economic relationship with North Korea has also been conditioned by developments wholly unanticipated in the "Agreed Framework." In the wake of Pyongyang's unprecedented 1995 formal international appeal for emergency food relief, the United States has assumed a role as a donor of humanitarian aid to North Korea. In comparison with other U.S. relief and food aid programs past and present, the current American initiatives under way for North Korea can be described as modest.[2] Yet in mobilizing what is by now hundreds of millions of dollars through private charities and taxpayer monies for the relief of a country to which Washington has never extended diplomatic recognition—and against which American troops in fact have long been deployed to defend U.S. allies—the American effort can nonetheless be regarded as strikingly new.

Commercial contacts between the United States and the DPRK seem to have started up in March 1995, with the U.S. Department of Commerce's approval of a 55,000-ton corn sale to North Korea by an American grain dealer.[3] Since that commencement, American authorities have approved a number of other transactions on a case-by-case basis, including telecommunications linkups, tourist excursions, airline overflight payments, purchases of North Korean magnesite, and a grain-for-DPRK-zinc barter deal.[4] In addition, representatives of some of America's largest businesses—including Coca-Cola, Boeing, and General Motors—have visited North Korea to explore possibilities for merchandizing arrangements, joint ventures, or direct investments.[5]

Given all those unexpected—some might once have said unimaginable—changes in the character of the American approach toward economic cooperation with North Korea over the past few years, we may well ask, What lies in store for this new U.S.–DPRK relationship in the period ahead? Do today's tentative and episodic American–North Korean business contacts presage a commercial relationship that will ultimately, in some meaningful sense, be "normalized"? Presuming a continuation of the DPRK's regime and system, how substantial an expansion of American–North Korean economic ties can we realistically envision? No less important, would a blossoming U.S.–DPRK economic relationship avail North Korea of the resources, markets, and managerial expertise that would at last permit Pyongyang to stabilize and revitalize its apparently badly faltering domestic economy?

Assessing the U.S.–DPRK Trade Outlook

To anyone seriously considering them, those are daunting questions. Each of those outcomes will be affected by a complex, quite likely changing, and very possibly unstable array of economic and political factors, not all of which can necessarily be identified beforehand and about many of which reliable information is currently unavailable.

How, then, does one approach the task of assessing the outlook for U.S.–DPRK commercial and financial relations? Three contrasting possibilities are suggested by the three different types of information now available for use in such an undertaking: prospective quantitative estimates; current expectations of concerned participants; and the DPRK's historical record of international economic performance.

Prospective Estimations. Some bold analysts have offered quantitative estimates of the potential and scope of U.S.–North Korean trade under more "natural" terms of intercourse. In South Korea, for example, the Korea Trade and Investment Promotion Agency reportedly concluded in 1994 that a full lifting of the U.S. trade embargo, in conjunction with improved North-South relations, could result in an immediate 10 percent increase in DPRK exports[6] (implying, roughly, a $100 million boost in DPRK sales abroad). Unfortunately, the reasoning and method underlying that calculation have not been fully explained.

In a much more methodologically transparent study on the North Korean economy, the American economist Marcus Noland has offered rather detailed computations bearing on a possible transition to a more normal trade regime for the DPRK.[7] As one may readily appreciate, U.S. economic sanctions against the North would presumably not be part of that more normal set of arrangements. Using a standard "gravity model" that does well predicting trade volumes elsewhere in the Asia-Pacific region, Noland concludes that, as of the early 1990s, roughly 7 percent of the DPRK's total trade turnover would have been expected to

Table 5-2 Actual and "Natural" North Korea Trade Shares (percent)

Actual Trade Shares		"Natural" Trade Shares	
China	26	South Korea	35
Japan	18	Japan	30
Russia	11	China	13
Iran	9	United States	7
Rest of world	36	Rest of world	15
Total trade in GDP	15	Total trade in GDP	71

Source: Marcus Noland, "Economic and Regional Cooperation in Northeast Asia," Joint U.S.–Korea Academic Studies, vol. 6 (1996), p. 162.

occur with the United States. (See table 5-2.) On the basis of that same model and the clearly tentative estimates of North Korean GNP used in it,[8] the implied total "natural" volume of U.S.–DPRK trade would be around $1 billion a year. Against the DPRK's estimated annual total trade turnover of under $2.5 billion in the mid-1990s,[9] that would look like a consequential sum.

Using economic techniques for assessing "revealed comparative advantage" within existing trade patterns, Noland further indicated a variety of product areas in which North Korean exports might, under more "normal" trade arrangements, be internationally competitive (and thus potentially attractive to American purchasers, among others). In that reckoning, North Korea's "prospective comparative advantage" would lie in the sale of such things as seafood, semiprocessed mineral products, and textiles or apparel. (See table 5-3.)

Noland is careful to remind his readers that all his calculations hinge on assumptions that are currently contrafactual. The calculations are offered not as predictions of the future, but rather as numerically denominated illustrations of one hypothetical alternative for the North Korean economy. And as it happens, that is really the most that can reasonably be demanded of positive econometric techniques under such circumstances. For better or worse, when it comes to specifying the prospects for U.S.–DPRK trade, the limits of the cliometric sciences are both immediate and completely unyielding. Computational procedures and econometric models could, of course, be harnessed to the manufacture of additional "estimates" or "scenarios" for U.S.–DPRK

Table 5-3 Prospective Sectors of Comparative-Advantage Analysis of North and South Korean Data

Standard International Trade Classification	Description
342	Fish—frozen (excluding fillets)
360	Crustaceans and mollusks—fresh, chilled frozen
542	Beans, peas, lentils, and other legumes
545	Other fresh or chilled vegetables
2613	Raw silk—not thrown
2731	Building and monumental stone—not further worked
2733	Sands—natural, of all kinds, whether or not colored
2786	Slag, dross, scalings, and similar waste—not elsewhere specified
2815	Iron ore and concentrates—not agglomerated
2816	Iron ore agglomerated (sinters, pellets, briquettes)
2881	Ash and residues—containing metals/metallic compounds
2911	Bones, horns, ivory, hooves, claws, coral, shells, etc.
3221	Anthracite—whether or not pulverized, not agglomerated
5621	Mineral or chemical fertilizers—nitrogenous
6512	Yarn—wool or animal hair (including wool tops)
6672	Diamonds—unworked cut/otherwise worked not mounted/set
7611	Television receivers
8421	Men's overcoats and other coats
8422	Men's suits—textile fabrics
8423	Trousers, breeches, etc.—textile fabrics
8429	Other outer garments—textile fabrics
8431	Coats and jackets—textile fabrics
8451	Jersey, pull-overs, twinsets, cardigans—knitted
8897	Basketwork, wickerwork, etc.—plaiting materials
9410	Animals—live, not elsewhere specified (including zoo animals)

Source: Marcus Noland, "Economic and Regional Cooperation in Northeast Asia," *95 Joint U.S.–Korea Academic Studies,* vol. 6 (1996), p. 163.

trade and finance in the years to come, but those would likely be little more than exercises in false precision.

Authoritative Expectations. The fact that economic studies and statistical methods can provide only a broad and general impression of a few of the possible directions for U.S.–DPRK commerce, of course, has not prevented some observers and principals from developing firmly held and sometimes elaborate views about that very outlook. Such expectations, of course, can sometimes be informative in and of themselves. Of particular interest in that regard are the views and arguments of DPRK officialdom.

Apart from the long-standing denunciation of America's sanctions, North Korea's official media offer few comments on U.S.–DPRK economic relations. When addressing American audiences directly, however, leading figures from North Korea have been more forthcoming—and revealing.

On at least three occasions over the past several years, highly placed DPRK officials or diplomats have expounded on the problems in U.S.–DPRK economic relations at seminars or public gatherings in the United States.[10] In each of those instances, the North Korean speakers asserted that American economic sanctions stood as a major—if not the major—obstacle preventing greater DPRK participation in the international economy. Those officials also commonly indicated that they expected a full lifting of U.S. economic sanctions to result in a dramatic upsurge of trade and direct foreign investment for their country. A press report on one of those seminars captured the essence of the other presentations as well:

> North Korea seems to think that the lifting of the U.S. economic sanctions is the most urgent task at present. . . . The North Korean delegates insisted that lifting the economic sanctions would affect other countries and greatly contribute to North Korea's economic revival.[11]

Coming as they do from personalities intimately familiar with the DPRK system, the informational value of those perspectives might be taken as nonnegligible. Yet compelling grounds also exist for discounting those opinions heavily, even if they happened to be volunteered in all sincerity. North Korean authorities, after all, to date have demonstrated something less than a masterly understanding of the opportunities inherent in the international trade system (or for that matter, of the therapies necessary for inducing economic recovery in their own country).

Past DPRK Trade Performance. The DPRK's established record of performance in its international commercial and financial transactions may in fact afford greater insight into the prospects for U.S.–North Korean economic relations than any other data currently available. Given the distinctive nature of the DPRK system and the strong continuities that may be said to have characterized the state's economic policies and practices over the past decades, past North Korean trade patterns may well offer some guidance into the constraints that could continue to trouble the U.S.–North Korean economic relationship after sanctions were fully lifted.[12] Given the extraordinary scarcity of reliable information on North Korea's economic situation, moreover, a review of North Korean trade performance has the additional benefit of providing one of the rare apertures through which the broader performance—and problems—of the DPRK domestic economy can be observed.

Reconstructing North Korean
Trade Patterns, 1970–1997

North Korea does not regularly release detailed information about its trade relations with other countries. For that reason, North Korea's trade patterns must be reconstructed from "mirror statistics": that is to say, from the reports of North Korea's trading partners on their sales to, and purchases from, the DPRK. The painstaking procedures involved are fairly straightforward[13] but should be briefly reviewed nonetheless.

Detailed "mirror statistics" on North Korea's foreign trade can be drawn from four separate sources: the United Nations Statistical Office's International Commodity Trade Database, into which as many as 170 countries report; Soviet and Russian trade statistics (Moscow did not until 1996 contribute to the UN trade database); ROK statistics on its post-1988 North-South trade (which are specifically excluded from the "international" trade data Seoul regularly transmits to the UN); and for a few years in the 1980s when China was not participating in the UN trade database, Chinese customs returns.

To reconstruct DPRK trade patterns from those data, we must use a common system for classifying the merchandise traded and a common medium for the valuation of transactions. The UN database provides its maximum coverage under the familiar commercial taxonomy known as Standard International Trade Classification (SITC), rev. 1. Detailed Chinese trade data (available for 1982 onward) have also been presented in terms of the SITC framework, and the ROK's North-South trade can be harmonized with that format. Soviet trade data are more of a problem: they were presented in accordance with the Council for Mutual Economic Assistance's own Standard Foreign Trade Classification (SFTC). Fortunately, researchers at the U.S. Census Bureau's International Programs Center have already converted Moscow's accounts on its trade with Pyongyang to SITC, rev. 1, for the period 1972 to 1995.[14] From those sources, we can obtain a detailed breakdown on the reported composition of North Korea's international trade.

By contemporary international convention, foreign trade is usually valued in current U.S. dollars. The UN database, Chinese customs statistics, and ROK reports on the North-South trade all measure trade in current dollars. Soviet trade volumes, however, were reported in current rubles; the aforementioned International Programs Center study on Soviet–DPRK trade, fortunately, used official dollar-ruble exchange rates to present that commerce in nominal dollar terms. From those sources, we can reconstruct a detailed "global" picture of North Korea's export and import patterns for the years 1970 to 1997.[15]

We should, however, recognize a number of problems with that reconstructed trade picture.[16] First, several of North Korea's major or potentially major trading partners (for example, Iran, Iraq, Ukraine, and Taiwan) do not report on their trade with the DPRK or are omitted from the UN database for other reasons. Second, since the DPRK's external commerce has been disproportionately geared toward items often excluded from standard trade accounts (for example, weapons and contraband), a portion of North Korea's trade with reporting partners may be excluded. By the same token, some of the barter trade along the China–DPRK border is probably not captured in Chinese trade accounts. Third, "mirror statistics" contain spurious entries—South Korean products, for example, may be miscoded as "North Korean"[17]—not all of which are likely to be detected. Finally, it is by no means clear that calculating transactions in "nonconvertible" currencies (for example, the Soviet ruble) on the basis of official dollar rates of exchange will provide a realistic valuation of that aspect of the DPRK's commerce.

When all is said and done, though, "mirror statistics" nevertheless provide a reasonably good approximation of the level, trends, and composition of North Korea's foreign trade. Used with care, they may illuminate otherwise obscure features of North Korea's international economic performance—and perhaps more than that alone.

DPRK International Economic Performance, 1970–1997

In examining North Korean trade patterns over the period 1970 to 1997 as reflected by "mirror statistics," we may discern a number of striking, unusual, and consistent patterns. Each of them arguably has a bearing on the prospects for U.S.–DPRK economic relations.

Extraordinarily Weak Long-Term Trade Development. If we go by the indications from "mirror statistics," North Korea had one of the world's poorest performance records in international trade over the quarter century between 1970 and 1997. Just how weak the DPRK's showing may have been is suggested by figure 5-1, which contrasts estimated export earnings for North Korea with those for other areas. Note that all those export earnings are measured in current U.S. dollars. We have no reliable means of converting current trade rubles into constant dollars and thus no obvious method for devising a "constant" index for North Korea's total imports or exports.[18]

Figure 5-1 Comparative Export Earnings: World, Asia, Africa, and DPRK, 1970–1997 (1970 = 1)

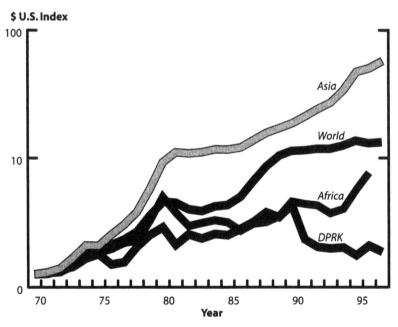

Sources: Derived from IMF, *International Financial Statistics Yearbook* (Washington, D.C.: IMF, 1996); UN commodity trade statistics; China customs statistics; ROK Ministry of Unification; U.S. Bureau of the Census.

Between 1970 and 1997 the nominal volume of total international exports, by the IMF's reckoning, increased by a factor of eighteen or more. For the DPRK, by contrast, that estimated nominal value did not quite triple. No other Asian country for which data are available fared nearly so poorly in the world economy over that period; for Asia as a whole (excluding industrial Japan), the corresponding increase in nominal dollar exports during those years was over sixtyfold. Even troubled Africa substantially outperformed North Korea's export record. Although we lack any proper method for estimating "real" changes in DPRK exports, it appears possible that North Korea's absolute constant-dollar level of exports might actually have been lower in 1997 than it had been in 1970.

It is true, of course, that North Korea suffered severe "trade shocks" from the final crisis of the Union of Soviet Socialist Republics and the loss of its preferential Soviet arrangements for subsidized trade and other aid. Yet even before the end of the cold war, North Korea's trade record was worse than mediocre. Between 1970 and 1989, for example, the estimated tempo of increase in export earnings was not only far lower than for the world as a whole (or of course for Asia), but also somewhat lower than for Africa.

And North Korea's long-term trade picture is actually even worse than those summary figures and comparisons suggest. For our reconstructed DPRK trade totals are buoyed by a pronounced expansion of Soviet–DPRK commerce in the USSR's final decade—an upturn dictated by Moscow's foreign policy and financed accordingly.

If its trade with the USSR is excluded from the ledger, North Korea's trade performance is nothing short of dismal. Between 1980 and 1989, for example, the estimated nominal value of DPRK exports to the non-Soviet world actually appears to have declined.[19] By the same token, in terms of current dollars, the DPRK's total foreign exports in 1997 may have been lower than its non-Soviet exports had been in 1980. Non-Soviet imports, for their part, seem to have stagnated in nominal terms during the 1980s and 1990s. Taken in real terms, North Korea's absolute trade turnover with the non-Soviet world was likely higher in 1975 than in 1985—and also higher in 1975 than it would be in 1995.[20]

Over the past two decades, Pyongyang has repeatedly enunciated an interest in promoting its commerce abroad and in attracting capital from overseas. In 1980, at the Sixth Congress of the Korean Workers' Party, the goal of tripling the DPRK's trade turnover during the 1980s was formally promulgated as state policy.[21] In 1984, the DPRK's first

Joint Venture Law was officially unveiled.[22] Throughout the early 1990s, North Korea introduced a succession of laws, administrative regulations, and procedural clarifications ostensibly intended to enhance the country's attractiveness as a venue for foreign investment and a partner for trade.[23] And in 1994, in his annual New Year's Day address, Kim Il Sung personally announced that the expansion of foreign trade had been embraced as one of the DPRK's three top economic priorities.[24]

Those formalistic statements and documents, however, contrast starkly with North Korea's actual record of achievements and results and beg the question of the gap between rhetoric and policy. Over long periods of time, after all, the trade patterns of individual countries are strongly shaped by their own economic policies and commercial practices.

To judge by DPRK performance between 1970 and 1997, the corpus of policies and practices that constituted the DPRK's "trade regime" would appear to have been not simply indifferent to but rather positively unreceptive toward the opportunities for mutually beneficial exchange inherent in the international marketplace. In practice, the broad contours of the DPRK's overall trade record by themselves would strongly seem to suggest that the regime has maintained an abidingly suspicious, if not actively hostile, posture toward commerce with other countries. Without deliberate, forceful, and sustained policy intervention, after all, it is difficult to imagine how a country in North Korea's circumstances could have so resisted the general international tendency over the past generation for robust expansion of foreign trade.[25] Given North Korea's particulars, moreover, the country's absolute levels of per capita trade turnover would seem to require specific explanation.

At this juncture, the DPRK's overseas sales of merchandise, on a per capita basis, apparently amount to less than $50 a year.[26] That is a remarkably low figure.[27] It is all the more striking when one considers some of the DPRK's defining developmental characteristics. With a population of barely twenty million people, North Korea's is exactly the sort of economy that might expect significant gains through participating, by means of international trade, in a more specialized division of labor. Insofar as North Korea has already made the transition to an urbanized, nonagricultural economy,[28] such a low level of demonstrated export capability appears all the more anomalous.

The most obvious explanation for such severe and long-standing structural distortions, of course, is the policy environment established by Pyongyang itself. For over forty years, the DPRK has set its economic policy against two continuously extolled imperatives: *juche* (usually translated as "self-reliance") and the correlative quest to build an "independent socialist economy." Philosophically and operationally, those imperatives may be said to lie at the very core of the DPRK system (unlike the irregular and essentially superficial official pronouncements about the desirability of expanding trade).

North Korea's foreign trade performance over the past generation not only appears to be entirely consistent with the doctrines of *juche* and the "independent socialist economy" but may even provide a faithful reflection of them. Indeed, paradoxical as it may sound, it is entirely possible that responsible authorities in Pyongyang may regard their country's trade patterns—with the extraordinarily delimited degree of economic contact with the outside world—not as a failure, but rather as a positive "achievement."

The Quest for External Subsidies. If Pyongyang's policies and practices have revealed a fundamental reluctance to pursue businesslike commercial relationships in the international marketplace, they have demonstrated no similar reticence about seeking economic assistance from abroad. Quite the contrary: North Korea's efforts to wrest aid and subsidy from foreign governments and overseas organizations have been persistent, focused, and arguably highly skillful. One of the distinguishing features of North Korea's foreign policy and international diplomacy, in fact, is the high and consistent priority assigned to the quest to secure inflows of concessional foreign capital.

We need recapitulate the DPRK's history as an aid recipient—or extractor—only briefly. Immediately after the Korean War, the DPRK enjoyed a massive aid effort—underwritten by the entire "socialist camp"—aimed at rebuilding its devastated economy.[29] In the decades following the Sino-Soviet rift, North Korea managed to continue to obtain economic assistance from both Moscow and Beijing simultaneously (no mean feat, considering the circumstances).[30] In the early 1980s, following the death of Leonid Brezhnev, Pyongyang revitalized its relations with Moscow and secured substantial increases in concessional Soviet aid as a consequence.[31] After the collapse of the USSR, North Korea leaned on China for increased "fraternal assistance."[32] Pyongyang has also assiduously cultivated concessional transfers from the noncommunist world. For many decades, it has mobilized remittances from ethnic Koreans in Japan through the General Association of Korean

Residents in Japan (known by the abbreviation *Chosen Soren* in Japanese, or *Chochongnyon* in Korean). More recently, under the terms of the "Agreed Framework," Pyongyang's nuclear negotiations with Washington concluded in a multilateral commitment that could provide North Korea with energy infrastructure and supplies worth $5 billion or more. Following its 1995 official appeal for emergency food relief, moreover, North Korea has received hundreds of millions of dollars in "humanitarian aid" from the governments of Japan, the ROK, and the United States, among others.

One consequence of North Korea's concentration on securing sources of external subsidy has been the regime's success in running a seemingly permanent balance-of-trade deficit. (See figure 5-2.) Between 1970 and 1997, according to my reconstructions, there was not a single year in which North Korea did not manage to import more from abroad than it sold overseas. Measured in current dollars and at official exchange rates, North Korea's cumulative trade deficit with the outside world—a measure of implicit net transfers to the DPRK—amounted to nearly $12.5 billion between 1970 and 1997. We may appreciate the role those implicit transfers played in augmenting North Korea's

Figure 5-2 DPRK Trade Balance (Deficit), 1970–1997

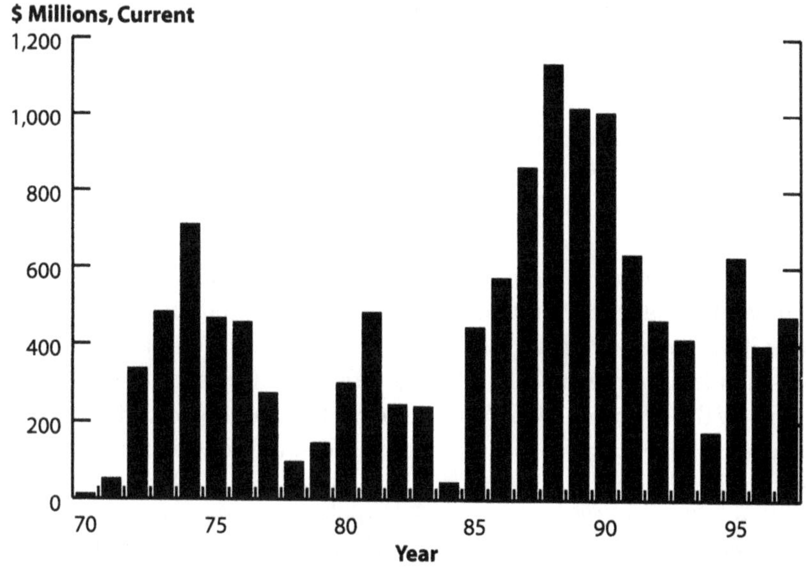

$ Millions, Current

Sources: Derived from UN commodity trade statistics; China custom statistics; ROK Ministry of Unification; U.S. Bureau of the Census.

capacity to obtain overseas provisions when we consider that North Korea's cumulative nominal exports over the same period appear to have totaled less than $30 billion.

North Korea's trade patterns may be said to depict a regime possessed of a fundamentally political conception of international economic relations, wherein goods and services are understood to flow not so much through voluntary commercial exchange between contractually equal partners but through a struggle between states and systems. For the "self-reliant" state that North Korea strives to be, we may thus view concessional transfers from abroad as winnings from that international struggle—or, given Korea's history, perhaps even as a sort of tribute from abroad.[33]

Like the South Korean government of an earlier era, North Korea today appears to be guided by an "aid-maximizing" economic strategy.[34] Yet an earlier generation of South Koreans decisively discarded "aid-maximizing" economic policies because they judged those to place their country under unacceptable economic and political constraints. Those same constraints continue to limit the scope of the possible for the DPRK.

Three overarching problems beset an "aid-maximizing" strategy. First, no matter how consummate one's officials may be in maximizing it, concessional aid is, in the final analysis, always a political transaction and thus is subject to the vagaries of sudden and unpredictable political change. From the DPRK's standpoint, the collapse of the Soviet bloc may be the most vivid illustration of that grim truth, but it is hardly the only one: remittances from North Korea's supporters in Japan appear to have fallen precipitously since the early 1980s,[35] and China's aid seemed surprisingly grudging once Beijing was no longer obliged to compete with Moscow for influence in Pyongyang.[36]

Second, no matter how "self-reliant" an aid-bolstered polity may fashion itself to be, a regimen financed by subventions from abroad is ultimately a dependent regimen. North Korea learned just how dependent it was on external largesse in 1994, when Beijing cut its shipments of "friendship grain" to 300,000 tons (from 800,000 tons the previous year): by the spring of 1995, North Korean officials were forced to launch their emergency appeal for international food aid, implicitly acknowledging that their regime was unable to feed its people.[37] For about $400 million to $500 million a year in grain imports, according to some estimates,[38] this new "food problem" could be made to vanish; the DPRK's "aid-maximizing" international economic regimen, unfortunately, has been incapable of dealing with such a problem on its own.

Third, no matter how successful one may be at the quest for aid, the scope for obtaining foreign resources through concessional transfers is incomparably smaller than through commercial trade. As much is indicated by the broad outlines of the contemporary world economy, in which annual trade turnover is estimated to be well over 100 times greater than yearly net disbursements of official development assistance.[39] More to the point in North Korea's case, in the economic race between the two Koreas was a time when the DPRK's absolute volume of imports exceeded the ROK's.[40] Today, however— in the wake of its 1997 financial crisis—South Korea imports an average of about $8 billion in goods and services every month,[41] and it finances those imports through its own export earnings. To judge by figure 5-2, the DPRK has yet never succeeded in extracting more than $1.2 billion in aid in a single year from foreign benefactors. What are the chances that North Korea could ever muster concessional aid flows of $8 billion a year (let alone $8 billion a *month*)?

North Korea may have an additional, incalculable drawback from an "aid-maximizing" orientation: North Korea's dealings with the outside world betray a lingering confusion about the difference between business-based transactions and charitable bequests.

Pyongyang's economic relations with Western countries remain seriously damaged to this day by Pyongyang's de facto default on almost $1 billion in commercial loans in the mid-1970s. Many other countries, of course, have fallen behind on their scheduled international debt repayments at some point during the past two decades; North Korea appears to have been unique, however, in insisting that it should not have to make good on any portion of its outstanding obligations. Although banking circles have treated the precise details of North Korea's behavior as proprietary information, many observers believe that the DPRK has made virtually no interest or amortization payments toward those debts over the past twenty-plus years.[42]

Pyongyang's defiant stance toward repayment of those Western debts has long puzzled financial specialists. Students of North Korean affairs have offered a variety of plausible hypotheses to explain it;[43] a possibility seldom discussed, however, is that the DPRK never intended to repay those monies in the first place. Yet that possibility would be entirely in keeping with North Korea's previous posture toward loans extended to it by Soviet-bloc countries: according to a number of Soviet sources, those were simply never repaid.[44]

Given its fundamentally political interpretation of its international commercial and financial dealings, it may be that the North Korean government views nonperformance on its Western debts as not only justifiable but deft. The consequence of treating those loans as if they were gifts, however, has been to undermine the DPRK's international creditworthiness, to preclude regular trade finance, and to reduce the country to barter for most of its transactions in the world marketplace.

Chronic Underinvestment in Foreign Machinery and Equipment. Given the "investment fetish" common to all communist economies[45] and evident in the DPRK in an extreme form, it may seem counterintuitive to suggest that the North Korean government has spent too little on capital goods of any sort. Yet "mirror statistics" on North Korean trade reveal a long-term pattern of skimping on expenditures for foreign machinery and other productive equipment that could modernize the economy's capital stock and improve its industrial infrastructure.

As figure 5-3 indicates, the share of North Korean imports allocated to the purchase of capital equipment has markedly and steadily declined over the past two decades. Even during the upswing in its economic relations with the USSR in the late 1980s—when Pyongyang presumably had some say over the composition of its growing aid from the USSR—the share of capital goods within total imports continued to drop.

By any international benchmark, North Korea has been a persistent and extreme underinvestor in foreign capital goods. (See table 5-4.) Over the past generation, the DPRK's share of capital goods within imports and its absolute level of capital goods imports per capita have been lower—typically, far lower—than in other communist economies. They also contrast sharply with patterns in the noncommunist, low-income world. By the early 1990s, in fact, per capita imports of machinery and equipment for the "developing" regions as a whole may have averaged about ten times the North Korean level.[46]

While economies throughout the rest of the world were incorporating ever more foreign machinery and equipment into their domestic capital stock, North Korea's imports of those goods were stagnating—or worse. The year 1975 may actually have been the high-water mark for DPRK imports of capital equipment, even in nominal dollar terms.

Although the figures necessary for such calculations are not available, it seems quite possible that the DPRK may have had the lowest proportion of imported capital goods within gross domestic capital for-

Figure 5-3 Capital Goods as a Percentage of Total DPRK Merchandise Imports, 1972–1997

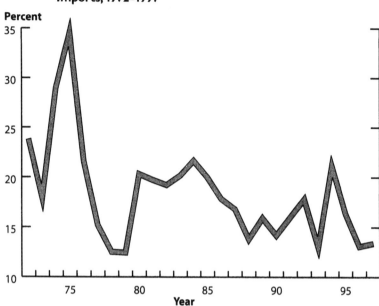

Sources: Derived from UN commodity trade statistics; China custom statistics; ROK Ministry of Unification; U.S. Bureau of the Census.

mation—or within its endowment of fixed reproducible capital—of any country in the world by the early 1990s. From the standpoint of the architects of North Korea's "independent socialist economy," that may have appeared to be an accomplishment in its own right. Yet the economic implications of that fateful policy determination have been almost unremittingly adverse.

Absent the option of replacing old equipment with updated machinery from abroad, North Korea finds itself locked into an aging industrial infrastructure that embodies generally obsolescent technologies; any prospects for innovation correspondingly rest largely with the DPRK's own *juche* R&D community. Since imported capital goods are typically less expensive and more productive than domestically manufactured alternatives,[47] North Korea's strictures against foreign machinery and equipment have consigned the economy to wasteful expense in its own investment sector and to unnecessarily slow economic growth. Chronic underinvestment in foreign machinery and equipment has had a pronounced and constricting impact on North Korea's ability to export—an impact in some measure independent

Table 5-4 DPRK Capital Goods Trade in International Perspective

Country/Region	Capital Goods as a Proportion of Trade (percent)			Capital Goods Trade per Person (current $ value)		
	Imports					
	1970s	1980s	1990s	1970s	1980s	1990s
USSR	35.9	37.1	—	45	18	—
CMEA Europe	35.7 [a]	31.7 [b]	—	175 [a]	303 [b]	—
Cuba	26.6	31.7	21.0	97	237	77
China	21.8 [c]	28.6	37.8	2 [c]	10	28
DPRK	20.9 [d]	18.5	16.4	14 [d]	18	12
ROK	28.8	30.2	35.1	68	238	774
Developing economies	27.4	32.1	46.5 [e]	27	57	114 [e]
	Exports					
	1970s	1980s	1990s	1970s	1980s	1990s
USSR	18.4	14.6	—	24	49	—
CMEA Europe	42.3 [a]	46.7 [b]	—	192 [a]	455 [b]	—
Cuba	negl.	negl.	negl.	negl.	negl.	negl.
China	3.7 [c]	3.3	13.9	negl. [c]	2	11
DPRK	2.9 [d]	7.6	11.1	1 [d]	6	6
ROK	14.8	32.3	45.0	32	294	922
Developing economies	4.8	12.8	27.4 [e]	4	23	67 [e]

Notes: Trade volumes are estimated in current dollars at official exchange rates: imports c.i.f. (except developing economies), exports f.o.b. "Developing economies" are defined per UN taxonomy (less China). Per capita trade volumes are calculated according to 1975, 1985, 1990–1995 populations.

a. Data are from 1970 and 1973–1979.
b. Data are from 1980–1988.
c. Data are from 1970 and 1975–1979.
d. Data are from 1972–1979.
e. Data are from 1990–1994.

Sources: For Cuba and USSR: U.S. Central Intelligence Agency, *Handbook;* Eastern Europe: U.S. Central Intelligence Agency, *Handbook;* ROK: *Korea Statistical Yearbook;* developing countries: *International Trade.* Populations are derived from United Nations, *World Population Prospects 1990.*

of, and in addition to, other export-restricting factors in the North Korean trade regimen.

Unsustainable Militarization of Trade. The North Korean economy has undergone an extraordinary degree of militarization over the past generation, a transformation presumably reflecting Pyongyang's strategy for reunification of the Korean peninsula on its own terms.[48] In its contest with Seoul for claim to the entire peninsula, however, that wholesale militarization posed problems and offered potential solutions. Indeed, North Korea's enormous military burden handicapped the North in its long-term race against the South. No less troubling, innovations in military technology were rapidly changing the terms of battle, and North Korea's defense industries could not produce the sorts of advanced munitions and materiel that would be available to its adversaries.

Pyongyang seems to have attempted to resolve that dilemma by militarizing its international trade. Through its tilt toward Moscow in the 1980s, North Korea managed to obtain massive amounts of Soviet military hardware—thereby improving the "correlation of forces" against the South. At the same time, North Korea made a push into the international weapons market as an arms supplier by selling the sorts of products its defense sector could produce to clients willing to purchase them.

Figure 5-4 depicts the military consequence of Pyongyang's revitalized ties with Moscow. The figure quantifies the unidentified residual in the USSR's reported exports to the DPRK; those "commodities and transactions not classified according to kind" (in the SITC taxonomy), we surmise, present a reasonably good approximation of the volume of Soviet weaponry shipped to North Korea.

Between 1974 and 1984, at official ruble–dollar exchange rates, that unexplained residual remained well under $100 million a year. It jumped to $400 million in 1985 and continued to climb thereafter. Over the years 1985 to 1990, those unidentified shipments would have amounted to $5 billion at official ruble–dollar rates. Those imports, moreover, came to dominate not only the DPRK's trade with the Soviet Union but the DPRK's entire trade profile. Between 1988 and 1990, for example, imports of Soviet weaponry appear to have accounted for nearly a third of North Korea's total imports from the outside world.[49]

Estimating North Korea's arms exports is more problematic, insofar as those illicit transactions generally do not show up in "mirror statistics." The U.S. Arms Control and Disarmament Agency (ACDA),

Figure 5-4 DPRK Imports of SITC 9 Items from USSR/Russia, 1972–1995

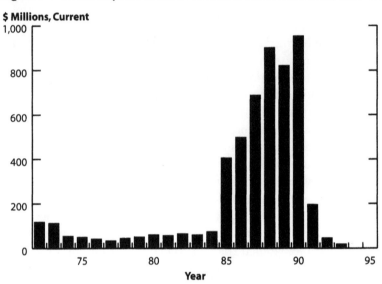

Source: U.S. Bureau of the Census, Center for International Research.

however, has offered estimates of that commerce; although those num-bers should not be treated as exact, they may be illustrative nonethe-less. (See figure 5-5.)

According to the ACDA, the DPRK entered modestly into arms exports in the mid-1970s and became an arms supplier of some conse-quence in the early 1980s. Between 1981 and 1989, by the ACDA's reckoning, North Korea exported almost $4 billion in weaponry (princi-pally to Iran for its war against Iraq). If those numbers are roughly cor-rect—and it should be emphasized that we have no means of determin-ing whether they are—weapons sales would have accounted for nearly 30 percent of North Korea's total exports during that period.

Ultimately, however, the militarization of North Korean trade proved to be an unsustainable policy. With the collapse of the Soviet Union, the transfer of military goods from Moscow to North Korea also collapsed; by 1994–1995, those flows had apparently ceased altogether. North Korea's weapons exports, for their part, apparently also collapsed after 1988, evidently a casualty of the end of the Iran-Iraq war, the end of the cold war, and international nonproliferation efforts. If the ACDA's fig-ures are correct, the nominal dollar value of North Korea's weapons sales in 1996 was just $50 million a year—lower than it had been in the late 1970s.

Figure 5-5   Arms Control and Disarmament Agency Estimates
of DPRK Arms Exports, 1975–1996

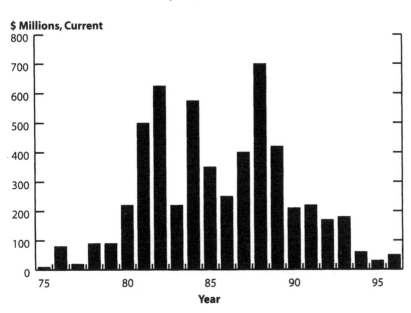

Source: U.S. Arms Control and Disarmament Agency, WMEAT database.

Until and unless Pyongyang completely recasts its reunification strategy, the DPRK's desire for foreign weaponry should be expected to grow. Imported weaponry, after all, would seem to offer the DPRK one of the very few available "quick fixes" to its increasingly unfavorable strategic position vis-à-vis South Korea. But because of other policies the regime has long pursued, the country could not now afford to purchase the materiel necessary for redressing the strategic balance, even if suppliers for such merchandise could be found. By the same token, the apparent erosion of the DPRK's industrial infrastructure, and the increasingly antiquated technology undergirding it, would limit prospects for weapons sales by North Korea today—even if the changes attendant on the end of the cold war had not done so already.

Inability to Penetrate Nonembargoed Western Markets. A final characteristic of North Korean trade patterns worth mentioning has been the country's rather limited success in merchandizing its products in the very large markets in which no standing sanctions exist against its trade.

Up to this writing, Washington's apparatus of sanctions has indeed denied North Korea access to the largest single market in the world. Yet the American market accounts for only a modest fraction of the total imports by "industrialized countries." Nearly four-fifths of the international purchases of merchandise by the OECD grouping, in fact, come from countries other than the United States. In 1997 the total imports of those same countries exceeded $2.7 trillion. None of those countries, moreover, maintains economic sanctions against North Korea.

Lack of legal obstacles against entry notwithstanding, North Korea has yet to make any appreciable inroads into those enormous markets. North Korea's indifferent performance is highlighted in figure 5-6, which contrasts the growth of those non-American OECD markets with changes in North Korea's exports to them. Between 1975 and 1997, the nominal dollar value of the imports of the non-American OECD grouping increased by a factor of about 5.5; North Korean exports to those countries, in contrast, did not quite triple. In relative terms, North Korea's share of the non-American OECD import market was barely half as great in 1997 as it had been in 1975. In absolute terms, North Korea's exports to those markets are estimated to have been lower in the 1990s than they were in 1980—even in nominal dollar terms.

That lackluster record, to repeat, cannot be explained in terms of hostile economic policies toward North Korea. It is instead to be understood as a largely predictable consequence of the distinctive characteristics of North Korea's trade that have already been described.

North Korea's performance in the non-American OECD market may actually be even poorer than figure 5-6 suggests, for with the collapse of the USSR and the virtual termination of Moscow-Pyongyang trade, one might have expected export capacity that had previously serviced Soviet markets to be redirected toward hard-currency sales. Such an adjustment, however, does not yet seem to have taken place. That much is underscored by the performance of North Korea's principal export products and commodities. (See figures 5-7 through 5-11.)

In the late 1980s and early 1990s, roughly half the DPRK's identifiable export revenues were generated by five kinds of products: iron and steel; cement; textiles and clothing; magnesite; and gold. With the possible exception of textiles, all those products are fairly homogeneous and thus in theory should have been salable in markets in which an articulated demand for them already existed. (The relatively small volumes involved, furthermore, should have obviated any potential pressures posed by inelastic international demand.) Yet, as figures 5-7

Figure 5-6 Changes in Trade: Total Imports of Non–U.S. Industrial Countries vs. DPRK Exports to OECD, 1970–1997 (1975 = 1)

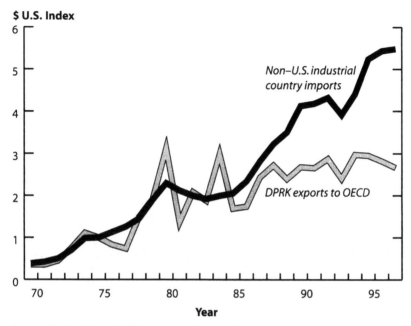

$ U.S. Index

Non–U.S. industrial country imports

DPRK exports to OECD

Year

Sources: Derived from IMF, *International Financial Statistics Yearbook,* 1996; UN commodity trade statistics; China customs statistics; ROK Ministry of Unification; U.S. Bureau of the Census.

through 5-11 all attest, North Korea appears to have had precious little success in redirecting its Soviet produce into non-Soviet markets.

To some degree, North Korea's apparent inability to maintain aggregate exports for particular products at their previous levels after the Soviet "trade shock" may speak to the shock itself (to constraints posed, for example, by a sudden shortage of necessary inputs or intermediate goods). But as the divergent post-Soviet export experiences of the DPRK and Vietnam should demonstrate, not every socialist economy heavily dependent on Soviet trade at the time of the USSR's collapse was equally affected by the loss. (See figure 5-12.) Whereas North Korea's exports, measured in nominal dollars, were only half as high in 1997 as they had been in 1989, Vietnam's had more than quadrupled. We can understand the difference here largely in terms of differences in trade regimes: Vietnam's successfully adjusted to competition beyond the confines of captive markets; North Korea's to date has not.

Figure 5-7 DPRK Export Performance: Steel, 1984–1997

$ Millions, Current

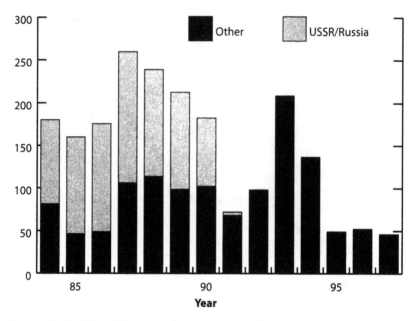

Sources: Derived from UN commodity trade statistics; China customs statistics; ROK Ministry of Unification; Korea International Trade Association; U.S. Bureau of the Census.

Concluding Observations

We cannot predict the future of the U.S.–DPRK economic relationship with any great precision. If the DPRK's past trade patterns, policies, and practices offer guidance into what we may expect from Pyongyang in the immediate future, three general observations about this new prospective relationship are in order.

First, under the DPRK's current policy regimen, even a complete and summary remanding of all restrictions against U.S.–DPRK trade should be expected to result in only modest volumes of commerce. After "normalization" of trade relations, the primary constraints against expansion of U.S.–North Korean trade would lie in the nature of the North Korean trade regime itself.[50] That trade regime may, of course, change— but for reasons already mentioned, it currently seems to reflect the core values and objectives of the North Korean state and thus may be "reformed" only with the utmost reluctance.

Figure 5-8 DPRK Export Performance: Cement, 1982–1997

$ Millions, Current

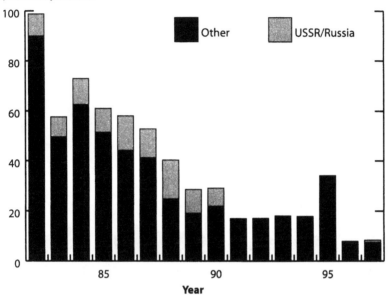

Sources: Derived from UN commodity trade statistics; China customs statistics; ROK Ministry of Unification; Korea International Trade Association; U.S. Bureau of the Census.

Figure 5-9 DPRK Export Performance: Textiles, 1980–1997

$ Millions, Current

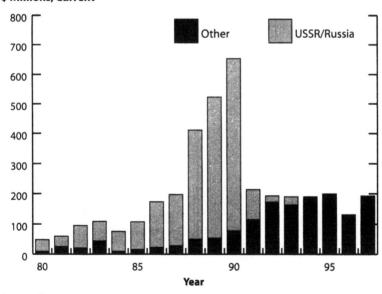

Sources: Derived from UN commodity trade statistics; China customs statistics; ROK Ministry of Unification; Korea International Trade Association; U.S. Bureau of the Census.

Figure 5-10 DPRK Export Performance: Magnesite, 1980–1997

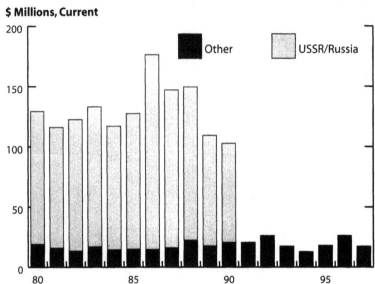

Sources: Derived from UN commodity trade statistics; China customs statistics; ROK Ministry of Unification; Korea International Trade Association; U.S. Bureau of the Census.

Figure 5-11 DPRK Export Performance: Gold, 1978–1997

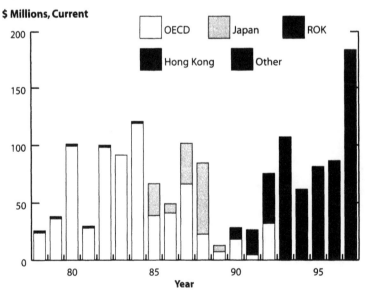

Sources: Derived from UN commodity trade statistics; China customs statistics; ROK Ministry of Unification; Korea International Trade Association; U.S. Bureau of the Census.

Figure 5-12 Export Performance: Vietnam vs. DPRK (1989 = 100)

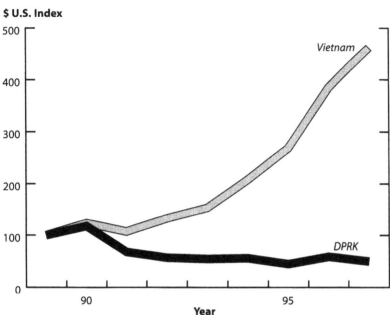

Sources: Derived from UN commodity trade statistics; China customs statistics; ROK Ministry of Unification; Korea International Trade Association; U.S. Bureau of the Census.

Second, notwithstanding the expressed expectations of leading North Korean officials, it would seem highly unlikely that a normalization of U.S.–DPRK trade relations, in and of itself, could provide the impetus for arresting North Korea's economic decline, much less alleviating its current economic woes. The economic resources that might be unleashed by such a relaxation would likely pale next to the requirements for such tasks, presuming the current policy regimen remains in place. North Korea's economic difficulties might arguably be remedied without enormous outlays of external economic resources under a very different economic regimen—but to speculate about radical changes in North Korean economic policies is tantamount to begging the question of the continued existence of the state itself.

Finally, if past North Korean policy provides any guidance, Pyongyang's interest in a normalized economic relationship with the United States lies less in the prospects for expanded commerce than in the potentialities of unlocking new sources of aid. In that regard, the hopes and expectations of North Korean authorities might not be unfounded. Under a more normalized diplomatic and economic relationship, the United States could arrange for substantial inflows of aid to North Korea even if Washington committed few funds of its own.

Washington could, for example, pave the way for a more successful international appeal for "humanitarian relief" for the DPRK; it could provide the opening for North Korea for concessional assistance from multilateral institutions such as the World Bank and the Asian Development Bank;[51] it could even be influential in facilitating the long-sought financial "settlement" from Japan.

For North Korea today, the search for new patrons may be a more familiar and attractive challenge than the trials of learning to compete in international markets. Pyongyang may correctly judge its relationship with the United States to be critical to its prospects for securing aid flows from other Western sources. Whether North Korean foreign policy can satisfy the conditions for a more favorable U.S. disposition toward Western aid for the DPRK—and whether such aid could resuscitate the ailing North Korean economy—are questions that can only be answered at a future date.

6

Beyond the DPRK:
Can Korean Unification Promote
Stability in Northeast Asia?

I n world affairs today, the division of the Korean peninsula into two
separate and irreconcilable political entities is taken as a basic fact
of life. Although the Koreans are a single, distinct people and had
lived under a single government for more than a thousand years before
the Allies' fateful August 1945 partition of their land, the continuing
existence of two suddenly formed and mutually hostile states in one
unhappy nation has come to be an established feature of the international order that has emerged since World War II. Indeed, in the view of
many sober analysts of foreign relations and experienced practitioners
of diplomacy, the division of Korea may be a characteristic feature of
the postwar global order: a fundamental reality in its own right—and
one integral to the "equilibria" that have been painfully attained both
within the Northeast Asian region and beyond it.

It is easy enough to see why students of foreign policy and international security would take divided rule in Korea to be a durable, lasting
phenomenon. Korea's fifty-plus-year division, after all, has been sufficiently sturdy to survive the death of the Soviet state: unlike the partition of Germany, which came to an end with the "end of the cold war,"
the contest in Korea between the communist regime in the North and
the pro-Western government in the South continues to this day. By
the same token, it is not difficult to explain why informed and prudent

specialists would contemplate any upending of the existing Korean political formula with the deepest of misgivings. As is known all too well,
the most nearly successful attempt to date to overturn Korea's two-state
arrangement—North Korea's surprise attack against the South in June
1950—happened to culminate in the Korean War, a horrendous multinational conflict that claimed millions of lives and brought the great
powers to the brink of world war.[1]

The international security framework that has evolved in Korea
since the 1953 Korean War cease-fire is predicated on an expectation
that the division of the peninsula will continue. Although it may seem
too obvious to require comment, the long-standing U.S. policy of deterrence in Korea—the basis for the U.S. military commitment to the Seoul
government—implicitly presumes that there will be a North Korea
against which South Korea must be defended. While the Korea policies
of Northeast Asia's other great powers—Japan, China, and Russia—
naturally differ from Washington's in both means and proximate objectives, all of them lend support in their own way to the preservation of a
two-state system for the Korean peninsula, since they all judge that
modus vivendi conducive to the preservation of peace and stability in a
vital but volatile region.

One may indeed argue that fundamental developments in Korea,
and throughout Northeast Asia, over the past four decades demonstrate
the soundness of the current two-state formula for Korea. Commercially,
the region has been transformed from an impoverished backwater into
an engine of progress within the world economy; rapid growth, rising
living standards, and burgeoning trade now typify the area. Although
military forces in Korea remain poised for a resumption of hostilities
at any moment, war has been avoided for nearly two generations. Not
only Korea but all of Northeast Asia has enjoyed a long peace, albeit a
tense one; and relations among the four great powers around Korea have
gradually improved and are arguably better today than at any point
in the past century.

Yet whatever may be said in its favor, the two-state system in Korea, to which the modern world has grown so accustomed, will not last
indefinitely. The permanent political partition of the Korean nation is,
quite simply, an unsustainable proposition. Indeed, the events unfolding in the peninsula over the past decade have been signaling, with
mounting pitch and power, that the division of Korea has already reached
the limits of its viability. At some point in the years ahead, the Democratic People's Republic of Korea, which rules North Korea, will likely

disappear from the political stage, and Korea will then reenter the international community as a united nation.

The final failure of the North Korean state is not something that external actors could forestall, even if they were so inclined. But the manner in which the DPRK departs can be influenced—and how it departs world politics matters greatly, both within Korea and beyond.

With its enormous army, its arsenal of ballistic missiles and chemical weapons, and its suspected nuclear capability, the DPRK is in a position to inflict fearsome collateral damage on all its neighbors— not just the Republic of Korea—during its death throes. Depending on the circumstances of its demise, North Korea's ultimate crisis could also imaginably provoke crises in or among some of the region's great powers. Humanitarian, economic, and even strategic catastrophes from which Northeast Asia would not soon recover are thus all too conceivable.

Korean reunification, however, is not foreordained to be a time of tragedy. To the contrary, with the proper preparations, and a bit of luck, a free and largely peaceful unification of the peninsula might also be consummated. The benefits from such a reunion could be enormous and wide-ranging and would not accrue solely to Koreans.

Despite its seemingly imposing financial requirements, reunification could actually enhance long-term prospects for prosperity and economic health. It could help to alter the quality of governance in the region by placing further weight behind the forces promoting openness, accountability, and civil order. No less significant, a successful Korean reunification would dramatically alter the region's military logic, mitigating rather than reinforcing the pressures for nuclear proliferation and arms buildup. In all, it is quite possible to think of a Korean unification in which rewards outweigh diverse costs. It is further possible to think of a Korean unification that serves to stabilize the regional order: of a Korean unification that contributes to the structure of stability for Northeast Asia.

If the nature of Korea's eventual reunification can indeed be influenced, just what sorts of steps can be taken to maximize the likelihood of a benign outcome—and by whom? In trying to answer that question, we must consider the prospects for the failing state that still rules North Korea, the desirability of a rapid as opposed to a more gradual reunification, and the instruments at the disposal of various governments and populations for affecting the pace and tenor of Korean reintegration.

North Korea's Grim Endgame

For at least a decade—some would say rather longer—the self-styled contest between Korea's two states has not been much of a contest at all. By almost any conventional measure of performance one might choose— economic development, domestic human rights, international legitimacy and recognition—South Korea's state and system look not only vastly superior to North Korea's but increasingly so. In that particular competition, of course, South Korea's clear-cut victory does not put an end to the race. As long as North Korea is capable of functioning as a state, it can pursue its grim duel against the South—no matter how poorly the DPRK fares in any given comparison with the ROK. Today, however, the DPRK's very ability to function indefinitely as a sovereign state is open to doubt. It must be emphasized that the outside world's knowledge about conditions within North Korea is woefully limited—a tribute of sorts to a secretive government that seems to regard strategic deception as an indispensable instrument of statecraft. Nevertheless, available information strongly suggests that the North Korean system has entered into a phase of grave decline. The weight of evidence further suggests that North Korea's continuing decline is unlikely to be reversed, insofar as the options for revitalizing the DPRK are few and the particular therapies that might restore the regime to health also threaten to destroy the system at its command.

By the late 1980s, the DPRK was already a structure evidencing severe strain. Economically, North Korea was an island of stagnation in a sea of East Asian growth. The regime's commitment to hypermilitarization (near total war mobilization since at least the early 1970s) and its insistence on an especially idiosyncratic variant of central economic planning had taken their predictable toll. If North Korea watchers from the former Warsaw Pact are correct, the actual levels of production for key items in the DPRK economy—electricity, steel, and the like—not only were far lower than official claims or targets, but were declining in absolute terms.[2] To the extent that North Korea's leaders tried to relieve the constraints posed by the economy's performance, they demonstrated a preference for circumventing central problems through *deus ex machina* solutions. Perhaps the most important of those opportunistic but temporary fixes was the rejuvenation of Pyongyang's relationship with Moscow after the death of Leonid Brezhnev: the new closeness in Soviet–DPRK ties seems to have translated into billions of rubles in aid and military materiel for North Korea over the 1984–1990 period.[3] Thanks to those blandishments, North Korea was able to persevere on its unsustainable course through the close of the Soviet era.

While the DPRK managed to weather the immediate collapse of the Soviet empire, the end of Soviet socialism nevertheless came as a direct and heavy blow to an already ailing project. Suddenly deprived of aid and highly subsidized trade with its then main commercial partner, North Korea's economy suffered sharp dislocations. External pressures on the economy intensified after the Soviet collapse, as China and pro-Pyongyang Korean ethnics in Japan—the two major remaining sources of concessional assistance to the DPRK—apparently tightened their purse strings, each for its own reasons.[4] With foreign supplies of critical production inputs (for example, oil and spare parts)—or the hard currency that could be used to purchase them—no longer secured, even stagnation began to look like an ambitious and unattainable goal for many sectors of the economy. In fact, North Korea now seems to be trapped in a self-perpetuating spiral of economic degeneration.

The most vivid manifestation of those systemic woes was the eruption of widespread food shortages in North Korea in 1995. Although the precise dimensions of that problem have been impossible for outsiders to ascertain, the prevalence and severity of privation can be inferred from Pyongyang's unprecedented diplomatic appeal that year for emergency food aid from abroad—a call that continues to be sounded to this day. While North Korean officialdom publicly insists that the country's current agricultural woes are of the "one time only" variety, precipitated in their reading by freak weather, a less optimistic assessment would conclude that food shortages lie ahead for the DPRK as far as the eye can see. Quite simply, it appears that the North Korean system, as it currently operates, no longer maintains a capacity to feed its own population.

When one considers how hard it is for a tightly disciplined and largely industrialized society to lose the capacity to feed itself, one begins to appreciate the magnitude of the DPRK's predicament. Severe and extended reductions in agricultural output are anomalous enough for such societies. Yet, even so, North Korea could totally prevent nutritional hardship at home through relatively modest purchases of grain from abroad. If Western estimates of North Korea's crop shortfall in 1996 are roughly correct, about $400 million to $500 million would be needed to fill that gap entirely through supplies from the world cereal market[5]—hardly an outlandish sum to scrape together, one might think, in a country of over 20 million people. The DPRK, however, has not yet managed to do so—and on its current trajectory is unlikely to be able to do so in the foreseeable future.

North Korea's food problem, like its other major economic problems, is the direct consequence of the policies that Pyongyang has carefully selected and relentlessly enforced. After all, North Korea's policy is to assign top priority in all resource allocations to its huge and unproductive military machine; to siphon off state investment into expensive showpiece projects of political rather than economic merit; to throttle the ideologically suspect consumer sector; to minimize the role of financial incentives in the workplace; to smother the transmission of price signals within and among domestic sectors; to divorce the local currency as much as possible from the actual process of economic exchange; to ignore the country's sorry international credit standing; and to avoid any unnecessary contact with the world economy. Little wonder that output is heading down.

It is probably safe to say that the economic environment in the DPRK at this time is more severely, and deliberately, distorted than anywhere else on earth. Yet, despite the obvious benefits that Pyongyang could grasp almost immediately by moderating its extremist regimen, the North Korean government has resolutely rejected the option of charting a new course. The reasoning behind that posture is straightforward and has been spelled out by DPRK leadership: the regime is unwilling to unleash the turbulent and unpredictable political forces that current arrangements still keep well under control.

North Korean post-mortems of the Soviet denouement assign the "inoculation" of "corrupt bourgeois culture" that is said to have infected the Soviet body politic with considerable responsibility for the USSR's eventual downfall. They also point to what they see as soft and vacillating leadership. In the words of Kim Jong Il, the DPRK's current ruler, "One-step concessions and retreat from the socialist principles ha[ve] resulted in ten and a hundred step concessions and retreat, and, finally, invited grave consequences of ruining the working class parties themselves."[6] Commentary by the DPRK's party paper recently made the same point even more sharply: "[I]f one discards socialism, it is death. This is a bloody lesson that the people learned again from social historic realities in the nineties."[7] By all indications, North Korea's leadership does not intend to repeat what it judges to have been the Soviet bloc's lethal mistakes. To the best of its abilities, the leadership plans instead to quarantine the population against the Western contagion and to do battle against the pressures for "reform."

From that perspective, it should not be a surprise that North Korea has tolerated only half-hearted and peripheral modifications of state policy despite the country's increasingly desperate economic straits. Although some acute observers of the Asian scene have speculated that North Korea might be able to evolve into a more open but still essentially autocratic polity,[8] indications are that the DPRK's own leaders are not at all sure that their state could survive such a transition. Irremediable economic decline is now the price for preserving what Pyongyang calls "our own style of socialism"—but it is a price North Korea's authorities are evidently willing to pay.

If the outlook for the DPRK's hierarchy from the pinnacle of its enterprise is thus inherently dark, recent developments in the South have made it even more menacing. In the ROK, 1996 witnessed the trial and conviction on charges of treason, mutiny, and corruption of two South Korean former presidents, Roh Tae Woo and Chun Doo Hwan. Although each was eventually granted clemency, both were sentenced to heavy punishments for their actions while in power; Chun received the death penalty. North Korean authorities may now reasonably expect that they will be held to the same strict standard of ROK justice if unification should occur on Seoul's terms, insofar as ROK law, like the DPRK's own, claims authority over Koreans throughout the entire peninsula. As the specter of systemic failure in North Korea grows closer, the penalties that DPRK leadership stands to face through such a failure look to be growing as well.

Under such circumstances, what can North Korea's leaders do to protect themselves and rescue their system? Outside observers who speculate about such things sometimes mention two radical measures: a renunciation of the state's claim to rule the Korean South that leads to a peace treaty with Seoul, a redirection of DPRK military resources, and significant foreign assistance; or a reconfiguration at the top that thrusts the ruling Kim "dynasty" aside and implements its own version of de-Stalinization—or both. Unfortunately for North Korea's elite, such seemingly bold and pragmatic steps look to be at least as likely to shorten the lifespan of their state as to lengthen it.

The claim to dominion over the entire Korean peninsula, and to the mission of reunifying Korea, is a cornerstone on which the legitimacy of DPRK rule leans—perhaps even more heavily in these austere times than it has at junctures in the past. Although reunification on North Korean terms may now be nothing but a fantasy, formal repudiation of that dream would undermine a primary justification for "our own style of socialism" in the DPRK—and beg the purpose of the bitter sacrifices that that system routinely requires of its subjects. By the same token, any power struggle that challenges the DPRK's official hagiography concerning the late Kim Il Sung and his descendants is more likely to weaken than to strengthen the foundations of North Korean rule. In no other modern country has the identity between a state and its ruling family been so purposely fused. Every putsch must have a raison d'être. If some government of national salvation should depose the members of the Kim circle and expose the deep shortcomings of their reign, it will simultaneously be revealing and acknowledging unacceptable flaws of the state those individuals now command. North Korea's present rulers clearly believe that their system cannot withstand a campaign of sustained *glasnost;* they may not be wrong.

None of the policy alternatives can look extremely attractive to the DPRK's leaders. Yet, one stratagem may seem decidedly more promising than any other. That is to continue to augment their potential to inflict devastation on neighboring or more distant adversaries. The international community, they may correctly calculate, can be expected to take rather less interest in the survival of their state if the "North Korean question" is construed as a purely humanitarian problem than if it is framed as an issue in international arms control. To extend the life of their state, by that reasoning, it is not only desirable but absolutely essential to enhance still further the strength of the DPRK's conventional forces and to upgrade progressively the threat posed by its "weapons of mass destruction." As best can be told, that is exactly what North Korean policymakers are attempting to do.

Despite North Korea's severe economic difficulties, the country's ambitious military program continues to move ahead. The Western intelligence community has yet to identify a "build down" in the North Korean People's Army troop strength; it notes instead continuing efforts at improvements in the quantity and quality of armaments at its disposal.[9] The severe and progressive decline of the North Korean economy is thought by many informed specialists to have restricted and perhaps even reduced the capabilities of North Korean conventional forces in the late 1990s.[10] But, if so, that would reflect simple exigence—not intentions or priorities of the Pyongyang elite. To the contrary, although that quantity is extremely difficult to calculate for any Soviet-type economy, it seems possible that North Korea's "military burden"—the ratio of the DPRK's defense expenditures to national output—may actually have *risen* over the course of the 1990s.[11] North Korea's program for developing nuclear weaponry has for now been suspended, it is widely supposed, through the "Agreed Framework" signed by Pyongyang and Washington in October 1994, but North Korea had already reportedly established a nuclear warfare command before that juncture,[12] may now have one or more atomic bombs in its possession, and could quickly resume its nuclear program by departing from the terms of that framework. And since the capabilities for outside detection of surreptitious North Korean nuclear activity are not perfect—in early 1999 a South Korean foreign ministry official reportedly stated that there are as many as 8,000 potential underground sites in the DPRK for a surreptitious program[13]—foreign observers can never be absolutely certain that North Korea has put its quest for atomic weaponry on hold, even when Pyongyang swears that to be so.

That nuclear program, in any case, is only one component in the DPRK's program for developing weapons of mass destruction. North Korea has established extensive capabilities for manufacturing chemical weapons, including nerve gas; according to some reports, the DPRK may have the world's third-largest inventory of those compounds.[14]

North Korea has also been working feverishly for decades on long-range missiles. The story of North Korea's missile development program has become fatefully familiar of late.[15] By the late 1980s, Pyongyang was making its own replicas of Soviet Scuds with a range of about 300 kilometers; by the early 1990s, the DPRK was at work on the No Dong class of missiles, with a range estimated at 1,000 to 1,300 kilometers. Today, it is developing the Taepo Dong, which, when perfected, may have a range of up to 10,000 kilometers;[16] according to some analysts, that intercontinental ballistic missile could be ready as early as the year 2000.

The latest milestone in North Korea's missile program, of course, was the August 1998 firing, without advance warning, of a three-stage Taepo Dong-1 rocket over the main island of Japan. Although Pyongyang subsequently insisted that it was harmlessly sending aloft a satellite for the broadcast of DPRK revolutionary hymns, the launch itself demonstrated that Pyongyang had (in the words of rocketry specialists) "progressed toward developing a multistage missile with a potential of between 3,800 and 5,900 km, approaching intercontinental ballistic missile range"[17]—a capability possessed by only a handful of countries in the world today. Although that surprise rocket launch provoked an international storm of criticism and alarm, North Korean authorities responded by insisting that it was their "sovereign right as a nation" to develop rocket technology and by indicating that there would be more launches to come.[18]

In 1994 North Korean negotiators famously warned their South Korean counterparts that the DPRK could turn Seoul into a "sea of fire." The previous year, North Korean media alerted the Japanese public to the possibility of "an unpredictable grave consequence from which Japan will never escape"[19] if Tokyo joined into the then-ongoing North Korean nuclear dispute. In 1998, when Japan protested the firing of the Taepo Dong-1 rocket over its territory and began to examine its options of defensive response, Pyongyang threatened that "Japan's hostile policy toward our republic will only bring about its own catastrophe."[20]

If and when the DPRK perfects a missile capable of reaching the American mainland, it may engage Washington in a similar dialogue— or it may not. It is possible, however, that we have already had a foretaste of what lies in store. In December 1998—after the Taepo Dong-1 launch and during negotiations with Washington over access to a particular underground site that had aroused nuclear suspicions[21]—North Korean military officials pointedly announced that "'Surgical operation'–style attack and 'preemptive strike' are by no means the exclusive option of the United States. The mode of strike is not a U.S. monopoly, either."[22] Departing from past formulations, they now advised that the United States was susceptible to an "annihilating blow" by North Korean forces and further proclaimed that they could "strike the enemy's positions and plunge them into a sea of fire no matter where they may be located on the planet."[23]

Regardless of the precise tenor of its diplomatic tactics, the DPRK will wish to convince all foreign powers it possibly can that they have a direct and personal stake in helping Pyongyang survive. Deliverable weapons of mass destruction and the thousands of emplaced artillery tubes already capable of targeting Seoul provide what Pyongyang may view as its best long-term bet for securing such support from abroad. Indeed, while prolonged decay of the national economy will eventually compromise the effectiveness of a conventional army, the killing force of those particular instruments should be much more insulated from those same adverse trends.

North Korea's endgame thus exposes all of Northeast Asia, and even possibly countries outside the region, to immediate and mounting peril. As the economic base beneath the North Korean state falters and the prospect of state failure draws closer, the lethal power in the hands of the regime and the leadership's incentives to exploit it continue to increase.

Will Delayed Reunification Be "Stabilizing"?

Whatever their particular differences, the North Korea policies of the five governments that must contend most directly with the DPRK—Seoul, Washington, Beijing, Tokyo, and Moscow—all appear today to be formulated around the assumption that a rapidly effected Korean reunification in the near future would not be in their own national interest. Implicitly or explicitly, their policies all seem to posit that a gradual drawing together of the two Koreas, conducted over a time horizon extending far into the future, would be optimal for financial or geopolitical reasons.

Not surprisingly, pronouncements about unification have been most detailed in South Korea. In 1991 then–President Roh Tae Woo declared that "our people do not want an accelerated unification." Despite his subsequent fall from grace and the perennial differences of opinion on the point within the Seoul government, that sentiment continues to guide policy. Despite President Kim Dae Jung's many differences with his immediate predecessors and their policies, his approach to Korean unification—his "sunshine policy of engagement"—marks a continuation of, not a departure from, Seoul's hesitant attitude toward "accelerated reunification." One of the three basic principles of Kim's policy, indeed, was that South Korea had "no intention" to "absorb North Korea";[24] President Kim has further declared—or assured—that he does not expect to achieve Korea's unification during his five-year term of office.[25] Research from the Korea Development Institute, the ROK's leading quasi-governmental economic think tank, succinctly expresses the mainstream viewpoint in Seoul. The institute's studies have argued that "the German experience demonstrates that national unification involves enormous costs, and, going forward, this is probably the most critical concern for South Korea"[26] and further that "the experience of German national unification convinced a large number of South Koreans that sudden economic integration in Korea . . . will result in disaster."[27] Rather than risk derailing South Korea's ascent to affluence, the prevailing Seoul consensus counsels, the ROK should try to plan for a reintegration with the North over a period of several decades, during which time the DPRK might reform its polity and transform its economy. It would appear that economic calculations bear heavily on that attitude.

Parallel calculations apparently lead the four great powers of Northeast Asia to a similar evaluation of the merits of a gradual and distant

Korean reunification. Although President Bush declared in Seoul in 1992 that "the day will inevitably come" when "Korea will be whole again,"[28] and the Clinton administration subsequently affirmed "the long-run objective" of an "ultimately reunified [Korean] Peninsula,"[29] American policy does not anticipate that advent any time soon. To the contrary, Washington's "Agreed Framework" with Pyongyang envisions a prolonged and expanding American engagement with the DPRK; the measures outlined in the document are not to be fulfilled for years to come.[30] Although positively disposed to Korean unification in the abstract, American policy includes no positive designs for hastening that event. In addition to its consideration for ROK anxieties about a rapid reunification, the U.S. position is shaped by its own concerns: specifically, the possibility that a Korean unification might mean the end of America's special security ties with (and forward bases in) the ROK—an arrangement that has, in Washington's estimate, helped both to stabilize the entire region and to extend American influence in Asia.

China, Japan, and Russia have their own grounds for reluctance about a rapid Korean reunification. In each instance, a continuing and long-term division of the Korean peninsula is viewed as being, at the very least, consistent with national interests. "The Chinese," as Chae-jin Lee has noted, believe that they "have no compelling reason to push for Korea's immediate political reintegration, even by peaceful means," insofar as they "view North Korea as a useful buffer zone that contributes to their national security" and at the same time enjoy a thriving commercial relationship with South Korea.[31] Japanese foreign policy remains more opaque than that of most other Westernized countries, so that divining its underlying rationales is often a challenge; one ingredient in Japan's approach to the two Korean states, though, seems to be an abiding apprehension that a united Korea might pose greater economic and diplomatic challenges to Tokyo.[32] Russia, for its part, is all but overwhelmed at the moment with its own internal troubles and in this time of extreme weakness might not be expected to welcome the possibility of a new rising regional power along its border.[33]

The fact that the viewpoints of a multiplicity of concerned governments about the preferable pace for Korean unification should be in rough alignment, unfortunately, is no guarantee that those judgments are correct. Our century provides repeated examples of shared misperceptions and collective miscalculations in foreign policy—as the prologues to World War I, World War II, and even the Korean War attest.

Tragic miscalculations about one's own national interests, one may note, seem to be more common in periods when a regional balance is undergoing fundamental change—and as we have just seen, the Korean peninsula is at precisely such a juncture today.

Closer inspection of particulars suggests that the concordance in question may indeed reflect a pervasive misassessment of national interests. In a diverse but systematic manner, one may argue, both the risks inherent in a delayed Korean reunification and the opportunities available from a more immediate reunification are being underestimated.

Consider first the economics of a Korean reunification. No doubt, the reintegration of the two Koreas, however it ultimately occurs, will involve major economic dislocations and will place immediate financial burdens on the working-age population of South Korea (the first cohort of Koreans in recorded history, incidentally, to be unfamiliar with privation and unexpected material sacrifice). Moreover, the equalization of incomes in northern and southern Korea will inevitably be a long historical process—like the enforced separation that brought today's disparities about. But can a "go-slow" policy realistically promise to reduce the dislocations and expenses attendant on unification?

The vision of a gradual and protracted reintegration of the two Korean economies so fondly entertained by so many South Koreans today hinges on a huge assumption. It implicitly holds that North Korea's government will someday embrace a program of economic liberalization—and would somehow survive to complete the decades of transformation that such a program would entail. Yet, as we have already seen, Pyongyang has to date vigorously opposed any liberalization of economic policies worthy of the name. Apart from wishful speculation, nothing as yet suggests that North Korea is contemplating any such reorientation. The weight of evidence, furthermore, indicates that Pyongyang's leadership believes that economic liberalization would be lethal for the regime. Viewed dispassionately, the notion that North Korea might meet the conditions that the "slow reintegration" scenario would demand of it can only be said to look remote—if not utterly fanciful.

If the DPRK does not conform to that idealized pattern of future behavior but instead cleaves to a more traditional policy direction, the most likely outlook is continued economic decline. For the ROK, by contrast, the most reasonable prognosis for the decades ahead would look to be steady and perhaps substantial economic growth. Under such circumstances, both the relative and the absolute gap in per capita income between North and South Korea will continue to widen.

On such a trajectory, the longer the North Korean state survives, the greater the economic chasm that will separate North and South. Other things being equal, that means that the "cost of unification" (if we understand that to be the investment needs of North Korea in relation to South Korean output) will grow steadily, perhaps even swiftly, every year that reunification is delayed. And while it is technically possible to imagine mathematical conditions under which the increased "costs" of a deferred unification might seem less onerous to the South Korean public, a more common-sense reading of the dynamic would be that a growing divergence between the two systems implies greater economic burdens the longer reunification is postponed.

The eventual economic "cost of reunification" in Korea, however, is not a mechanistically predetermined sum. To the contrary, it will be contingent on as yet unspecified human actions and government policies. If the specter of German-style unification expenses terrifies some South Korean policymakers today, they tremble before a false analogy.

As any number of careful studies have already pointed out, the great bulk of West German transfers to the "new Federal States" since 1990 have been for social welfare payments—*not* for investment.[34] In eastern Germany, as it happened, most of the "costs of unification" to date were incurred through a collision between politically popular but overgenerous wage increases (which priced a huge portion of the *"Ossi"* work force out of the job market) and an extravagant, newly installed social insurance apparatus (which paid qualifying beneficiaries on the established *"Wessi"* scale). There is no reason for these particular expenses to be replicated elsewhere—much less in the ROK, which for better or worse still lacks most of the adornments of a full-fledged "welfare state."

Moreover, we should remember that a Korean reunification—even a sudden, unexpected one—will result in benefits as well as costs. Enlightened and foresighted policy could systematically augment those benefits.

In the short run, reunification with a poorer partner could have a number of potentially beneficial effects: it could, for example, help relieve South Korea's incipient labor shortage, reduce pressures on wages and production costs, and thereby enhance Korea's international competitiveness. While South Korean workers may not relish that particular prospect, it is not inconceivable that a fusion of the two Korean work forces could actually increase purchasing power and living standards for the great majority in both the North and the South.[35]

Over the long run, as northern Korea's infrastructure and industrial capacity are renovated, all of Korea could experience dynamic "supply-side effects" from the newly installed capital stock in the North. The flip side of North Korea's current infrastructural obsolescence—of the likely need to scrap almost all the DPRK's extant production facilities—is the coming opportunity to replace decrepit plants with state-of-the-art equipment embodying the latest technology.

As was learned in postwar Japan and West Germany, wholesale reconstruction of an industrial base can bring unexpected economic advantages: it can lower production costs, stimulate work-force skills, dramatically enhance potential productivity, and lay foundations for sustained long-term economic growth. Those advantages, we may recall, accrued not only to Japan and West Germany, but also to the economies with which they were integrated. While the analogy is clearly inexact, the prospective modernization of the North Korean economy will undoubtedly offer the possibility of enormous spillover benefits to southern Korea. Nor would the spillover benefits of a successful modernization of northern Korea be limited to Korean nationals. Success in that venture would strengthen—not weaken—the entire framework for prosperity in Northeast Asia and the Pacific; it would directly spur international economic development through the favorable investment opportunities, the expanded domestic market, and the improved quality of exportable goods and services that would, in such an outcome, accompany Korean reunification.

In the final analysis, we can liken Korea's future reunification to a single gigantic investment project: if the rates of return to that project are high, the costs of the project will take care of themselves. Achieving and maintaining the necessary rates of return will not be easy, we can be sure. But at the same time, that is surely not the hopeless task that some in Seoul today implicitly take it to be. Through prudent and coordinated preparations by the ROK and its allies, the chances that a Korean reunification will be an economic success—even if it takes place at very short notice—can be greatly increased.

If the economic potentialities of a more immediate and more intentional Korean unification look to be decidedly less menacing than so often depicted, what of its possible political and strategic ramifications? Does deferring the settlement of the "Korean question" seem likely to purchase security—or at least decrease external tension and turbulence—for the other countries in the region? Once again, the answer is less self-evident than current policies seem to presume.

In great power politics and in international relations more generally, deferring the resolution of difficult or contentious issues—and the "Korean question" assuredly qualifies as one of those—can sometimes have merit. If the costs of maintaining an unstable balance are low, or if the problem under consideration is likely to grow less onerous with time, pushing the issue off into the future can sometimes serve a country's national interests. Unfortunately, from the standpoint of the great powers in Northeast Asia, neither of those conditions obtains in the Korean *problematik*.

Over the foreseeable future, as we have seen, North Korea's economic circumstances are likely only to worsen, even as the killing power of its weapons of mass destruction waxes. On the current trajectory, then, the magnitude of the potential shocks to the region that the demise of the North Korean state might trigger is unlikely to be intrinsically mitigated simply by securing a later date for that event. By diverse criteria—including mass loss of life—the potential for damage to the region may actually increase the longer North Korea's endgame continues.

In the meantime, the various costs of maintaining the unstable balance in the Korean peninsula—already nonnegligible for the United States—stand only to rise over time. From a financial standpoint, in addition to underwriting military deterrence in Korea, Western governments now envision substantial outlays to Pyongyang for economic and humanitarian aid in the years to come: the "Agreed Framework" is only one of several mechanisms for such transfers. To the extent that the great Pacific powers conceptualize "Korean security" in a two-state framework, they will be ineluctably drawn toward subsidizing the Northern system as its internal crises mount.

On a separate ledger, given the DPRK's constantly improving arsenal of weapons of mass destruction, the extended survival of the North Korean regime will raise both the probability and the expected intensity of "out-of-theater" security threats facilitated by DPRK sales or transfers of arms to extremist governments or terrorist groups in other parts of the world. Although such threats would likely prove most burdensome to the United States—the only one of the four Pacific powers with truly global interests and obligations—none of the others could realistically expect to be left unaffected by destabilization abetted by weapons of mass destruction in distant venues (say, for example, the Middle East).

For the Pacific powers, the "Korean question" is no longer a problem that can be postponed and then muddled through. Ironically, by their current approaches to that conundrum, the great powers of Northeast Asia have commonly embraced a "strategy" whose ultimate impact may actually be to reduce the security and well-being that each of them will enjoy.

And what of the alternatives? The notion of purposely working to prepare for, and thereby perhaps to hasten, Korea's reunification may seem fraught with risk—and indeed it is. For such a strategy can offer no absolute guarantee that the reunification of Korea it would usher in will be a peaceful one.

But that is posing and answering the wrong question. In the perilous years ahead, there is no strategy that can honestly promise perpetual peace in the Korean peninsula—or Northeast Asia, for that matter. Indeed, the entirety of East Asia, in Aaron Friedberg's telling phrase, is now "ripe for rivalry"[36] and will be for many years to come. Under the circumstances, the only meaningful criterion for contending strategies is a comparative assessment of their potential risks and benefits. By that criterion, a policy that deliberately prepares for and attempts to expedite the coming of a free, peaceful, and united Korea looks decidedly superior to its alternatives. To appreciate the difference, one may begin by imagining how the character of international relations in Northeast Asia would be altered if Korea were governed by a single, democratic state.

Two great imponderables tower over that variant of a thought experiment: the future evolutions of China and Russia. All specific and subsidiary implications for the region of a free and united Korea will depend on the course that events will take in those two countries—and those courses are as yet largely unclear. Irrespective of particulars yet to unfold in China and Russia, however, a free and united Korea can be seen as a force for stability and prosperity in the region. In a variety of ways, unification of the Korean peninsula under an open and liberal order could be expected to reduce potentially destabilizing tensions and to add to inducements for peaceful cooperation.

For Northeast Asia, perhaps the most dramatic implications of a successful Korean reunification would be military. At the moment, nearly 2 million Korean troops confront each other in that divided land. A free and united Korea could commence a far-reaching demobilization, releasing hundreds of thousands of military personnel for economically productive undertakings, retiring armaments that were once trained across the DMZ, and decommissioning the peninsula's weapons of mass destruction. Such disarmament could still leave Korea as a power to reckon with. But a far-reaching demilitarization in Korea would also recast the conventional and nuclear logic of Northeast Asia.

For one thing, a major demobilization would stand in contraposition to the arms buildup that has been underway in East Asia since the 1980s and has continued there unabated since the end of the cold war.[37] While a major disarmament in Korea would not alter the ambitions of other governments—a major factor in any true "arms race"—it could substantially change the nature of "risk perception" and "defense sufficiency" in the region and in that respect attenuate pressures for further buildup.

Whereas a continuing division of Korea invites a competitive proliferation in Northeast Asia—with the ROK and Japan, in one reading, eventually opting for nuclear defense to counter ominous tendencies in the DPRK—a united Korea could make good on Seoul's standing pledge to foreswear possession or development of atomic weaponry. Moreover, by eliminating Korea as a possible purveyor of weapons of mass destruction, unification would strike a double blow against international proliferation: for that not only would end all Korean activities in that market but would also tangibly complicate China's surreptitiously merchandizing weapons of mass destruction.

A successful Korean unification would also bear on the tenor of international relations in Northeast Asia. With a single and democratic government on the Korean peninsula, many of the current regional sources of tension would simply cease to be. While it is reasonable to suppose that the interests of the great powers of the Pacific will diverge in important respects after Korean unification, just as they do today, a successful reunification not only would affect the balance of power in the region, but could also influence the manner in which regional disputes and frictions tend to be handled. While a united Korea's chosen alliances and alignments might matter greatly to the great powers of the Pacific, a united and democratic Korea's alliances and alignments are most unlikely to constitute a *casus belli*. With open and accountable governance, civilian rule, and enthusiasm for commercial progress, a united and free Korea's foreign policy is likely to be moderate in outlook and problem-solving in nature—very much, indeed, like South Korea's own foreign policies today. United Korea's domestic arrangements could also be a factor in international politics; the very fact of a solid civil society in Korea, for example, would lend support to neighboring Russia's continuing quest for stable civil institutions and might provide additional (if highly indirect) encouragement for such changes in China as well.

Finally, as we have already noted, the project of Korean reunification stands to offer spillover benefits to all economies in the region. Apprehensions already expressed in some circles in Russia and China about being "crowded out" by the economic reconstruction of a united Korea are almost certainly misplaced. The global capital market is enormous and growing rapidly: in 1997 alone—the most recent year for which data are available—it financed over $1.7 trillion in international borrowings and facilitated an over $350 billion flow of foreign direct investment.[38] In a system of that size and sophistication, the additional demand for external finance produced by a Korean reunification is quite unlikely to compromise Beijing's or Moscow's access to international capital or to affect significantly the terms on which capital is secured. On the other hand, the boom in domestic demand that would follow a successful Korean reunification would likely offer wide-ranging and lucrative business opportunities to all the Pacific powers. One of the most intriguing economic implications of a successful reunification involves integration of the Chinese, Russian, and Korean markets. To date, *juche* economics has effectively precluded the development of infrastructural or commercial linkages between the DPRK and nearby areas of China and Russia; with an ROK-style "business climate" in northern Korea, however, a "growth triangle" worthy of the name could at last join the three countries.

In the end, the prospects for both stability and conflict in Northeast Asia will depend heavily on the nature of the states in the region, the sorts of linkages that bind them, and the relative costs and benefits of hostilities.[39] From that perspective, a free and unified Korea would clearly seem to weigh as a "stabilizing" force for the region. Attempting to postpone Korea's reunification, moreover, is unlikely to improve the ultimate chances of successful reunion. In fact, as we have seen, just the opposite is likely to be true. For, sadly, the vision of a gradual and orderly drawing together of the two Koreas, cherished as it may be, looks today at bottom to be little more than a fantasy.

For every state in Northeast Asia that must currently deal with the DPRK, preparing for the post–DPRK era is not only a prudent task but an urgent one. The striking point about a successful Korean reunification is that *all* populations in Northeast Asia would stand to benefit from it. Those dividends are by no means yet assured, but with careful and concerted effort, they may be brought within grasp.

Preparing for Reunification

Every government in Northeast Asia can help improve the chances of a free and peaceful reunification in Korea through its actions today and in the years ahead. That much is self-evident. But just what should the various countries in the region be doing and planning for, if they want to enhance the prospects for a successful unification? And is it realistic to expect them to embrace those requisite measures?

As one contemplates the possibilities for influencing events in the peninsula, two current constraints on future policies loom large. The first is the fact that neither China nor Russia can, at least as yet, be counted on to cooperate in any multilateral deliberations about post–DPRK Korea. The second is that the allies most likely to cooperate in those preparations—the ROK, Japan, and the United States—have already restricted their freedom of maneuver through the "Agreed Framework" that they entered with Pyongyang in 1994. Both those complications deserve further comment.

For all the obvious historical reasons, Washington's security relationships with Beijing and with Moscow are vastly different from its relationships with Seoul and Tokyo. For equally obvious reasons, we can expect both China and Russia to regard an "American" design for a new Korea with considerable suspicion, not only now but in years to come. China, in particular, has reason to appreciate the Korean status quo: given what are now its close ties to both Korean governments, its booming trade with the South, and the "socialist buffer" that the DPRK still provides, one may argue that the Chinese state enjoys a more favorable position in Korea today than at any point in the past century and a half.

Weighing against the impediments to cooperation, though, is a single and compelling fact: the current order in Korea cannot last. It is in both China's and Russia's interests to help shape the order that replaces it. Moreover, when one carefully examines Chinese and Russian interests in the peninsula, it is apparent that they coincide with ROK–Japan–U.S. interests in fundamental respects—both now and in years to come.

If oil flows from the Middle East are disrupted tomorrow by a crisis involving North Korean–made weapons of mass destruction, for example, China—which is becoming a major global oil importer—will suffer directly. Conversely, as we have seen, both Russia and China stand to reap commercial and security benefits from a successful Korean reunification.

From a pure national interest standpoint, both China and Russia have strong incentives for approaching the challenge of Korean reunification together with the ROK–Japan–U.S. alliance, not apart from it. The task for U.S., Japanese, and South Korean diplomacy, then, is not to convince Russian and Chinese leaders to submit to a Western strategy for Korea, but rather to encourage them to think clearly and realistically about where their own interests in Korea actually lie.

The "Agreed Framework" poses a rather different set of problems to Western diplomats and strategists. That complex document outlines an extended schedule of financial, material, and diplomatic benefits that Pyongyang may obtain from a U.S.–led international consortium if and when the DPRK passes a variety of milestones—mainly concerning compliance with the Nuclear Nonproliferation Treaty but also involving such things as detente with South Korea and arms control.

As negotiators on both sides have pointed out, the document is not an agreement: in formal terms, it is simply a sort of road map. Others, however, have observed that the ambiguous nature of the document exposes America and her allies to the worst of two diplomatic worlds: obliging Washington to behave as if it were bound by treaty while permitting Pyongyang to decide when and whether it would honor its corresponding obligations.[40] Furthermore, the range of Western–DPRK engagements envisioned under the "Agreed Framework" could ultimately be read as placing restrictions on the range and scope of Western reunification strategies for Korea.

If Western governments are not to be ensnared by that nonagreement in the years ahead, they must honestly recognize the "Agreed Framework" for what it is. For one thing, the "Agreed Framework" (representations to the contrary notwithstanding) does not "solve the North Korean nuclear problem." Quite the contrary, it merely postpones the resolution of the issue, by permitting both sides to resolve to settle the matter later on. The North Korean nuclear "problem," for its part, does not derive from the technical specifications of the DPRK's Soviet-style reactors, but rather from the nature and intentions of the North Korean state. The DPRK *is* the North Korean nuclear problem—and unless those intentions change, that problem will continue as long as the North Korean state holds power.

If Western governments believe that they have some small chance of influencing the nature of that state through the "Agreed Framework," they should assess such progress—or the lack of it—carefully and unflinchingly. But to allow that document to compromise preparations for

Korean unification, or to substitute for them, would be a grave mistake.

The Western countries with the greatest prospective influence on Korea's ultimate reunification are, of course, the ROK, the United States, and Japan. What sorts of things could each of them do, bilaterally or multilaterally, to raise the odds for a free, peaceful, and successful Korean reunification?

The Republic of Korea. Let us begin with the ROK, the government that will be most affected by the outcome. As a first but still necessary step, Seoul would make clear that preparing for a successful unification is an immediate national priority but is a matter that will also require long-range policies. Political leadership in the ROK must increase the South Korean public's awareness of the tests that lie ahead and must make the case that those tests can be successfully surmounted only by sensible strategy and concerted, collective effort.

As they contemplate the coming trials of unification, South Koreans may recognize that, paradoxically, their most important agenda may actually center on domestic reform within the ROK. If a free and peaceful reunification is indeed consummated, the subsequent success of that project will depend greatly on the dynamism of the ROK economy, the resilience of ROK society, and the stability of the ROK polity. Despite the ROK's great strides in all those areas over the past generation, each of them had unfinished business.

Very generally speaking, policy-induced distortions throughout much of the South Korean economy continue to constrain productivity and flexibility[41]—qualities sure to be required in a reintegration with the North. They also hinder prospective reintegration more directly. As is well known in international business circles, the ROK's "climate" for foreign direct investment is not famously hospitable—but in reconstructing the North, the alternative to foreign direct investment will be higher exactions from South Korean taxpayers.

As it happens, further economic liberalization will bring tangible and immediate benefits to the population of South Korea. In that sense, it is a sound and worthy objective in its own right. The approaching reunification with the North, however, transmutes economic reform from a sound objective into an urgent one.

The same may be said of civil and legal reforms. Despite the ROK's achievement of constitutional, civilian rule, progress in civil and administrative law has lagged. Incontestible guarantees to the rights of the individual (including property rights) and to accountable, transparent governance are intrinsically desirable and beneficial. With unification impending, however, the importance of civil and legal reform only rises: in North and South alike, the credibility of a united Korea's political system will depend on openness, impartiality, and equality before the law. What ROK President Kim Young Sam once called the "Korean disease" could become a virulent illness if it is not cured before reunification.

In the domestic realm, preparing for reunification mainly means doing what the ROK should already be doing anyway. But preparing for reunification also has a bearing on South Korean defense policy and its posture toward the North.

Preventing war and forging a successful reunification will require close cooperation with all the ROK's allies, including ally Japan. Although Seoul's ties to Tokyo have been deepening and warming for decades, ample room for improvement still exists. The 1996 squabble over the disputed Tokdo-Takeshima islands—which culminated in an ROK military landing on those barren rocks—is exactly the sort of distraction that a defense policy for South Korea cannot afford. If deterring North Korea is the objective, moreover, the merit of South Korea's costly current program for developing a submarine fleet is hardly self-evident.[42] Korea and Japan, it is true, have a long and tortured historical relationship. In a successful Korean reunification, however, there will be deep, extensive, and growing cooperation between the ROK and Japan. Absent such cooperation, a successful reunification will be so much less likely.

With regard to North Korea, the ROK must begin to think not only about deterrence, but about reconciliation. Healing the wounds of divided Korea promises to be a monumental task—one that may take generations to complete. But the process can begin now. Committing the ROK to a "malice toward none" policy after Korean unification and to guaranteeing ordinary Northerners the same civil and political rights as Southerners would send an important and stabilizing message.

The United States. The United States can shape the prospects for Korea's reunification through a diversity of instruments, but its unique and indispensable contribution is in the realm of security. Just as the U.S. military commitment to the ROK has been the sine qua non for deterrence in the peninsula, a vibrant U.S.–ROK security relationship in a united Korea will be critical to the success of reunification.

That assertion is not based on an ominous reading of geopolitical prospects for the region. In fact, portents of dark developments are not necessary to make the case. The case instead rests on the economics of reconstruction in Korea after a free and peaceful unification.

Although analysts cannot yet calculate exact sums, rebuilding the economy of northern Korea will obviously require tremendous amounts of money. It is just as obvious that the process will proceed more rapidly and place less of a burden on Korean taxpayers, if the international capital markets can be harnessed to the project. Private capital, however, must be attracted—and the attractiveness to overseas investors of the "investment climate" of postunification Korea will depend on perceptions of the risks and potential rewards in that country.

Undoubtedly, prospective foreign investors and international financial markets will regard a strong American security commitment to the Republic of Korea in the period after unification as a factor reducing—not raising—risk for Korean undertakings. If that security commitment attenuates, however, or if America should disengage from Korea on even the friendliest of terms, Korea will have to pay a commensurately higher "risk premium" for any capital it does manage to attract—and its ability to attract international capital will almost surely be compromised. Strong security ties to the United States, simply put, are essential if the project of Korean unification is to "pay off." It is not too much to suggest that the fate of reunification could ultimately depend on them.

For Washington, however, preparing for Korean reunification will mean more than thinking about "bases and places"—much more. As the world's predominant economy and as the presumptive leader of any strategic Western initiative in Northeast Asia or other regions of the globe, the United States will almost naturally be responsible for coordinating an international approach to Korean unification. Managing such an effort wisely and effectively will be a tremendous task—a task no less taxing or delicate than the historic endeavor that united Germany in 1990.[43] The events that precipitated Germany's reunification, however, were largely unexpected; Korean reunification, by contrast, can—and should—be anticipated.

Japan. To consider Japan's prospective influence on Korean unification is to beg the question of Japan's role in the world. In our century, Japan has never had a "normal" foreign policy: before World War II, it was an insatiable and revisionist power; since its terrible defeat, it has acted as a meek, one-legged giant. To this day, it is difficult for the Japanese to discuss their "national interests"—even in the

Korean peninsula, where those interests are so directly and dramatically affected.

For better or worse, until such time as Japan can play on the international stage in the same manner as other industrial democracies, its potential contributions to a successful Korean reunification are most likely to conduce through the two diplomatic channels in which Tokyo is most comfortable: international finance and multilateral institutions.

Fortunately, much can be done through both those channels. If Korean reunification is to succeed, it will presage a significant expansion of trade and will require very substantial commitments of foreign capital (through both direct investment and portfolio lending). Japan's government and the Japanese business community can begin now to focus on the potentialities of mutually beneficial economic cooperation in a united Korea and on the problems that must be avoided or resolved if such cooperation is to bear fruit. The Japanese business and financial community may also be well placed to participate in the major infrastructural development projects that could draw together the economies of northern Korea, China, and Russia.

Much can also be done in multinational forums, both now and in the future. Preventing North Korean sales of weapons of mass destruction or nuclear-capable missiles, for example, is an immediate problem that multilateral diplomacy can address; Japan could be a persuasive lobbyist for a UN resolution empowering members to interdict such materials from Nonproliferation Treaty violators. In the years ahead, Japan could use its growing influence at the World Bank and other multilateral development banks to encourage those institutions to devote their technical expertise and their financial resources to meeting the challenges that will be entailed in Korea's coming reunification. Indeed, throwing themselves into the economic rebuilding of the northern portion of a unified Korea is arguably a more productive and constructive assignment for the World Bank and other multilateral development banks than most projects in which they are engaged today.

A list of possible initiatives and policies could be extended. The point, however, is succinct. Northeast Asia can live with a united Korea—in fact, it could be considerably more comfortable with a single free Korea than with the present arrangements. It is time for statesmen in the Pacific and beyond to think about how to make Korean reunification a success—because success or no, a Korean reunification lies in store in the years ahead.

Postscript: Has the South Korean
Financial Crisis of 1997 Changed Everything?

Readers of the preceding chapter will note—and may well object—that its analysis makes no great mention of the ROK's momentous 1997 financial upheaval: or more specifically, of the impact of that economic setback on prospects for North-South relations. That question deserves extended examination, not only because of its importance in its own right, but also because of the strong opinions that seem to be forming today regarding its answer.

In Washington, Seoul, Tokyo, and perhaps elsewhere, something like a consensus seems to be emerging about the impact of the Republic of Korea's recent travails on the outlook for relations between divided Korea's two governments—and by extension, on the prospects for reunification of that tormented land. According to that nascent consensus, South Korea's crisis of international liquidity in late 1997, and the economic slowdown subsequently provoked by it, have altered not only the economic but also the political landscape of the Korean peninsula, making possible—if not positively forcing—a new direction for North-South interactions.

In such an interpretation of events, the Democratic People's Republic of Korea, in the wake of South Korea's abrupt and even humiliating comeuppance, now regards the South Korean system as a somewhat less fearsome adversary and the Seoul government as a somewhat less menacing interlocutor. Thus, in that telling, South Korea's difficulties have lessened Pyongyang's resistance both to inter-Korean dialogue and to the sorts of economic cooperation the North so clearly needs today. The South, for its part, is seen as having been rudely awakened from an overweening confidence by the drama that drove it to seek massive assistance from the International Monetary Fund and the international community. Wholesale absorption of the North, previously a cherished objective in many South Korean circles, is now said to be recognized as an impractical dream. The newly limited capabilities of the ROK economy and the South Korean state, according to that consensus, argue for a much more gradual, incremental approach to the drawing together of the two Korean systems. The net result, consequently, is said to be a significant shift in the dynamics and underlying calculus of relations between the two Koreas.[44]

In the pages that follow, I argue that this emerging consensus is fundamentally unpersuasive. I attempt to demonstrate that its analysis (or more specifically, key assumptions on which that analysis rests) cannot be squared with important facts already at hand—some of them basic and self-evident.

To be sure, perceptions in the South—and possibly also in the North, although for outsiders that is mere guesswork—have been shaken, if not overturned, by recent events very much in the news. And in politics perceptions can matter greatly. Yet, at the end of the day, neither North Korea's prospects for regime survival nor Pyongyang's interests in "inter-Korean affairs" have been altered appreciably by South Korea's newfound financial and economic difficulties. Conversely, while South Korea's problems have clearly constrained the resources from which its government may draw in pursuing overall policy objectives, it is much less clear that those resource constraints have any great bearing on the conduct of an appropriate policy toward the North. Looking to the longer horizon, it is paradoxically possible that South Korea's economic crisis may in some ways actually enhance Seoul's capacities for consummating an eventual and successful unification of the Korean peninsula on its own terms.

Consider the North Korean *problematik* for a moment. As has already been emphasized, we know woefully little about the DPRK: state, economy, or society. That officially contrived "data famine" notwithstanding, it is safe to say that the prospects for regime survival in North Korea are principally shaped today by Pyongyang's own policies and that the DPRK has doggedly clung to and relentlessly implemented a regimen of ultimately ruinous economic policy for what is now many long years.

It is no longer a state secret that the DPRK economy has entered into steep decline or that the country is suffering from severe food shortages: the DPRK's top leadership now officially acknowledges as much. But, contrary to protestations by Pyongyang, neither bad weather nor bad luck can explain away the disastrous performance of the contemporary North Korean system. In the main, that economic system has suffered—and continues to suffer—from self-inflicted injuries.

Indeed, Pyongyang has a distinctive approach to economic affairs:[45]

• its insistence on underwriting an astonishing degree of militarization
• its penchant for "planning without facts"
• its fetish for what it labels "investment," irrespective of the productive returns on such expenditures

- its continuing attempt to delink price relations from resource allocation decisions and its largely successful quest to demonetize its domestic distribution of goods and services
- its protracted war against its own consumers
- its promotion of a highly eccentric variant of "food self-sufficiency"
- its proclivity for treating foreign loans as if they were non-repayable presents from afar
- its allergic reaction to generating export earnings through mutually beneficial commerce

It is not difficult to understand the pattern of economic failures the DPRK has thus far experienced.

Barring a radical reorientation of the North Korean regime's economic policy—convincing signs of which, incidentally, are still not in evidence,[46] despite the country's desperate and apparently still worsening material conditions[47]—Pyongyang's economic dealings constitute a prescription for eventual system failure. The plight of the South Korean *won* and of the South Korean GDP would seem to have only the most incidental bearing on the trajectory on which the DPRK is currently embarked.

More immediately, North Korea's approach to inter-Korean affairs is arguably not just informed by, but deeply animated by, the regime's own interpretation of "unification policy." For Pyongyang, as I argue in chapter 2, "unification" has long meant unification on its terms—and its terms alone: the transformation of the entire Korean peninsula into what the DPRK leadership would describe as a "single independent socialist nation."

The quest for unconditional unification is deeply embedded within the logic of the DPRK regime—indeed, one might even say indispensable to it. To relinquish the claim to mastery of the entire Korean peninsula would be to beg the rationale behind the terrible suffering the North Korean populace has endured over the past half century. Explicitly abandoning its long-standing "unification policy" could be deeply subversive of the authority and legitimacy of the North Korean state.

For that reason, when it has to deal peaceably with the South, North Korea finds itself in a straitjacket. Yet the straitjacket is hardly of the IMF's making.

Now, let us turn for a moment to the ROK. South Korea is not so prosperous in 1999 as it was in 1997, and its government has less wherewithal at its disposal. But in what way does that basic fact constrain Seoul in implementing its policies toward Pyongyang? Do financial limitations now prevent South Korean leadership from embarking on what would otherwise be demonstrably superior paths of inter-Korean policy?

What, for example, of inter-Korean economic cooperation? Given the inviolability of what Pyongyang terms "our own style of socialism" *(urisik sahoejuui)*, North Korea's ability to absorb genuinely productive development assistance is extraordinarily limited—indeed (one may argue) entirely negligible, at least for the moment. And given the funhouse mirror that is its domestic price structure, North Korean leadership today, as I argue in chapter 4, in fact lacks any objective basis for determining the potential benefit of any commercial exchange with outside partners.

For its part, from the very inception of its *Nordpolitik* in 1988, South Korea's approach to commerce with the North has been governed—and distorted—by political considerations. Early in 1998, however, the Kim Dae Jung government announced a departure from that approach as part of the new "sunshine policy of engagement": an injunction to "separate business from politics." Thenceforth, inter-Korean commerce was to be based on purely businesslike calculations: reward versus risk, and the potential for profit. It may well be that South Korea's new approach to North-South economic relations has been influenced by its government's newly felt austerity—but irrespective of the motivating factors, Seoul's policy in that regard promises now to be on sounder ground than it was before.[48]

What, then, of the "Agreed Framework," the Korean Peninsula Energy Development Organization, and the impending financial burdens entailed in building two light-water reactor nuclear power plants for the North?

All other things being equal, the weakness of the *won* and the South Korean economy imply greater strains in meeting that particular objective. But all other things are *not* given, as the very structure of the "Agreed Framework" itself implicitly recognizes.

As the diplomats who crafted it went to great lengths to explain, the "Agreed Framework" is not a treaty; it is not a contract; and it is not even an *agreement*. If it were any of those things, after all, Pyongyang would be in default on its existing obligations: conspicuously refraining as it has over the past five years from any meaningful steps toward a resumption of its interrupted dialogue with the ROK,[49] to cite just one case in point![50]

The essence of that curious document is that the "road map" outlined within it is inherently—and almost inevitably—subject to continued reexamination and emendation by the negotiating parties involved. Strictly speaking, the ROK is not a party to those negotiations, insofar as the document was signed only by representatives of Washington and Pyongyang. Yet, although South Korea is not a signatory to the "Agreed Framework," it is very much a presence within it—not least because the South Koreans are expected to foot most of the bill for the light-water reactor nuclear power plants that would be presented to North Korea under the current reading of the accord.

If South Korean taxpayers and their representatives should feel hard pressed by the ROK's budgetary austerity and should they notice that nonnuclear plants happen to be much less expensive to construct than lightwater reactors, the "Agreed Framework" might possibly prove sufficiently elastic to encompass those concerns. For those who doubted the original wisdom of providing a violator of the Nuclear Nonproliferation Treaty with new sources of potentially fissile material, a nonnuclear arrangement with the Korean Peninsula Energy Development Organization would speak not only to budgetary issues but to issues of peninsular security.

And what about the troubled "Four-Party Talks" among Seoul, Pyongyang, Washington, and Beijing? Their ultimate purpose, we have been told, is to replace the 1953 Korean War cease-fire with an architecture for a lasting peace. Yet, if I have accurately described North Korea's "unification policy," such a framework would be utterly inimical to Pyongyang's own vital interests. Such a conjecture may help to explain why so very little progress has been made in those talks since 1996. Again, it would seem that South Korean financial woes have had precious little impact on Seoul's options for its policies toward Pyongyang.

Fourth, the ROK defense policy looms large in inter-Korean policy, if only implicitly. South Korea's defense budget has been slashed since the IMF accord,[51] and the pace of military modernization has been shifted to a decidedly lower gear. Yet, despite a presumed erosion of the capabilities of the North Korean People's Army, the population of Seoul and other South Korean locales remains exposed to the continuing threat of devastating artillery barrages, chemical weapons assaults, and other preventable hazards.

But why? Is it really impossible for the ROK Ministry of Defense to scrape together any additional funds for counterbattery radar, Patriot-style missiles, or chemical weapons countermeasures?

Even a cursory examination of the ROK budget suggests otherwise, for South Korea continues to invest in the construction of a submarine fleet[52]—an expensive project whose contribution to the defense of the population of Seoul is less than fully obvious.

Policymakers and military planners in South Korea might justify their growing submarine fleet—the seventh submarine became operational—on the basis of some potential future threat, albeit one as yet invisible.[53] Prudential statecraft, however, would seem to militate for dealing with real risks at hand before speculating on debatable contingencies of some future world very different from our own.

If military modernization in the ROK is suffering today, it is a victim of priorities—not immutable budget pressures. So here, once again, South Korea's economic crisis does not seem to pose the limiting constraint on the optimal conduct of inter-Korean policy.

Finally, let us consider what South Korea's present economic circumstances portend for an eventual, hypothetical, Korean reunification. Just how does the situation worsen the odds for a successful reintegration of Korea's two economies and societies?

The ostensible answer, of course, would be that South Korea will have less income and wealth at its disposal, now and in the years immediately ahead, for underwriting the tasks of unification than would economic forecasts offered in, say, the summer of 1997 have expected. That much is surely true. But it is important here to distinguish between income and wealth per se and the institutional arrangements and human capabilities that generate income and wealth. Economists can mechanistically estimate the present value of the projected growth potential South Korea appears to have forgone because of its current economic troubles—the pure windfall loss, so to speak. But it is not self-evident that the fate of Korean unification should rest on that sum—those few percentage points of current ROK output—as the emerging consensus noted above implicitly assumes.

South Korea's predicament at the end of 1997 was a liquidity squeeze. But that squeeze highlighted serious structural or institutional problems in the ROK economy. It vividly illuminated the weaknesses in the government, corporate, and financial sectors—and within all those sectors, weaknesses in the legal system.

Those weaknesses were hardly a secret: foreign observers had been writing about them for years. More important, though, South Korea's top political leaders have been writing about those same shortcomings for years. President Kim Dae Jung's *Mass Participatory Economy*, for example, provides a penetrating critique of the inefficiencies and inequities of the "Korea, Inc." system.[54] And, as it happens, Dr. Cho Soon, the former president of the ROK's current opposition party, has offered a similar—and if anything, an even more detailed—critique in his book, *The Dynamics of Korean Economic Development.*[55]

The broad outlines of the framework required for continuing ROK development—for propelling the ROK from its latecomer status toward world economic leadership—is widely known; until now, though, the wrenching changes that implementing such a framework would entail have also been widely resisted. If South Korea's current economic problems have a single virtue, it is that much of the ROK public and most of its political leadership now recognize that they no longer have the luxury of indefinitely postponing that transition.

If the reforms now under discussion are thoroughly enacted, South Korea will finally put in place a framework not just for recovery, but for sustainable material advance. That framework, moreover, offers greater hope for an eventual Korean reintegration than anything the old "Korea, Inc." system could ever have proposed. The eventual economic reconstruction of the North, after all, promises to be an enormously expensive undertaking, necessitating vast amounts of foreign capital; the framework of reforms now under consideration at last offers a plausible hint as to how those monies might some day be attracted from abroad.

South Korea's economic crisis has had an additional effect that would seem to bear positively on the prospects of success for an eventual Korean reunification. While that factor is less tangible, it may eventually prove to be scarcely less consequential.

Until now, the younger generation in contemporary South Korea has been unfamiliar with privation and unexpected sacrifice. One may argue, indeed, that it is the first generation in Korea's long history to be personally unfamiliar with such things. Until now, those young people have taken financial success and rapid economic growth very much for granted—perhaps even as the natural state of affairs.

Today's economic troubles in South Korea have dramatically altered that climate of expectations. That is not necessarily such a bad thing from the standpoint of Korea's eventual reunification.

There is some merit, after all, in being reintroduced to the age-old truths that success is not foreordained, that great achievements are not automatic, and that worthy goals are worth struggling for. When one considers the great tasks of reconciliation awaiting a reunified Korea, it may also be no bad thing that young South Koreans have been introduced to pervasive financial setback before they were introduced to their brothers and sisters from the North.

Notes

Chapter 1: Introduction

1. Kim Il Sung, *With the Century* (Pyongyang: Foreign Languages Publishing House, 1992). Kim died before those reminiscences could be completed.

2. Kevin Sullivan and Mary Jordan, "U.S. Wrestles with Policy on N. Korea; Famine, Nuclear Threat Raise Stakes in Debate," *Washington Post*, March 13, 1999, p. A1.

3. Juliet Hindell, "Secret Film Shows Plight of Starving Children in North," *Daily Telegraph* (London), December 19, 1998, p. 17.

4. Robert A. Scalapino, *The Politics of Development: Perspectives on Twentieth Century Asia* (Cambridge: Harvard University Press, 1988), p. 47.

5. For more details, see Nicholas Eberstadt, *Korea Approaches Reunification* (Armonk, N.Y.: M. E. Sharpe, 1995), chap. 1.

6. *Chungang Ilbo* (Internet version), April 14, 1999 (reprinted as "DPRK Said to Set up 500 Mobile Phone Circuits in Najin," in *U.S. Foreign Broadcast Information Service Daily Report: East Asia* (hereafter, FBIS/EA), April 14, 1999). The report was issued by the ROK Ministry of National Unification.

7. I derived that estimate from my North Korea international commodity trade database.

8. In May 1999 North Korean officials released information indicating that the country's crude death rate had jumped by almost three-eighths between 1995 and 1998. Initially, commentators took that revelation to imply that over 200,000 persons had succumbed to "excess mortality" in North Korea since the emergency appeal for international food aid commenced. *Korea Times* (Internet version), May 10, 1998 (reprinted in *FBIS/EA* as "DPRK

Statistics Show Famine Killed Hundreds of Thousands," May 11, 1999).

That may or may not prove to be an accurate assessment. Insufficient information is available at the moment to estimate North Korea's recent mortality trends with any confidence. Nevertheless, the revelation was significant insofar as it marked the first official North Korean acknowledgment that the food crisis in the country had taken a toll in terms of human lives.

9. Pyongyang Korean Central Broadcast Network, broadcast December 8, 1993 (translated in *FBIS/EA* as "Communique Issued on Plenum," December 9, 1993).

10. For a detailed exposition of North Korea's deft and highly rational calculations in the international arena, see Chuck Downs, *Over the Line: North Korea's Negotiating Strategy* (Washington, D.C.: AEI Press, 1999).

11. A single vignette makes the point. In early 1998, an official from the World Bank visited Pyongyang to explain the purpose and functions of the World Bank and other international financial institutions. At the DPRK's central bank, his presentation was interrupted by one of the bank's governors, who asked him to explain briefly the difference between "macroeconomics" and "microeconomics." At the DPRK ministry of finance, he was similarly asked by a senior official to explain the difference between a "market economy" and a "centrally planned economy."

12. *People's Korea*, February 15, 1992; cited in Hy Sang Lee, "Economic Factors in Reunification," in Young Whan Kihl, ed., *Korea and the World: Beyond the Cold War* (Boulder, Colo.: Westview Press, 1994), pp. 205–6.

13. Korea Central News Agency Radio (Pyongyang), broadcast March 4, 1993 (reprinted in *FBIS/EA* as "Kim Chong-Il Rejects 'Renegades' of Socialism," March 5, 1993, p. 10).

14. "Let Us Adhere to Line of Building Independent National Economy"; joint article of *Nodong Sinmun* and *Kulloja*, September 17, 1998. This article was translated in *FBIS/EA*, but apparently never appeared in its Internet version. I am indebted to Randolph Fleitman of the U.S. Embassy in Seoul for bringing it to my attention.

15. *Nodong Sinmun*, May 24, 1997, p. 6 (translated in *FBIS/EA* as "North Korea: Daily Warns against Ideological 'Infiltration,'" June 26, 1997).

16. "Let's Make This Year a Turning Point in Building a Powerful Nation," joint editorial in *Nodong Sinmun, Choson Inmingun,* and *Chongnyon Jonwi,* January 1, 1999. I rely here on the unpublished *FBIS/EA* translation of the text, which Randolph Fleitman of the U.S. Embassy in Seoul graciously forwarded to me.

17. *Nodong Sinmun*, May 24, 1997, p. 6 (translated as "North Korea: Daily Warns against Ideological 'Infiltration,'" June 26, 1997).

18. I derived that estimate from my North Korea international commodity trade database.

19. I derived that from ROK National Statistical Office data. Available at

NSO website, <http://www.nso.go.kr/search/data/e-stat9901.pdf>; accessed March 30, 1999.

20. I derived that estimate from my North Korea international commodity trade database.

21. "Hyundai Announces Broad Accord with North Korea," *New York Times*, November 2, 1998, p. A14.

22. *Korea Times* (Internet version), April 16, 1999 (reprinted in *FBIS/EA* as "Hyundai Moving to Make Foreigners' Kumgang Tour Possible," April 16, 1999).

23. Sheryl WuDunn, "South Koreans on Vacation Try out the North," *New York Times*, April 25, 1999, sec. 1, p. 6.

24. *Korea Times* (Internet version), April 23, 1999 (reprinted in FBIS/EA as "Lim Accents S-N Detente to Remove Cold War Legacy," April 23, 1999).

25. *Nodong Sinmun*, April 22, 1999 (translated in *FBIS/EA* as "Daily Lambasts ROK Minister for N-S Cooperation Remarks," April 22, 1999).

26. I derived those estimates from my North Korea international commodity trade database.

27. Ibid.

28. Korea Central News Agency (Pyongyang), "DPRK's Military Warns of 'Annihilating Blow' to US," December 2, 1999. Available at *People's Korea* website, <http://www.korea-np.co.jp/pk/72nd_issue/98120206.htm>; accessed April 1, 1999.

29. The preamble of the September 1998 DPRK Constitution designated "the great leader comrade Kim Il Sung"—then dead over four years—as "the eternal President" of North Korea. Currently, Kim Jong Il's formal state appointment is as chairman of the DPRK National Defense Commission (NDC). In his speech nominating Kim Jong Il for chairman of the National Defense Commission, SPA Standing Committee chairman Kim Yong Nam declared, "The NDC Chairman is the highest post of the state." "General Secretary Kim Jong Il Elected State Head—Constitution Altered," *People's Korea*, September 7, 1998. Available at <http://www.korea-np.co.jp/pk/62nd_issue/98092412.htm>; accessed March 1, 1999.

30. *Minju Choson*, October 24, 1998. Cited in Pak Hon-ok, "North Korea's Effort to Become a Military Power and Kim Chong-il's Choice," *Pukhan* (Seoul), December 1998, pp. 56–65 (translated in *FBIS/EA* as "North Korea: DPRK Pursuit of Military Power Examined," December 24, 1998).

31. American officials insisted that there was no connection between the two announcements; North Korean officials referred to the food pledge as a "fee." In this case, North Korea's claim was closer to reality than Washington's—for without that food pledge, there surely would have been no "visit" granted.

32. Korea Central News Agency (Pyongyang), "KPA Will Answer U.S. Aggression Forces' Challenge with Annihilating Blow—Statement of KPA General Staff Spokesman," December 2, 1998. Available at *People's Korea*

website, <http://www.korea-np.co.jp/item/9812/news12/02.htm>; accessed March 1, 1999.

33. For a contemporary report, see Sheryl WuDunn, "North Korea Fires Missile over Japanese Territory," *New York Times*, September 1, 1998, p. A6.

34. Korea Central News Agency (Pyongyang), "Nobody Can Slander DPRK's Missile Policy—KCNA Commentary," June 16, 1998. Available at *People's Korea* website, <http://www.korea-np.co.jp/9806/news06/16.htm#2>; accessed March 1, 1999.

35. "U.S. Ends Talks in N. Korea; North Resists Halt to Missile Exports," *Washington Post*, April 1, 1999, p. A16.

Chapter 2: North Korea's Unification Policy

1. The speed and apparent nonchalance with which American officials drew their line across a map of Korea is depicted in Bruce Cumings, *The Origins of the Korean War*, vol. 1: *Liberation and the Emergence of Separate Regimes, 1945–1947* (Princeton: Princeton University Press, 1981), pp. 120–22. For obvious reasons, less information is available on the deliberations within Stalin's government on the issue of partition; we do know, however, that the Soviets immediately and without amendment accepted the American proposal for demarcating Korea along the thirty-eighth parallel. See, for example, Erik Van Ree, *Socialism in One Zone: Stalin's Policy in Korea, 1945–1947* (Oxford: Berg Publishers, 1989), pp. 62–63.

2. This is translated in Sung Chul Yang, *The Northern and Southern Korean Political Systems: A Comparative Analysis* (Boulder, Colo.: Westview Press, 1994), p. 907. The translation is for the text of the most recent (sixth) revision of the KWP charter, which was promulgated in 1980; earlier versions of the charter's preamble, however, also highlight that same objective if with somewhat different wordings.

3. The relevant passage is Article 103 of the 1948 constitution. See Robert A. Scalapino and Chang-sik Lee, *Communism in Korea*, pt. 2 (Berkeley: University of California Press, 1973), pp. 1319–30 for the entire constitution; the quotation is on p. 1330. In 1972 a revised DPRK constitution finally named Pyongyang the official capital of North Korea.

4. The best account to date of North Korea's methodical preparations for its 1950 offensive against the ROK may be Sergei N. Goncharov, John W. Lewis, and Xue Litai, *Uncertain Partners: Stalin, Mao, and the Korean War* (Stanford: Stanford University Press, 1993). Additional relevant information may be found in Kathryn Weathersby, "Soviet Aims in Korea and the Origins of the Korean War, 1945–1950," Cold War International History Project Working Paper No. 8, 1993.

5. Goncharov, Lewis, and Xue, *Uncertain Partners*, pp. 136–37, 154–55; Weathersby, "Soviet Aims in Korea," pp. 24–26.

6. Radio speech to the "entire Korean people," July 8, 1950, cited by Byung Chul Koh, "Unification Policy and North-South Relations," in Robert A. Scalapino and Jun-yop Kim, eds., *North Korea Today: Strategic and Domestic Issues* (Berkeley: University of California Institute of East Asian Studies, 1983), p. 264.

7. For useful background on the theory and practice of *maskirovka*, see Brian D. Dailey and Patrick J. Parker, eds., *Soviet Strategic Deception* (Lexington, Mass.: D. C. Heath, 1985).

8. John Merrill, *Korea: The Peninsular Origins of the War* (Newark, Del.: University of Delaware Press, 1989), p. 176. As Merrill observes, this was "part of a carefully orchestrated campaign designed to show continuing movement on the northern side."

9. Ibid., p. 177.

10. One of the fullest accounts of the evolution of North Korea's formal diplomatic posture on reunification can be found in Hakjoon Kim, *Unification Policies of South and North Korea, 1945–1991: A Comparative Study* (Seoul: Seoul National University Press, 1992).

11. I do this to describe the DPRK's unification policy according to the principle of parsimony, so that "assumptions introduced to explain a thing not be multiplied beyond necessity."

12. For a good introduction to that idea, see Julian Lider, *Correlation of Forces: An Analysis of Marxist-Leninist Concepts* (New York: St. Martin's Press, 1986).

13. The following section draws upon Nicholas Eberstadt, "National Strategy in North and South Korea," *NBR Analysis* (Seattle, Wash.), vol. 7, no. 5 (1996).

14. See Merrill, *Korea: The Peninsular Origins.* As Merrill concludes: "North Korean hopes of achieving unification by forming a united front with southern opponents of Rhee, by infiltrating ROK security forces, and by armed guerilla struggle had all been dashed. . . . [B]y the summer of 1950, an attack across the [thirty-eighth] parallel was the only alternative Pyongyang had left" (p. 184).

15. For details of the DPRK's formal positions and proposals, see H. Kim, *Unification Policies,* pp. 161–241; and Byung Chul Koh, *The Foreign Policy of North Korea* (New York: Frederick A. Praeger, 1969), pp. 124–42.

16. One of the best efforts made to date to quantify the DPRK's economic performance is Fujio Goto, "Indexes of North Korean Industrial Output, 1944–1975," *KSU Economic and Business Review* (Kyoto), no. 9 (1982).

17. See Masao Okonogi, "North Korean Communism: In Search of Its Prototype," in Dae-sook Suh, ed., *Korean Studies: New Pacific Currents* (Honolulu: University of Hawaii Press, 1994).

18. Interestingly enough, Kim Il Sung's doctrine of *juche* (usually translated as "self-reliance") was formally expounded during those very years. The

international arrangements just described might be said to illustrate *juche* in action. In essence, they could be seen as a complete inversion of the Yi Dynasty's doctrine of *sadae:* there would be no bowing to the great powers with which Pyongyang had to contend; instead, tribute (in the form of more-or-less permanent flows of concessional aid) would be exacted from *them.*

19. For those rumors, see Scalapino and Lee, *Communism in Korea*, p. 983.

20. For estimates of the growth of North Korean military manpower, see Nicholas Eberstadt and Judith Banister, "Military Buildup in the DPRK: Some New Indications from North Korean Data," *Asian Survey*, vol. 31, no. 11 (November 1991), pp. 1095–1115.

21. The Fourth KWP Congress in September 1961, for example, had publicly proclaimed a "war of national liberation in south Korea"; the Second Party Conference in October 1966 revealed the policy of "the arming of the entire people and the fortification of the whole country" then already well under way; and the DPRK's posture of increasing military confrontation with the ROK and its U.S. allies—which reached its crescendo in 1968–1969 with the infiltration into Seoul of a commando team to assassinate President Park, the capture of the U.S. spy ship *Pueblo*, and the downing of an American EC-121 spy plane—could hardly fail to be noticed.

22. Cited in Jung Ha Lee, "The Impact of the Nixon Doctrine on South Korea: A Critical Analysis of U.S.–South Korean Relations, 1969–1976," Ph.D. dissertation, Catholic University of America, 1980, pp. 263–64. Perhaps significantly, those remarks in Beijing were not reprinted in Kim's *Collected Works*, published roughly ten years later.

23. Brezhnev happened to be quite familiar with Kim and the DPRK on his accession to general secretaryship of the Communist Party of the Soviet Union in 1964. Earlier in his career, Brezhnev had served, among other capacities, as the party's delegate to the KWP's 1956 Congress. His speech to the congress implicitly criticized both Kim and North Korean policy. See Erik van Ree, "The Limits of *Juche:* North Korea's Dependence on Soviet Industrial Aid, 1953–76," *Journal of Communist Studies*, vol. 5, no. 1 (1989), pp. 50–73, especially p. 60.

24. Henry A. Kissinger, *White House Years* (Boston: Little, Brown, 1979), p. 1251.

25. For estimates, see Soo-young Choi, "Foreign Trade of North Korea, 1946–1988: Structure and Performance," Ph.D. dissertation, Northeastern University, 1991.

26. Many explanations have been tendered by Western specialists for North Korea's seemingly self-defeating behavior during that financial drama; seldom mentioned is the possibility that Pyongyang viewed the loans as a form of aid in the first place and thus never really intended to pay them back.

27. For more details, see Peter Hayes, *Pacific Powderkeg: American Nuclear*

Dilemmas in Korea (Lexington, Mass.: D. C. Heath, 1991), especially pp. 71–86.

28. For a quite different interpretation of post-1980 DPRK unification policy, see Byung Chul Koh, "North Korea's Strategy toward South Korea," *Asian Perspective*, vol. 18, no. 2 (1994), pp. 37–53. Koh discerns a "change in Pyongyang's strategic thinking" around 1980 (p. 41) "aim[ed] at the preservation of parity or equality for the North" (p. 43). Koh's assessment is informed primarily by a careful reading of official DPRK pronouncements on inter-Korean relations; as already noted, however, the formal diplomatic record is a problematic lens through which to view North Korea's actual efforts and objectives in that realm.

29. Eberstadt and Banister, "Military Buildup," p. 1104.

30. See, for example, Hans Maretzki, *Kimismus in Nordkorea: Analyse des Lezten DDR–Botschafters in Pjoengyang* [*Kimism in North Korea: Analysis of the Last GDR Ambassador to Pyongyang*] (Boeblingen, Germany: Anita Tykve Verlag, 1991); and Marina Trigubenko, "Industrial Policy in the DPRK," paper presented to the Korea Development Institute–*Korea Economic Daily* conference on the North Korean economy, September 30–October 1, 1991.

31. Such thinking was revealed, for example, in N. V. Ogarkov, *Vsegda v Gotovnosti k Zashchite Otechestva* [*Always in Readiness for the Defense of the Motherland*] (Moscow: Voenizdat, 1982). For an informative discussion of those issues, see Dale R. Herspring, "Nikolay Ogarkov and the Scientific-Technical Revolution in Soviet Military Affairs," *Comparative Strategy*, vol. 6, no. 1 (1987), pp. 29–59.

32. For one analysis and critique of the distinctive nature of the North Korean planned economy, see Mitsuhiko Kimura, "A Planned Economy without Planning: *Su-ryong*'s North Korea," Discussion Paper Series F-074, Faculty of Economics, Tezukayama University, March 1994.

33. Those estimates are based on analysis of officially reported Soviet trade data. For more details, see Nicholas Eberstadt, Marc Rubin, and Albina Tretyakova, "The Collapse of Soviet and Russian Trade with the DPRK, 1989–1993: Impact and Implications," *Korean Journal of National Reunification*, vol. 4 (1995), pp. 88–103.

34. For more information, see ibid.

35. For more details, see Nicholas Eberstadt et al., "China's Trade with the DPRK, 1990–1994: Pyongyang's Thrifty New Patron," *Korean and World Affairs*, vol. 19, no. 4 (1995–1996), pp. 665–85.

36. For details, see Hong Nack Kim, "Normalization Talks between Pyongyang and Tokyo," in Young Whan Kihl, ed., *Korea and the World: Beyond the Cold War* (Boulder, Colo.: Westview Press, 1994), pp. 111–29.

37. Quoted in the *Korea Herald*, September 12, 1991, p. 1 (reprinted in *U.S. Foreign Broadcast Information Service Daily Report: East Asia* (hereafter *FBIS/EA*), September 12, 1991, p. 29).

38. For a translation of the DPRK's April 1992 Constitution, see Sung Chal Yang, *The North and South Korean Political Systems*, pp. 871–74; the relevant

emendation is in Article 3.

In September 1998 the DPRK Constitution was officially revised once more. In the latest version of the constitution, no mention is made of Marxism-Leninism. An official translation of the full text of the 1998 constitution is available at *People's Korea* website, <http://www.korea-np.co.jp/pk/61st_issue/98091708.htm>; accessed March 28, 1999.

39. The announcement appeared in a KWP communiqué on the status of the fulfillment of the Third Seven-Year Plan (1987–1993), broadcast in Pyongyang on December 8, 1993 (translated in *FBIS/EA* as "Communiqué Issues on Plenum," December 9, 1993, pp. 12–19); the quotation is on p. 13.

40. Kim Il Sung's address to the Supreme People's Assembly, May 24, 1990, broadcast on Pyongyang Domestic Service, May 24, 1990 (translated in *FBIS/EA*, May 24, 1990, pp. 17–26); the quotation is on p. 24.

41. Detailed estimates of North Korea's export performance are provided in chapter 5. For 1998, South Korea's exports of goods and services were officially estimated to have totaled $132 billion. *Yonhap*, February 24, 1999 (reprinted in *FBIS/EA* as "ROK Registers Trade Surplus Totaling $39 Billion," February 24, 1999). Note incidentally, that 1998 was an "off" year for the South Korean economy, reflecting as it did the repercussions of the ROK's international financial crisis from late 1997.

42. For the full text of the "Agreed Framework," see the *Pyongyang Times*, October 22, 1994, p. 8.

43. Kevin Sullivan, "N. Korea Admits Selling Missiles; Move Seen as a Test of U.S. Embargo," *Washington Post*, June 19, 1998, p. A1.

44. Sonni Efron, "N. Korea Fires Ballistic Missile into Sea of Japan," *Los Angeles Times*, August 31, 1998, p. A8.

45. David E. Sanger, "North Korean Site an A-Bomb Plant, U.S. Agencies Say," *New York Times*, August 17, 1998, p. A1.

46. "N. Korea Says It's on 'Full Alert,'" *Atlanta Journal and Constitution*, December 3, 1998, p. A8.

47. David E. Sanger, "U.S. to Send North Korea Food despite Missile Launching," *New York Times*, September 10, 1998, p. A3.

48. Thomas E. Ricks, "North Korea Agrees to Let U.S. Inspect Suspected Nuclear-Weapons Site in May," *Wall Street Journal*, March 17, 1999, p. A4; and "Golden Potatoes," *Economist*, March 20, 1999, pp. 45–46.

49. Holger Jensen, "North Korea Knows the Code to Uncle Sam's Credit Card," *Denver Rocky Mountain News*, September 1, 1998.

50. Inaugural Address by President Kim Dae Jung as published in the *Korea Times*, February 26, 1998, p. 1.

51. For the full text of the program, as broadcast by Korea Central News Agency Radio (Pyongyang) on April 7, 1993, see *FBIS/EA*, April 7, 1993, pp. 17–18; the quotation is on p. 18.

52. Korea Central News Agency Radio (Pyongyang), "Motive Force Lead-

ing Whole Nation to Comprehensive Unity," broadcast May 12, 1993 (reprinted in *FBIS/EA* as "Daily Explains Tenth Point in Unity Program," May 13, 1993, p. 21).

Chapter 3: The DPRK under
Multiple Severe Economic Stresses

1. Nicholas Eberstadt, "'National Strategy' in North and South Korea," *NBR Analysis* (Seattle, Wash.), vol. 7, no. 5 (1996); Hans Maretzki, *Kimismus in Nordkorea: Analyse des Letztes DDR-Botschafters in Pjoengyang* [*Kimism in North Korea: Analysis of the last GDR Ambassador to Pyongyang*] (Boeblingen, Germany: Anita Tykve Verlag, 1991); and Marina Ye Trigubenko, "Economic Characteristics and Prospects for Development: With Emphasis on Agriculture," in Han S. Pak, ed., *North Korea: Ideology, Politics, Economics* (Englewood Cliffs, N.J.: Prentice Hall, 1996), pp. 141–59.

2. Nicholas Eberstadt, Marc Rubin, and Albina Tretyakova, "The Collapse of Soviet/Russian Trade with the DPRK, 1989–1993: Impact and Implications," *Korean Journal of National Unification*, vol. 4 (1995), pp. 88–103; and Hong-Tack Chun, "Economic Conditions in North Korea and Prospects for Reform," Korea Development Institute, KDI Working Paper No. 9603, March 1996.

3. *Tong-a Ilbo*, May 13, 1994 (translated in *U.S. Foreign Broadcast Information Service Daily Report: East Asia* (hereafter *FBIS/EA*) as "DPRK Reportedly Facing Worst Food Crisis," May 13, 1994, p. 23).

4. *Chungang Ilbo*, February 18, 1996 (translated in *FBIS/EA* as "ROK: D.P.R.K. Citizens 'Swarming' to Pyongyang for Food," February 20, 1996, pp. 44–45).

5. Digital *Choson Ilbo*, June 14, 1996 (reprinted in *FBIS/EA* as "ROK: N. Koreans Travel to Forage; Envoys Seek Food for Families," June 17, 1996, p. 56).

6. *Sankei Shimbun*, August 31, 1995 (translated in *FBIS/EA* as "Sources Say Cholera Outbreak Killed 230 People," September 1, 1995, pp. 30–31).

7. Digital *Choson Ilbo*, June 18, 1996 (reprinted in *FBIS/EA* as "ROK: 'At Least 100' Allegedly Die of Hunger in DPRK's Hamhung," June 19, 1996, p. 46).

8. For a representative selection of relevant reports from the Western press during the period, see Jasper Becker, "The Starvation of a Nation," *South China Morning Post*, February 4, 1996, p. 9; Nick Rufford, "Famine Threatens New Korean Crisis," *Sunday Times* (London), June 2, 1996; Barbara Slavin, "In North Korea, Isolation and Famine a Deadly Mix; Politics Makes Desperate Situation More Dangerous," *USA Today*, October 21, 1996, p. 14A; Steven Mufson, "Tales of Starvation Emerge from North Korea," *Washington Post*, April 17, 1997, p. A1; Andrew S. Natsios, "North Korean Famine Watch," *Christian*

Science Monitor, September 8, 1997, p. 20; Hilary Mackenzie, "'A Generation At Risk': From Inside North Korea, A Frightening Look at a Famine That's Robbing a Nation of Its Children," *Toronto Star*, September 28, 1997, p. A1; and Nicholas D. Kristof, "Invisible North Korea: Famine Isn't Always What It Seems," *New York Times*, October 12, 1997, sec. 4, p. 4.

9. See, for example, Barbara Slavin, "S. Korea Sends Grain to Starving North: But 50,000 Tons Is Called Too Little," *USA Today*, March 10, 1998; and Jasper Becker, "More Than 3.5 Million Feared Dead in Famine," *South China Morning Post*, September 28, 1998, p. 9.

10. *Yonhap*, March 14, 1999 (republished in *FBIS/EA* as "Hwang: Over 3 Million People Died of Starvation in DPRK," March 14, 1999). The defector in question is Hwang Jang-yop, formerly DPRK Korean Workers' Party secretary for international affairs and president of Kim Il Sung University. Reportedly one of the influential figures in developing North Korea's official *juche* ideology, he sought asylum in South Korea in February 1997 and arrived in the ROK two months later.

11. "Famine Kills 3M in North Korea," *Guardian* (London), February 18, 1999, p. 12; and Jenifer Veale, "Famine Cuts North Korean Population 'by Two Million,'" *Times* (London), February 19, 1999.

12. Global economic histories of the World War II period include Alan S. Milward, *War, Economy, and Society: 1939–1945* (Berkeley: University of California Press, 1977); and Richard James Overy, *Why the Allies Won* (New York: W. W. Norton & Co., 1996). On particular combatant economies, see John Barber and Mark Harrison, *The Soviet Home Front, 1941–1945: A Social and Economic History of the USSR in World War II* (New York: Longman, 1991); Jerome B. Cohen, *Japan's Economy in War and Reconstruction* (Minneapolis: University of Minnesota Press, 1949); and Richard James Overy, *War and Economy in the Third Reich* (New York: Oxford University Press, 1944). Studies of specific economic sectors of given warring states include Bruce F. Johnston, *Japanese Food Management in World War II* (Stanford: Stanford Food Research Institute, 1953); Susan Linz, ed., *The Impact of World War II on the Soviet Union* (Totowa, N.J.: Rowman and Allheld, 1985); Alfred C. Mierzejewski, *The Collapse of the German War Economy, 1944–1945: Allied Air Power and the German National Railway* (Chapel Hill: University of North Carolina Press, 1988); and Gunter J. Trittel, *Hunger und Politik: Die Ernahrungskrise in der Bizone (1945–1949)* (Frankfurt, Germany: Campus Verlag, 1990).

13. Milward, *War, Economy, and Society*; Overy, *Why the Allies Won*; and Barber and Harrison, *The Soviet Home Front*.

14. U.S. Central Intelligence Agency, *Handbook of International Economic Statistics* (Washington, D.C.: Government Printing Office, 1995), p. 28.

15. Barber and Harrison, *The Soviet Home Front*.

16. In perhaps the finest study to date on the economics of disaster and recovery, Hirshleifer defines *economic collapse* as "a failure in the mode of

functioning of the economic system, in essence, a breakdown in the division of labor. . . . [E]ssential connecting links in the economic system [are] broken, so that production [falls] even more rapidly than . . . the resources available." Jack Hirshleifer, *Disaster and Recovery: A Historical Survey*, Memorandum RM-3079-PR (Santa Monica, Calif.: RAND Corporation, April 1963). For all its virtues, even that careful definition seems problematic. It might seem to suggest, for example, that the United States circa 1933 was experiencing economic collapse.

17. Cohen, *Japan's Economy*; Johnston, *Japanese Food Management*; and Trittel, *Hunger und Politik*.

18. An initial search of the literature did not identify any studies that focused on the wartime and postwar breakdown of the German or the Japanese food systems. The details of those breakdowns, however, are included in the references in note 12. What may be especially noteworthy from those accounts are two features: the very uneven regional impacts of severe disruptions of the food system and the proximate role of sudden ration reductions in precipitating the food crises that ensued.

19. To cite just a few, see David A. Baldwin, *Economic Statecraft* (Princeton: Princeton University Press, 1985); Richard Ellings, *Embargoes and World Power: Lessons from American Foreign Policy* (Boulder, Colo.: Westview Press, 1985); Gary Clyde Hufbauer, Jeffrey J. Schott, and Kimberly Ann Elliott, *Economic Sanctions Reconsidered*, 2d ed. (Washington, D.C.: Institute for International Economics, 1990); Linda Martin, *Coercive Cooperation: Explaining Multilateral Economic Sanctions* (Princeton: Princeton University Press, 1992); and David M. Rowe, "The Domestic Political Economy of International Economic Sanctions," Harvard University Center for International Affairs Working Paper Series No. 93-1, 1993.

20. Two interesting, but by no means comprehensive, treatments are Edmund Burke III, ed., *Global Crises and Social Movements* (Boulder, Colo.: Westview Press, 1988); and Peter A. Gourevitch, *Politics in Hard Times: Comparative Response to International Economic Crises* (Ithaca: Cornell University Press, 1986).

21. Cf. Gerd Hardach, *The First World War, 1914–1918* (Berkeley: University of California Press, 1977). In real terms, for example, Germany's trade volume fell by about two-thirds between 1914 and 1917. Ibid., p. 25.

22. Cohen, *Japan's Economy*; Mierzejewski, *Collapse of the German War Economy*; Milward, *War, Economy, and Society*; Overy, *Why the Allies Won*; Overy, *War and Economy in the Third Reich*; and Alan S. Milward, "Restriction of Supply as a Strategic Choice," in Gordon H. McCormick and Richard E. Bissell, eds., *Strategic Dimensions of Economic Behavior* (New York: Praeger, 1984).

23. That perception, inter alia, was fateful fuel for the *Dolchstosslegende* of the pre-Hitler era—the notion that German troops, though "unbeaten on

the field" in World War I, had been "stabbed in the back" by domestic traitors and foreign foes.

24. Milward, *War, Economy, and Society*, p. 85.

25. Overy, *War and Economy in the Third Reich*, p. 367.

26. Hardach, *The First World War, 1914–1918*, p. 31.

27. Milward, "Restriction of Supply."

28. Of course, as Overy has pointed out, "There has always seemed something fundamentally implausible about the contention that dropping almost 2.5 million tons of bombs on tautly-stretched industrial systems and war-weary populations would not seriously weaken them." Overy, *Why the Allies Won*, p. 133. The question, however, is whether "economic warfare" per se was a decisive or merely a contingent factor in the eventual collapse of the Nazi economy and the Japanese imperial economy. After September 1944, as Mierzejewski has persuasively detailed, the German national railway system began to crumble under Allied bombing, and consequently the Third Reich's planned economy commenced an accelerating disintegration (Mierzejewski, *Collapse of the German War Economy*). But as Milward has shown, the success of the Allied air offensive at that precise time turned on the Luftwaffe's sudden inability to maintain supplies of aviation fuel for its fighter defense squadrons (Milward, *War, Economy, and Society*), and the shortage of high-quality aviation fuel, in turn, was a direct result of Germany's loss of control over Romanian oil fields to advancing Soviet forces. In that sense, the success of "economic warfare" may be said to have hinged on the success of military warfare.

29. Ellings, *Embargoes and World Power*, p. 25.

30. See, among others, Robert B. Ekelund and Mark Thornton, "The Union Blockade and Demoralization of the South: Relative Prices in the Confederacy," *Social Science Quarterly*, vol. 73, no. 4 (1992), pp. 890–902; Paul V. Gates, *Agriculture and the Civil War* (New York: Alfred A. Knopf, 1965); Mary Elizabeth Massey, *Ersatz in the Confederacy* (Columbia: University of South Carolina Press, 1952); and David George Surdam, "Northern Naval Superiority and the Economics of the American Civil War," Ph.D. dissertation, University of Chicago, Department of Economics, 1994.

31. Hirshleifer, *Disaster and Recovery*.

32. Ibid., pp. 37–38.

33. The adverse—and persistently adverse—role of policy on economic performance in the Southern states is suggested by the extraordinarily long time required to reattain antebellum levels of output per capita. For the South as a whole, per capita output may not have reached 1860 levels until the beginning of the twentieth century; for the states of the "Deep South," recovery by that measure may not have been achieved until the eve of World War I. Claudia D. Goldin and Frank D. Lewis, "The Economic Cost of the American Civil War: Estimates and Implications," *Journal of Economic History*, vol. 35, no. 2 (1975), pp. 299–326. War devastation by itself would not seem to explain such an ex-

tended hiatus: recall that per capita output had recovered to prewar levels within six years of defeat in West Germany and within nine years in Japan.

34. Hufbauer, Schott, and Elliott, *Economic Sanctions Reconsidered.*

35. Kenneth A. Rodman, "Public and Private Sanctions against South Africa," *Political Science Quarterly,* vol. 109, no. 2 (1994), pp. 313–34.

36. All figures are derived from International Monetary Fund, *International Financial Statistics Yearbook 1995* (Washington, D.C.: IMF, 1995), p. 697.

37. Nicholas Eberstadt, *The Tyranny of Numbers* (Washington, D.C.: AEI Press, 1995), chap. 7.

38. These are the official Vietnamese economic data as reported to the Asian Development Bank. See Asian Development Bank, *Asian Development Outlook,* 1996–98 ed. (Manila: Asian Development Bank, 1998).

39. George Irvin, "Vietman: Assessing the Achievements of Doi Moi," *Journal of Development Studies,* vol. 31, no. 5 (1995), p. 735. See also David Dollar, "Economic Reform, Openness, and Vietnam's Entry into ASEAN," *ASEAN Economic Bulletin,* vol. 13, no. 2 (1996), pp. 169–84.

40. U.S. Central Intelligence Agency, *Handbook of International Economic Statistics* (Washington, D.C.: Government Printing Office, 1996).

41. Manual Pastor, Jr., and Andrew Zimbalist, "Waiting for Change: Adjustment and Reform in Cuba," *World Development,* vol. 28, no. 5 (1995), p. 708.

42. Ann Wroe, "Heroic Illusions: A Survey of Cuba," *Economist,* vol. 339, April 8, 1996, p. S6.

43. Jorge Perez-Lopez, "The Cuban Economy in the Age of Hemispheric Integration," *Journal of Interamerican Studies and World Affairs,* vol. 39, no. 3 (1997), pp. 3–47; and Carmelo Mesa-Lago, "Assessing Economic and Social Performance in the Cuban Transition of the 1990s," *World Development,* vol. 26, no. 5 (1998), pp. 857–76.

44. See U.S. Central Intelligence Agency, *Handbook of International Statistics 1997* (Washington, D.C.: Government Printing Office, 1998), p. 158; and U.S. Central Intelligence Agency, *World Fact Book 1998* (Washington, D.C.: Government Printing Office, 1999), p. 122.

45. Carmelo Mesa-Lago, "Cuba: Un Caso Unico de Reforma Anti-Mercado. Retrospectiva y Perspectivas," *Pensamiento Iberoamericno,* no. 22/23 (1992–1993), pp. 56–100.

46. Edward Gonzalez and David Ronfeldt, *Storm Warnings for Cuba,* Memorandum MR-432-OSD (Santa Monica, Calif.: RAND Corporation, 1994); Douglas W. Payne, "Inside Castro's Mafia State," *Society,* vol. 33, no. 2 (1996), pp. 39–46; and Wroe, "Heroic Illusions."

47. U.S. Central Intelligence Agency, *Handbook of International Economic Statistics* (Washington, D.C.: Government Printing Office, 1995).

48. World Bank, *World Development Report 1996* (New York: Oxford Uni-

versity Press, 1996), p. 222. Note that all figures on national rates of illiteracy should be treated with caution.

49. Ibid., p. 200. Note, inter alia, that the World Bank places adult illiteracy at 9 percent for women and 4 percent for men in Vietnam, which seems to have coped well with its Soviet trade shock.

50. Patrick Clawson, "How Has Saddam Hussein Survived? Economic Sanctions, 1990–93," McNair Paper No. 22, National Defense University Institute for National Strategic Studies, 1993; Graham E. Fuller, *Iraq in the Next Decade: Will Iraq Survive until 2002?* Note N-3591-DAG (Santa Monica, Calif.: RAND Corporation, 1993); Ahmend Hashim, "Iraq: Fin de Regime?" *Current History*, vol. 95, no. 597 (1996), pp. 10–15; "Iraq: Down but Not Out," *Economist*, vol. 335, April 8, 1995, pp. 21–23.

51. One Iraqi official put it memorably: "Waiting for Saddam Hussein to go is like waiting for Godot to arrive" (Hashim, "Iraq," p. 14). Saddam's staying power, of course, reflects his skills in the international as well as the domestic arena—and, conversely, the shortcomings of the tactics and stratagems of his international adversaries. For a trenchant analysis and critique of those shortcomings, see David Wurmser, *Tyranny's Ally: America's Failure to Defeat Saddam Hussein* (Washington, D.C.: AEI Press, 1999).

52. Clawson, "How Has Saddam Hussein Survived?" p. 11.

53. Ibid., p. 14.

54. Cf. Eberstadt, Rubin, and Tretyakova, "The Collapse of Soviet/Russian Trade with the D.P.R.K."

55. Young Namkoong, "Trends and Prospects of the North Korean Economy," *Korea and World Affairs*, vol. 20, no. 2 (1996), pp. 219–35; and Marcus Noland, "The North Korean Economy," *Joint U.S.–Korean Academic Studies*, vol. 6 (1996), pp. 127–78.

56. Chun, "Economic Conditions in North Korea"; Eberstadt, "National Strategy"; Namkoong, "Trends and Prospects"; and Noland, "The North Korean Economy."

57. For an informative evaluation of North Korea's response to pressures for trade and investment liberalization, see Young Namkoong, "An Analysis of North Korea's Policy to Attract Foreign Capital," *Korea and World Affairs*, vol. 19, no. 3 (1995), pp. 459–81.

58. It should be remembered that both Cuba and Korea are currently embroiled in unification struggles. The boundaries of the struggle are self-evident in the Korean peninsula; for Cuba, the contending forces are located on the island proper and in Miami, Florida.

59. Nicholas Eberstadt, "The DPRK's International Trade in Capital Goods, 1970–1995: Indications from 'Mirror Statistics,'" *Journal of East Asian Affairs*, vol. 12, no. 1 (Winter/Spring 1998), pp. 165–223.

60. C. R. Bawden, *The Modern History of Mongolia*, rev. ed. (London: Kegan Paul International, 1989); Robert Rupen, *How Mongolia Is Really Ruled:*

A Political History of the Mongolian People's Republic, 1900–1978 (Stanford: Hoover Institution Press, 1978); Van Chi Hoang, "Collectivization and Rice Production," in P. J. Honey, ed., *North Vietnam Today: Profile of a Communist Satellite* (New York: Frederick A. Praeger, 1962), pp. 117–27; and Gerard Tongas, *L'Enfer Communiste au Nord-Vietnam* (Paris: E. Debresses, 1960).

61. Alain Blum, *Naître, Vivre, et Mourir en URSS, 1917–1991* (Paris: Librarie Plon, 1994); Robert Conquest, *The Harvest of Sorrow: Soviet Collectivization and the Terror-Famine* (New York: Oxford University Press, 1986); and Michael Ellman, "A Note on the Number of 1933 Famine Victims," *Soviet Studies*, vol. 43, no. 2 (1991), pp. 375–79.

62. Jasper Becker, *Hungry Ghosts: Mao's Secret Famine* (New York: Free Press, 1997); Chris Bramall, *In Praise of Maoist Economic Planning: Living Standards and Economic Development in Sichuan since 1931* (New York: Oxford University Press, 1993); Nicholas Lardy, "The Chinese Economy under Stress, 1958–1965," in Roderick MacFarquhar and Jon K. Fairbanks, eds., *The Cambridge History of China*, vol. 14: *The People's Republic*, pt. 1 (New York: Cambridge University Press, 1987), pp. 360–97; Justin Yifu Liu, "Collectivization and China's Agricultural Crisis in 1959–1961," *Journal of Political Economy*, vol. 98, no. 6 (1990), pp. 1228–52; and Dali L. Yang, *Calamity and Reform in China: State, Rural Society, and Institutional Change since the Great Leap Famine* (Stanford: Stanford University Press, 1995).

63. Karl Jackson, ed., *Cambodia, 1975–1978: Rendezvous with Death* (Princeton: Princeton University Press, 1989); and Yathay Pin, *L'Utope Meurtiere: Un Rescape du Genocide Cambodgien Temoigne* (Paris: R. Laffont, 1980).

64. William Moskoff, *The Bread of Affliction: The Food Supply in the USSR during World War II* (New York: Cambridge University Press, 1990).

65. On increases in procurement quotas in Ukraine, see Conquest, *Harvest of Sorrow*; on the Chinese communization of farms, see Liu, "Collectivization"; on communal dining, see Yang, *Calamity and Reform in China*; on Chinese increase in procurement, see Bramall, *In Praise of Maoist Economic Planning*; and on Cambodian Great Leap Forward techniques, see Jackson, *Cambodia*.

66. Ellman, "Note."

67. Judith Banister and E. Paige Johnson, "After the Nightmare: The Population of Cambodia," in Ben Kiernan, ed., *Genocide and Democracy in Cambodia: The Khmer Rouge, the United Nations, and the International Community* (New Haven: Yale University Southeast Asia Studies, 1993), pp. 65–139.

68. Judith Banister, *China's Changing Population* (Stanford: Stanford University Press, 1987).

69. Becker, *Hungry Ghosts*; and Yang, *Calamity and Reform in China*.

70. Bawden, *Modern History of Mongolia*.

71. Tongas, *L'Enfer Communiste*.

72. Lardy, "Chinese Economy under Stress"; and Yang, *Calamity and Reform in China.*

73. Alan S. Whiting, "The Sino-Soviet Split," in MacFahrquhar and Fairbank, eds., *The Cambridge History of China*, vol. 14: *The People's Republic*, pt. 1, pp. 478–538.

74. By no coincidence, the Soviet government had implemented an internal passport system for the USSR in 1932.

75. Banister, *China's Changing Population;* and Lardy, "Chinese Economy under Stress."

76. Nicholas Eberstadt and Judith Banister, *The Population of North Korea* (Berkeley: University of California Institute of East Asian Studies, 1992).

77. See, for example, *Nodong Sinmun*, May 28, 1994 (translated in FBIS/EA, June 28, 1994, pp. 28–30); *Minju Choson*, January 15, 1995 (translated in *FBIS/EA*, March 7, 1995, pp. 38–41); and *Nodong Sinmun*, January 21, 1995 (translated in *FBIS/EA*, March 1, 1995, pp. 43–45).

78. Some sources with first-hand experience in the DPRK, for example, have claimed that North Korean agriculture was already plagued by serious structural problems by the late 1980s and that agricultural output was already stagnating or declining by that time. See Maretzki, *Kimismus in Nord Korea;* Trigubenko, "Economic Characteristics"; and Yi U-hong, *Donzoko no Kyowakoku: Kita Chosen Husaku no Kozo* (Tokyo: Aki Shobo, 1989).

79. That appeal begs the question of the accuracy of the DPRK leadership's own assessment of the country's current food situation and food outlook. It is quite possible that top decisionmakers might lack accurate information about the magnitude and incidence of food shortfalls or might entertain unrealistic expectations about the relative ease with which the current food problem might be resolved. Communist directorates have certainly been subject to such misapprehensions during food crises in the past.

80. Hy-sang Lee, "Supply and Demand for Grains in North Korea: A Historical Movement Model for 1966–1993," *Korea and World Affairs*, vol. 18, no. 3 (1994), pp. 509–52; Chun, "Economic Conditions in North Korea"; and Namkoong, "Trends and Prospects."

81. Eberstadt and Banister, *The Population of North Korea.*

82. For some informed and penetrating speculations about the possible dynamics here, see Robert Collins, "The Pattern of Collapse in North Korea," research note (Seoul: CINUNC, 1996).

83. See Nicholas Eberstadt, "Demographic Shocks after Communism: Eastern Germany, 1989–1993," *Population and Development Review*, vol. 20, no. 1 (1994), pp. 137–52.

Chapter 4: Inter-Korean Economic Cooperation

1. Analysts and policymakers have been examinimg nonmilitary instru-

ments for diplomacy, in fact, for over a decade now. One may trace the evolution of that particular tendency in Western policy toward North Korea back to 1988, when South Korea's President Roh Tae Woo launched his *Nordpolitik*. *Nordpolitik* may be said to have represented the first major step beyond a policy of deterrence of, and toward a policy of engagement with, the DPRK.

2. South Korea is believed to have become North Korea's third-largest trading partner in 1994. Cf. *Korea Times*, November 29, 1995 (reprinted in *U.S. Foreign Broadcast Information Service Daily Report: East Asia* (hereafter *FBIS/EA*) as "South Becomes North's 3d Largest Trading Partner," November 29, 1995).

3. According to official South Korean figures, North-South trade turnover during the years 1989 to 1997 amounted to $1.54 billion. ROK Ministry of National Unification, *Nampuk Kyoyeok Tonggye Charyo* (Seoul: Ministry of National Unification, 1998), p. 3. In 1998 inter-Korean trade reportedly totaled an additional $222 million. *Yonhap*, January 28, 1999 (reprinted in *FBIS/EA* as "South Korea: ROK Sees $37.41 Million Surplus from Inter-Korean Trade," January 28, 1999). By the official South Korean tabulation, trade turnover between North and South Korea would have come to $1.76 billion over the 1989 to 1998 period.

Those official South Korean data on "economic exchange" with the North are idiosyncratic in a number of respects. See Nicholas Eberstadt, "Inter-Korean Trade, 1989–1997: A Decomposition in Accordance with SITC, Rev. 1," unpublished paper, December 1998, especially pp. 19–22. Questions about the data notwithstanding, it is probably correct to say that today the cumulative commerce between the two Koreas is approaching $2 billion.

4. Most important among those are the two light-water reactors on North Korean soil that are to be built and financed by the Korean Peninsula Energy Development Organization under the "Agreed Framework." Groundbreaking for that project commenced in August 1997, and construction is not envisioned to be completed before 2003 at the very earliest. The total cost of the project is currently estimated at $4.6 billion.

Although the Korean Peninsula Energy Development Organization is an international organization (with current membership of eleven sovereign governments plus the European Union), the light-water reactor project in North Korea is, in its essence, a South Korean venture. The ROK has committed to pay 70 percent of the total cost of the project, and the prime contractor for the project is KEPCO, South Korea's public utility company.

For a succinct description of the Korean Peninsula Energy Development Organization and the current status of the light-water reactor project, see "A Tiger by the Tail," *Energy Economist*, no. 203 (September 1998), pp. 2–5.

5. Most important is the October 1998 agreement between Hyundai founder Chung Ju-yung and North Korea's Kim Jong Il to develop the Kumgang-san region in the DPRK for inter-Korean tourism. In that deal Hyundai pledged

$906 million "to North Korea for the exclusive rights over the next six years to develop tourism projects in the scenic Diamond Mountains area, which lies near the border with the South and is famed in Korean folklore." Cf. John Burton, "Hyundai to Invest Billions in North Korea," *Financial Times*, November 2, 1998, p. 4.

6. The German formulation was *Wandel durch Annäherung*, "change through rapprochement."

7. *Pukhan*, October 1993, pp. 90–101 (translated in *FBIS/EA* as "North-South Economic Cooperation Discussed," December 10, 1993, pp. 48–54) (Korea Trade Promotion Center's analysis); Yeon Ha-cheong, "Economic Consequences of German Unification and Its Policy Implications for Korea," Korea Development Institute, KDI Working Paper 9303, April 1993; Japan External Trade Organization, *Kita Chosen no Keizai to Boeki no Tenbo*, 1993 ed. (Tokyo: Nihon Boeki Shinkokai, 1993); *Chungang Ilbo*, January 19, 1993, p. 2 (translated in *FBIS/EA* as "Russian Economic Institute Analyzes DPRK Economy," January 21, 1993, p. 28) (Russian Economic Research Institute). Some Soviet-bloc observers of the North Korean scene argue that the decline began during the 1980s. See, for example, Hans Maretzki, *Kimismus in Nordkorea: Analyse des Letzten DDR–Botschafters in Pjoengjang* [*Kimism in North Korea: Analysis of the Last GDR Ambassador to Pyongyang*] (Boeblingen, Germany: Anita Tykve Verlag, 1991), pp. 150, 155; and Marina Trigubenko, "Industrial Policy in the DPRK," paper presented at Korea Development Institute–*Korea Economic Daily* conference on the North Korean economy, September 30–October 1, 1991, p. 6.

8. Japan External Trade Organization, *Kita Chosen no Keizai to Boeki no Tenbo*, 1992 ed. (Tokyo: Nihon Boeki Shinkokai, 1992); see also Choi Soo-young, "North Korean Trade, 1946–1988: Structure and Performance," Ph.D. dissertation, Northeastern University, 1992.

9. Japan External Trade Organization, *Kita Chosen no Keizai*, 1992 ed.; and *Yonhap*, December 25, 1993 (reprinted in FBIS/EA as "DPRK's Negative Economic Growth Reviewed," December 27, 1993, p. 34).

10. Maretzki, *Kimismus in Nordkorea*, describes some of those arrangements. See also Valentin I. Moiseyev, "USSR–DPRK Economic Cooperation," paper presented at the Korea Development Institute–*Korea Economic Daily* conference on the North Korean economy, September 30–October 1, 1991.

11. See, for example, Nicholas Eberstadt, *Korea Approaches Reunification* (Armonk, N.Y.: M. E. Sharpe Co., 1995), chap. 1; and Mitsuhiko Kimura, "A Planned Economy without Planning: *Suryong*'s North Korea," Discussion Paper Series F-074, Faculty of Economics, Tezukayama University, January 1994.

12. Korea Central News Agency Radio (Pyongyang), broadcast December 8, 1993 (translated in *FBIS/EA* as "Communiqué Issued on Plenum," December 9, 1993, pp. 12–18).

13. Korea Central News Agency Radio (Pyongyang), broadcast January 1,

1994 (translated in *FBIS/EA* as "Kim Il Sung Delivers 1994 New Year Address," January 3, 1994, p. 18).

14. For enumeration and analysis, see Nicholas Eberstadt, "North Korea: Reform, Muddling Through, or Collapse?" *NBR Analysis Series* (Seattle, Wash.), September 1993; Eui-gak Hwang, "North Korean Laws for the Induction of Foreign Capital and Practical Approaches to Foreign Investment in North Korea," pts. 1 and 2, *Vantage Point*, March 1994, pp. 1–10, and April 1994, pp. 1–9; Jhe Seong-ho, "North Korea's Foreign Investment Inducement Laws: An Assessment and Analysis," pts. 1 and 2, *Vantage Point*, August 1993, pp. 2–10, and September 1993, pp. 2–10; and Lee Kye-man, "The Constitutional Basis of North Korea's Economic System," *Vantage Point*, July 1993.

15. That official translation of the 1998 DPRK Constitution is available at *People's Korea* website, <http://www.korea-np.co.jp/pk/61st_issue/98091708.htm>; accessed March 30, 1999.

16. That point was first made publicly, to my knowledge, by Lawrence H. Summers, then vice president for research at the World Bank, in his Research Institute for National Unification lecture of August 1992 in Seoul. For a version of that lecture, see *RINU Newsletter*, vol. 1, no. 4 (December 1992).

17. *Korea Economic Weekly*, March 25, 1992, p. 4 (reprinted in *FBIS/EA* as "Reunification Cost Estimated at $245 Billion," March 26, 1992, p. 23).

18. *Wall Street Journal*, May 17, 1994, p. 9.

19. Marcus Noland, Sherman Robinson, and Li-gang Liu, "The Economics of Korean Unification," Working Paper 97-5, Institute for International Economics, 1997. That particular estimate was predicated on an economic reintegration of the Koreas commencing in the year 2000.

20. Whether such escalating estimates present an accurate assessment of the costs and transfers that would be required in the event of reunification is another question altogether—and one that I address in chapter 6.

21. See *Yonhap*, December 17, 1993 (reprinted in *FBIS/EA* as "Measures to Reduce Reunification Cost Suggested," December 20, 1993, p. 31), for a report on an early South Korean Federation of Korean Industries proposal in that regard.

22. For one early and effusive assessment of that approach, see Dan C. Sanford, *South Korea and the Communist Countries: The Politics of Trade* (New York: St. Martin's Press, 1990).

23. For a detailed exposition on that phenomenon, see Alice H. Amsden, *Asia's Next Giant: South Korea and Late Industrialization* (New York: Oxford University Press, 1989), especially chap. 6.

24. See, for example, World Bank, *Korea: Managing the Industrial Transition* (Washington, D.C.: World Bank, 1987); Danny M. Leipziger and Peter M. Petri, "Korean Industrial Policy: Legacies of the Past and Directions for the Future," World Bank Discussion Paper No. 197, 1993; and Cho Soon, *The Dynamics of Korean Economic Development* (Washington, D.C.: Institute for

International Economics, 1994).

25. See, for example, Ha Dong-man, "Basic Steps to Internationalize Korea's Economy," *Korea Focus*, March–April 1994. Ha's arguments were all the more noteworthy in that he was at the time director for international economic policy for the Economic Planning Bureau.

26. Janos Kornai, *The Socialist System* (Princeton: Princeton University Press, 1992).

27. Ibid., p. 342.

28. Jan Winiecki, *The Distorted World of Soviet-Type Economies* (Pittsburgh: University of Pittsburgh Press, 1988), p. 141.

29. Kornai, *The Socialist System*, p. 348.

30. Korea Central News Agency Radio (Pyongyang), broadcast July 20, 1992 (translated in *FBIS/EA* as "*Nodong Sinmun* on Defense of Socialism," July 29, 1992, p. 11).

31. For one exposition, see Julian Lider, *Correlation of Forces: An Analysis of Marxist-Leninist Concepts* (New York: St. Martin's Press, 1986).

32. For a classic exposition, see Albert O. Hirschman, *National Power and the Structure of Trade* (Berkeley: University of California Press, 1945).

33. For an analysis of interwar Germany's economic diplomacy in that regard, see David M. Kaiser, *Economic Diplomacy and the Origins of the Second World War* (Princeton: Princeton University Press, 1980).

34. For a thorough inventory of those *Ostpolitik*-era financial transfers from Bonn to Berlin and a prescient assessment of their economic significance for the East German state, see Jerzy Lisiecki, "Financial and Material Transfers between East and West Germany," *Soviet Studies*, vol. 42, no. 3 (1990), pp. 513–34.

35. Timothy Garton Ash, *In Europe's Name: Germany and the Divided Continent* (New York: Random House, 1993), p. 186.

36. Ibid., pp. 188–89.

37. *DPA*, January 31, 1992 (translated in *U.S. Foreign Broadcast Information Service Daily Report: Western Europe* (hereafter *FBIS/WE*) as "Stoltenberg Reveals Warsaw Pact's Attack Plan," February 3, 1992, p. 18).

38. Federal Republic of Germany Ministry of Defense, Office of the Minister of Defense, "Militärische Planungen des Warschauer Paktes in Zentraleuropa: Eine Studie," Bonn, January 1992. I am indebted to Dr. Manfred Kehrig of the German Defense Ministry's Military Archives in Koblenz for this reference.

39. Even more ominously: "In [East German military] staff exercises the deployment of nuclear weapons as a 'first strike' had been acted out, [FRG Defense Minister] Stoltenberg said." See *DPA*, January 31, 1992 (translated in *FBIS/WE* as "Stoltenberg Reveals Warsaw Pact's Attack Plan," February 3, 1992, p. 18).

40. For an excellent analysis of that drama, see Jeffrey Gedmin, *The Hid-*

den Hand: Gorbachev and the Collapse of East Germany (Washington, D.C.: AEI Press, 1992).

41. Ash, *In Europe's Name*, p. 205.

42. For one prescient account, see Adam B. Ulam, *Dangerous Relations: The Soviet Union in World Politics, 1970–1982* (New York: Oxford University Press, 1983).

43. Henry S. Rowen and Charles Wolf, Jr., eds. *The Impoverished Super-power* (San Francisco: ICS Press, 1990).

44. See, for example, Anders Aslund, *Gorbachev's Struggle for Economic Reform*, rev. ed. (Ithaca: Cornell University Press, 1991).

45. Igor Birman, *Secret Incomes of the Soviet State Budget* (Boston: Martinus Nijhoff, 1981); and Igor Birman, "Sizing Soviet Military Expenditures," paper prepared for American Enterprise Institute conference "Comparing the Soviet and American Economies," April 17–20, 1990.

46. See, for example, Nicholas R. Lardy, *Foreign Trade and Economic Reform in China, 1978–1990* (New York: Cambridge University Press, 1992); World Bank, *China: Foreign Trade Reform* (Washington, D.C.: World Bank, 1994); Susan L. Shirk, *How China Opened Its Door: The Political Success of the PRC's Foreign Trade and Investment Reform* (Washington, D.C.: Brookings Institution Press, 1994); Joseph C. H. Chai, *China: Transition to a Market Economy* (New York: Oxford University Press, 1997); and Nicholas R. Lardy, *China's Unfinished Economic Revolution* (Washington, D.C.: Brookings Institution Press, 1998).

47. For at least two years before the elder Kim's death, his heir-designate Kim Jong Il was officially identified as the major decisionmaker behind DPRK domestic policies. Kim Il Sung himself spelled that out for a delegation from the *Washington Times* in an interview published on his eightieth birthday: "[Kim Jong Il] is already taking full responsibility for our country. In fact, all affairs of our country are run by him. As far as I am concerned, I am carrying out some external work. As far as the internal affairs of our country are concerned, everything is dealt with by him" (*Washington Times*, April 15, 1992, p. A11).

48. See Chong-Pin Lin, "Beijing and Taipei: Dialectics in Post-Tiananmen Interactions," *China Quarterly*, no. 136 (December 1993), pp. 785–86; and Tse-Kang Leng, "Dynamic–Mainland China Economic Relations," *Asian Survey*, vol. 38, no. 5 (1998), pp. 494–509.

49. *Renmin Ribao*, January 13, 1999, p. 5 (translated in *U.S. Foreign Broadcast Information Service Daily Report: China* as "China: Twenty Years of Cross-Strait Contact Marked," January 22, 1999).

50. *Hong Kong Wen Wei Po*, January 26, 1999, p. A5 (translated in FBIS/EA as "Commentary on 1998 Cross-Strait Relations," February 5, 1999).

51. World Bank, *China: Foreign Trade Reform*, p. xvi.

52. Lardy, *Foreign Trade and Economic Reform in China*, p. 39.

53. Ibid., p. 39.

54. *Chungang Ilbo*, November 22, 1992, p. 4 (translated in *FBIS/EA* as "128 DPRK Companies Involved in Foreign Trade," January 7, 1993, pp. 32–33).

55. *Chungang Ilbo* (Internet version), February 24, 1999 (reprinted in *FBIS/EA* as "KOTRA: DPRK Reduces Number of Trading Companies," February 24, 1999). Before a restructuring of the DPRK foreign trade structure in late 1998, according to that account, the number of DPRK foreign-trade companies had risen to "more than 300."

56. See Eberstadt, "North Korea: Reform, Muddling Through, or Collapse?" p. 12.

57. *Chungang Ilbo*, December 10, 1993, p. 4 (translated in *FBIS/EA* as "Daily Comments on DPRK Politburo Listings," December 10, 1993, p. 36).

58. According to one South Korean source, "North Korea has all but completely defaulted the reimbursement of its foreign debts since 1985." *Yonhap*, September 18, 1984 (reprinted in FBIS/EA as "DPRK Reportedly Fails to Pay Foreign Debts," September 18, 1984).

59. See, for example, *Yonhap*, February 13, 1994 (reprinted in *FBIS/EA* as "DPRK 'Turned Cold' on N-S Cooperation," February 15, 1994, p. 45).

60. *Choson Ilbo*, February 15, 1994, p. 1 (translated in FBIS/EA as "DPRK Reportedly Asks ROK to Invest in Port," February 15, 1994, p. 47).

61. *Hong Kong AFP*, September 24, 1998 (reprinted in *FBIS/EA* as "North Korea: AFP–DPRK Official Arrested, Not Executed," September 25, 1998).

62. *Chungang Ilbo* (Internet version), October 13, 1998 (reprinted in *FBIS/EA* as "South Korea: DPRK Reportedly Changes Name of Najin Trade Zone," October 14, 1998).

63. *Yonhap*, March 8, 1999 (reprinted in *FBIS/EA* as "Ministry: N-S Economic Cooperation at Virtual Standstill," March 9, 1999).

64. The phrase in question is from Article 37. The official translation of the DPRK 1998 Constitution is available at *People's Korea* website, <http://www.korea-np.co.jp/pk/61st_issue/98091708.htm>; accessed March 30, 1999.

65. *People's Korea*, February 15, 1992; and *Pyongyang Times*, November 7, 1992. Both quotations are cited in Hy Sang Lee, "Economic Factors in Reunification," in Young Whan Kihl, ed., *Korea and the World: Beyond the Cold War* (Boulder, Colo.: Westview Press, 1994), pp. 205–6.

66. Korea Central News Agency Radio (Pyongyang), broadcast March 4, 1993 (reprinted in *FBIS/EA* as "Kim Chong-il Rejects 'Renegades' of Socialism," March 5, 1993, p. 10).

67. "Korean Joint Venture Begins Operating," *Journal of Commerce*, August 20, 1996, p. 3A.

68. Kim Jong Il, "Let Us Exalt the Brilliance of Comrade Kim Il Sung's Idea on the Youth Movement and the Achievements Made under His Leadership," August 26, 1996. The official translation is available at *People's Korea*

website, <http://www.korea-np.co.jp/pk/62nd_issue/98082412.htm>.

69. Kim Jong Il, "On Preserving the *Juche* Character and National Character of the Revolution and Construction," June 19, 1997. The official translation is available at *People's Korea* website, <http://www.korea-np.co.jp/pk/62nd_issue/98092412.htm>; accessed March 30, 1999.

70. Kim Jong Il, "Let Us Reunify the Country Independently and Peacefully through the Great Unity of the Entire Nation," April 18, 1998. The official translation is available at *People's Korea* website, <http://www.korea-np.co.jp/pk/62nd_issue/98092412.htm>; accessed March 30, 1999.

Chapter 5: Prospects for U.S.–DPRK Economic Relations

1. For details, see Zachary S. Davis et al., "Korea: Procedural and Jurisdictional Questions Relating to a Possible Normalization of Relations with North Korea" (Washington, D.C.: Congressional Research Service, November 24, 1994); and Kim Kook Shin, "The Origins of the U.S. Aid Policy toward Korea and the Outlook for Its Future Development," *East Asian Review* (Seoul), vol. 8, no. 4 (1996), pp. 74–95.

2. Between September 1995 and July 1997, the U.S. government allocated or pledged a cumulative total of just over $60 million in food and medical aid for the DPRK. *Korea Times*, July 15, 1997 (reprinted in *U.S. Foreign Broadcast Information Service Daily Report: East Asia* (hereafter *FBIS/EA*) as "South Korea: U.S. to Provide Another $27 Million in New Food Aid to DPRK," July 15, 1997). Between 1994 and early 1999, U.S. food aid to North Korea, according to the Congressional Research Service, totaled $140 million with another $100 million pledged "in the pipeline." Douglas Farah and Thomas Lippman, "The North Korean Connection: U.S. Says Cash-Strapped Pyongyang Sponsors Heroin Production," *Washington Post*, March 26, 1999, p. A21.

Those donations would constitute only a small fraction of the official U.S. funds regularly allocated for such purposes. By way of perspective, between 1992 and 1995 America's bilateral aid programs spent an average total of about $1 billion a year on food aid and an additional $800 million a year on emergency and distress relief. Organization for Economic Cooperation and Development, *Development Cooperation 1995* (Paris: OECD, 1997), p. A36.

3. Kim, "Origins of the U.S. Aid Policy," p. 81.

4. For some details, see Nigel Holloway, "Don't All Jump at Once," *Far Eastern Economic Review*, August 3, 1995, pp. 55–56; Donna Marino, "Return to North Korea," *Travel News*, February 13, 1996, p. 41; "Seoul May Block N. Korean Air Deal," *Financial Times*, October 11, 1995, p. 6; and "Cargill Signs Metals Deal in North Korea," *American Metal Market*, April 15, 1997, p. 2.

5. See, for example, Steve Glain, "Unlikely Prize: Evolving North Korea Attracts Foreigners Seeking Business Deals," *Wall Street Journal*, September 20, 1995, pp. A1, A9.

6. As reported in the *Korea Times,* July 8, 1994, p. 8 (reprinted in *FBIS/ EA* as "Trade Group Reports Increase in North Exports," *FBIS/EA,* July 8, 1994).

7. Marcus Noland, "The North Korean Economy," *Joint U.S.–Korean Academic Studies,* vol. 6 (1996), pp. 127–78.

8. "Gravity models" of trade customarily require data on, among other things, the size of a country's GNP and its level of per capita income. For North Korea, Noland used figures published by the ROK Bank of Korea. Among available estimates for such things, those may be as good as any others and perhaps better than some. For obvious reasons, they are nonetheless problematic.

9. The ROK Ministry of National Unification, for example, has estimated North Korean trade turnover at $2.11 billion in 1994 and $2.06 billion in 1995. *Korea Times,* March 23, 1996, p. 6 (reprinted in *FBIS/EA* as "ROK: NUB Says DPRK Economy Shrank 6 Percent in 1995," March 26, 1996). Those particular estimates exclude inter-Korean trade, which totaled, very roughly, $200 million in 1994 and $300 million in 1995.

Later in this chapter I introduce my own estimates of DPRK trade volume. Those estimates will differ somewhat from the Unification Ministry numbers just cited; even so, the totals are broadly similar.

10. In August 1995, for example, DPRK Ambassador to the U.N. Han Song-yol addressed a seminar in Los Angeles on investment opportunities in North Korea for American firms; in April 1996 in Washington, D.C., Kim Jong U, then chairman of the DPRK Committee for the Promotion of External Economic Cooperation, offered remarks at a George Washington University seminar on the North Korean economy; and in March 1997 DPRK Vice Foreign Minister Kim Kye Kwan spoke in Washington to a gathering at the Heritage Foundation. For some details, see *Hanguk Ilbo,* August 5, 1995, p. 6 (translated in *FBIS/EA* as "Han Song-yol Hopes U.S. Will Lift Sanctions," August 7, 1995, p. 42); *Sisa Journal,* May 9, 1996, pp. 78–79 (translated in FBIS/EA as "ROK Weekly Examines DPRK's Reform, Opening Up," May 9, 1997); and *Seoul Sinmun,* March 14, 1997, p. 10 (translated in *FBIS/ EA* as "Daily Reports on DPRK Delegation's Washington D.C. Visit," March 14, 1997).

11. "Daily Reports on DPRK Delegation's Washington D.C. Visit."

12. In posing the problem in that manner, I have implicitly embraced three assumptions. First, North Korea's trade patterns to date strongly reflect, and have indeed been largely determined by, the DPRK's own political economy. Second, within that political economy is an embedded regime logic that is not highly sensitive to changes in domestic conditions or international events. Third, the primary determinant of the scope of a postsanctions commercial relationship between the United States and North Korea would be the DPRK's own political economy and internal regime logic. It is worth making those assumptions ex-

plicit, since it is by no means clear that every reader would agree with them.

13. There is a considerable literature drawing on such techniques. Specialists on communist economies, for example, made extensive use of "mirror statistics" to analyze the performance of earlier regimes subject to official "statistical blackouts" (for example, Stalin's USSR and Maoist China).

For the DPRK, one of the first efforts at reconstructing North Korean foreign trade through "mirror statistics" is to be found in Joseph Sang-hoon Chung, *The North Korean Economy: Structure and Performance* (Stanford: Hoover Institution Press, 1974). To date, perhaps the most comprehensive reconstruction and analysis of North Korea's trade is Soo-young Choi, "Foreign Trade of North Korea, 1946–1988: Structure and Performance," Ph.D. dissertation, Northeastern University, 1991.

14. Marc Rubin, "North Korea's Trade with the USSR and Russia, 1972–1995," U.S. Bureau of the Census, International Programs Center, November 1996.

15. An additional set of adjustments attempted to take account of the carriage, insurance, and freight (c.i.f.) charges that North Korea would pay in its purchases from abroad but that are not reported in its trading partners' accounts (and, conversely, included in their purchases from North Korea but not paid to the DPRK). Those c.i.f. costs, of course, are unknown. Following International Monetary Fund convention, I assumed that c.i.f. costs amounted to 10 percent of f.o.b. (free on board) values and scaled accordingly.

16. For a fuller exposition on those issues, see Nicholas Eberstadt, "The DPRK's International Trade in Capital Goods, 1970–1995: Indications from 'Mirror Statistics,'" *Journal of East Asian Affairs*, vol. 12, no. 1 (Winter/Spring 1998), pp. 165–223.

17. The UN database reports hundreds of millions of dollars in trade between "North Korea" and Saudi Arabia between 1974 and 1982, and hundreds of millions more between "North Korea" and Mexico in 1994 and 1995. I have taken those to be erroneous and have purged them from my reconstructed series. I have likewise stricken some other smaller but equally implausible records (for example, for Sikkim–DPRK transactions).

18. That issue is dealt with in greater detail in Nicholas Eberstadt, Marc Rubin, and Albina Tretyakova, "The Collapse of Soviet and Russian Trade with the DPRK, 1989–1993: Impact and Implications," *Korean Journal of National Reunification*, vol. 4 (1995), pp. 88–103.

19. Note, incidentally, that "non-Soviet" is not simply a euphemism for "Western economies." For the DPRK, consequential "non-Soviet" trade partners during those years included China, the countries of CMEA Europe, and the "Third World" grouping. I deal more specifically with North Korea's performance in Western markets later in this chapter.

20. If we deflate North Korea's estimated non-Soviet commerce by the price indexes for U.S. exports and imports, for example, the DPRK's real

exports to those regions would have declined by about 10 percent between 1975 and 1995; its real imports from them, by about 15 percent. The price indexes are taken from Organization for Economic Development and Cooperation, *National Accounts: Main Aggregates, 1960–1995*, vol. 1 (Paris: OECD, 1997), pp. 146–47.

21. For details, see Choi, "Foreign Trade of North Korea."

22. For details, see Eui-gak Hwang, *The Korean Economies: A Comparison of North and South* (New York: Oxford University Press, 1993); and Bonhak Koo, *The Political Economy of Self-Reliance: Juche and Economic Development in North Korea, 1961–1990* (Seoul: Research Center for Peace and Unification, 1992).

23. For one reading of those measures, see Nicholas Eberstadt, "North Korea: Reform, Muddling Through, or Collapse?" in Thomas L. Henriksen and Kyongsoo Lho, *One Korea? Challenges and Prospects for Reunification* (Stanford: Hoover Institution Press, 1994).

24. The two other priority areas mentioned were agriculture and light industry.

25. Political instability and eruptions of civil turmoil are factors that have prevented some contemporary countries from participating in the international upswing in trade. Suffice it to say that lack of firm political control by central authorities has not been the DPRK's problem.

26. My calculations would place per capita DPRK exports in 1995 at about $40 (presuming a 1995 population of about 23 million). While some North Korean exports for that year are doubtless not included in my series, the absolute value of that unmeasured commerce is probably not great.

27. In 1994 North Korea's estimated level of exports per capita was about $10 greater than in 1995 but was still only slightly above that of the Central African Republic and below that of Laos and Kenya. Those data are derived from International Monetary Fund, *International Financial Statistics Yearbook 1996* (Washington, D.C.: IMF, 1996).

28. For details, see Nicholas Eberstadt, *Korea Approaches Reunification* (Armonk, N.Y.: M. E. Sharpe, 1995).

29. For some details, see Karoly Fendler, "Economic Assistance from Socialist Countries to North Korea in the Postwar Years: 1953–61," in Han S. Park, ed., *North Korea: Ideology, Politics, Economy* (Englewood Cliffs, N.J.: Prentice Hall, 1996).

30. Some of that history is recorded in Chin O. Chung, *Pyongyang between Peking and Moscow: North Korea's Involvement in the Sino-Soviet Dispute, 1958–1975* (Birmingham: University of Alabama Press, 1978).

31. For details, see Eberstadt, Rubin, and Tretyakova, "The Collapse of Soviet and Russian Trade with the DPRK."

32. Those shifts are detailed in Nicholas Eberstadt et al., "China's Trade with the DPRK, 1990–1994: Pyongyang's Thrifty New Patron," *Korea and*

World Affairs, vol. 19, no. 4 (1995–1996), pp. 665–85.

33. It is interesting to note that *sadaejuui*—the historical doctrine that informed the tributary relations between the Yi court and the Chinese empire—is a term of the utmost opprobrium in the DPRK's political lexicon. One interpretation would suggest that *juche* simply stands *sadaejuui* on its head: demanding (or attempting to demand) tribute from abroad as the prerogative of an independent socialist Korean state!

34. That is the apt phrase of David C. Cole and Princeton N. Lyman. See their *Korean Development: The Interplay of Politics and Economics* (Cambridge: Harvard University Press, 1971), pp. 171–74.

35. See, for example, Nicholas Eberstadt, "Financial Transfers from Japan to the DPRK: Estimating the Unreported Flows," *Asian Survey,* vol. 36, no. 5 (1996).

36. Eberstadt et al., "China's Trade with the DPRK."

37. The correspondence between the drop-off of Chinese food shipments and the emergence of an officially acknowledged DPRK "food problem" is examined in Nicholas Eberstadt, "DPRK's International Trade in Food, Energy, and Motor Vehicles: Indications from 'Mirror Statistics,'" *Asian Survey,* vol. 38, no. 3 (March 1998), pp. 203–30.

38. Hong-Tack Chun, "Economic Conditions in North Korea and Prospects for Reform," Korea Development Institute, KDI Working Paper No. 9603, March 1996, pp. 7–9.

39. In 1997, international exports and imports were estimated to total over $11 trillion; official development assistance disbursements, by contrast, came to about $70 billion. *International Monetary Fund, International Financial Statistics Yearbook 1998* (Washington, D.C.: IMF, 1998); OECD, *Geographical Distribution of Financial Flows to Aid Recipients, 1992–97* (Paris: OECD, 1998).

40. That happened, for example, in the early 1960s. For details, see *Korea Approaches Reunification,* chap. 1.

41. According to ROK official statistics, imports in 1997 totaled about $145 billion—or just over $12 billion per month. The level of imports fell steeply in the wake of the financial crisis of late 1997. Even so, by the end of 1998, imports were flowing into the ROK at a rate of over $8 billion per month. Data are available at the ROK Ministry of Finance website, <http://www.mofe.go.kr/ENGLISH/Data/E_ECONO_TREND_SDATA/esd9902_5.html>; accessed March 30, 1999.

42. For background, see Hwang, *The Korean Economies;* and Choi, "Foreign Trade of North Korea."

43. See, for example, Joseph S. Chung, "Foreign Trade of North Korea: Performance, Policy, and Prospects," in Robert A. Scalapino and Hongkoo Lee, eds., *North Korea in a Regional and Global Context* (Berkeley: University of California, Institute of East Asian Studies, 1986).

44. See, for example, George Ginsburgs, "Soviet Development Grants and Aid to North Korea, 1945–1980," *Asia Pacific Community* (Tokyo), vol. 18, no. 4 (1982), pp. 42–63; and Erik van Ree, "The Limits of *Juche:* North Korea's Dependence on Soviet Industrial Aid, 1953–76," *Journal of Communist Studies*, vol. 5, no. 1 (1989), pp. 50–73.

45. For lucid expositions of the phenomenon, see Jan Winiecki, *The Distorted World of Soviet-Type Economies* (Pittsburgh: University of Pittsburgh, 1988); and Janos Kornai, *The Socialist System: The Political Economy of Communism* (Princeton: Princeton University Press, 1992).

46. For a fuller treatment, see Eberstadt, "The DPRK's International Trade in Capital Goods, 1970–1995."

47. For evidence to this effect, see Jong-Wha Lee, "Capital Goods Imports and Long-Run Growth," *Journal of Development Economics*, vol. 48, no. 1 (1995), pp. 91–110.

48. For a more detailed exposition of that interpretation, see chapter 2.

49. According to some military specialists, Soviet weapons shipments to North Korea during those years consisted of such things as avionics systems and high-performance aircraft—items the DPRK could not manufacture domestically.

50. The American business community, as it happens, is beginning to get a taste of North Korea's guerilla-style, "hit-and-run" approach to dealings in the international market. According to one State Department official, an American grain trading concern has already been left with $70 million in unpaid bills for produce it delivered contractually to the DPRK. C. Kenneth Quinones, "The Agricultural Situation in North Korea," *Korea's Economy 1997* (Washington, D.C.: Korean Economic Institute, 1997), p. 103. Furthermore, according to one news report, North Korean authorities unilaterally abrogated their breakthrough grain-for-zinc barter deal with Cargill Inc. after the price of zinc moved up by $100 a ton on the international spot market and it seemed possible that a more advantageous swap might be arranged. *Washington Times*, June 13, 1997, p. A9. Such practices, one may note, have been quite typical of DPRK international business techniques over the past generation.

51. American authorities have reportedly indicated that they would favorably view a DPRK application for admission to the Asian Development Bank. "Japan to Block N. Korea in ADB," *Financial Times*, May 10, 1997, p. 3.

Chapter 6: Can Korean Unification Promote Stability in Northeast Asia?

1. William Stueck, in fact, has argued that the Korean War was a *substitute* for World War III. See his *Korean War: An International History* (Princeton: Princeton University Press, 1995), pp. 348–53.

2. See, for example, Hans Maretzki, *Kimismus in Nordkorea: Analyse des Letzten DDR–Botschafters in Pjoengyang* [*Kimism in North Korea: Analysis by the Last GDR Ambassador to Pyongyang*] (Boeblingen, Germany: Anita Tykve Verlag, 1991); and Marina Trigubenko, "Industrial Policy in the DPRK," paper presented to the Korea Development Institute–*Korea Economic Daily* conference on the North Korean economy, September 30–October 1, 1991.

3. For further details, see Nicholas Eberstadt, Marc Rubin, and Albina Tretyakova, "The Collapse of Soviet and Russian Trade with the DPRK, 1989–1993: Impact and Implications," *Korean Journal of National Reunification* (Seoul), vol. 4 (1995), pp. 88–103.

4. For details, see Nicholas Eberstadt et al., "China's Trade with the DPRK, 1990–1994: Pyongyang's Thrifty New Patron," *Korea and World Affairs*, vol. 19, no. 4 (1995–1996), pp. 665–85; and Nicholas Eberstadt, "Financial Transfers from Japan to the DPRK: Estimating Unreported Flows," *Asian Survey*, vol. 36, no. 5 (1996), pp. 523–42.

5. Those calculations come from Hong-Tack Chun, "Economic Conditions in North Korea and Prospects for Reform," Korea Development Institute, KDI Working Paper No. 9603, March 1996, pp. 7–9. Chun's cost estimate, moreover, may be on the high side, insofar as it posits rice imports, which are much more expensive than comparable amounts of wheat or maize.

6. *People's Korea*, February 15, 1992.

7. *Nodong Sinmun*, February 13, 1999, p. 6.

8. See, for example, Robert A. Scalapino, *The Last Leninists: The Uncertain Future of Asia's Communist States* (Washington, D.C.: Center for Strategic and International Studies, 1992).

9. A 1995 U.S. Department of Defense policy paper summarized those findings:

North Korea continues to expend its national resources to:

• mechanize its huge, offensively postured ground forces;
• expand its already massive artillery formations;
• enhance the world's largest special operations force.

Office of International Security Affairs, *United States Security Strategy for the East Asia–Pacific Region* (Washington, D.C.: Department of Defense, February 1995), p. 18.

10. Cf. David A. Fulghum, "North Korean Forces Suffer Mobility Loss," *Aviation Week and Space Technology*, November 24, 1997, pp. 61–62; and Michael O'Hanlon, "Stopping a North Korean Invasion: Why Defending South Korea Is Easier Than the Pentagon Thinks," *International Security*, vol. 22, no. 4 (1998), pp. 137–70.

11. For a fuller treatment, see Nicholas Eberstadt, "Development, Struc-

ture, and Performance of the DPRK Economy: Empirical Indications," paper presented at the conference "Developing Social Infrastructure in North Korea for Economic Cooperation between the North and the South," Korea University, Seoul, November 9–10, 1998.

12. For details, see *Chugan Choson,* June 30, 1994, pp. 26–28 (translated in *U.S. Foreign Broadcast Information Service Daily Report: East Asia* (hereafter *FBIS/EA*) as "Weekly Assesses DPRK Nuclear War Preparations," June 30, 1994, pp. 38–41).

13. *Chungang Ilbo* (Internet version), February 11, 1999 (reprinted in *FBIS/EA* as "US Said to Supply 1 Million Tonnes of Grain to DPRK," February 11, 1999).

14. "Characteristics of DPRK Chemical Weapons Noted," *FBIS/EA,* May 12, 1995, p. 44.

15. For a chronology of that program, consult Center for Nonproliferation Studies, "Chronology of North Korea's Missile Trade and Developments." Available at <http://cns.miis.edu/research/korea/chron.html>; accessed March 30, 1999.

16. *Seoul Shinmun,* September 11, 1995, p. 3 (translated in *FBIS/EA* as "U.S. Reportedly within New North Missile Range," September 11, 1995, p. 49).

17. Center for Nonproliferation Studies, "31 August 1998 Launch of North Korean Rocket: Factsheet." Available at <http://cns.miis.edu/research/korea/factsht.htm>; accessed March 30, 1999.

18. *Chungang Ilbo,* February 12, 1999 (reprinted in *FBIS/EA* as "DPRK Publishes Magazine on Details of Satellite Launch," February 17, 1999).

19. Korea Central News Agency Radio (Pyongyang), broadcast April 19, 1993 (reprinted in *FBIS/EA* as *"Nodong Sinmun:* Japan Must 'Act Prudently,'" April 20, 1993, p. 12).

20. Korea Central News Agency (Pyongyang), "Disgraceful Behavior of Doughfaces," December 4, 1998. Available at *People's Korea* website, <http://www.korea-np.co.jp/item/9812/news12/04.htm#6>; accessed March 30, 1999.

21. For more details, see chapter 2.

22. Korea Central News Agency (Pyongyang), "DPRK's Military Warns of 'Annihilating Blow' to U.S.," December 2, 1998. Available at *People's Korea* website, <http://www.korea-np.co.jp/pk/72nd_issue/98120206.htm>; accessed March 30, 1998.

23. Korea Central News Agency (Pyongyang), "'Any Enemy Is Target of Our Strike': KPA Vice Marshal." Available at *People's Korea* website, <http://www.korea-np.co.jp/pk/72nd_issue/98120504.htm>; accessed March 30, 1999.

24. "Inaugural Address by Kim Dae-Jung, the 15th-Term President of the Republic of Korea," February 25, 1998, ref. no. 399. Available at ROK Blue House (Chong Wa Dae) website, <http://www.cwd.go.kr/index-eng.html>;

accessed March 30, 1999.

25. *Korea Times*, June 12, 1998, p. 2 (reprinted in *FBIS/EA* as "South Korea: Kim Not Expected to Realize Unification during Presidency," June 15, 1998).

26. Ha-Cheong Yeon, "Economic Consequences of German Unification and Its Policy Implications for Korea," Korea Development Institute, KDI Working Paper No. 9303, April 1993, p. 23.

27. Hong-Tack Chun, "A Gradual Approach toward North and South Korean Economic Integration," Korea Development Institute, KDI Working Paper No. 9311, November 1993, p. 4.

28. "Remarks to the Korean National Assembly in Seoul," January 6, 1992, in *Public Papers of the Presidents of the United States: George Bush (1992–93)*, vol. 1 (Washington, D.C.: Government Printing Office, 1993), p. 40.

29. U.S. Department of Defense (DOD), "The United States Security Strategy for the East Asia–Pacific Region 1998." Available at DOD website, < http://www.defenselink.mol/pubs/easr98.html >; accessed March 30, 1999.

30. If all goes exactly as planned, the third and final phase of that framework would be implemented some time after the year 2003. See Michael J. Mazarr, "Going Just a Little Nuclear: Nonproliferation Lessons from North Korea," *International Security*, vol. 20, no. 2 (1995), p. 98. Unanticipated delays would correspondingly extend the time horizon of the envisioned U.S.–DPRK arrangement, and such delays have already been experienced. See the report in *Korea World*, September 19, 1998 (reprinted in *FBIS/EA* as "South Korea: LWR Construction in DPRK Likely to Fall behind Schedule," September 22, 1998); and KBS-1 Radio (Seoul), broadcast January 14, 1999 (translated in *FBIS/EA* as "South Korea: KEDO to Delay LWR Construction in DPRK until 15 June," January 20, 1999).

31. Chae-Jin Lee, *China and Korea: Dynamic Relations* (Stanford: Hoover Institution Press, 1996), pp. 171–72.

32. As one analyst observed, "Considerations of this kind must remain speculative, but they probably lurk in the minds of long-term planners among Japanese bureaucrats." Wolf Mendl, *Japan's Asia Policy: Regional Security and Global Interests* (London: Routledge, 1995), p. 67.

33. Russian scholars and policymakers, it must be noted, usually profess that Russia favors an "early Korean unification." For one such presentation, see Alexander Zhebin, "Russia and Korean Unification," *Asian Perspective* (Seoul), vol. 19, no. 2 (1995), pp. 175–90.

34. See, for example, Gerlinde and Hans-Werner Sinn, *Jumpstart: The Economic Unification of Germany* (Cambridge: MIT Press, 1992); Organization for Economic Cooperation and Development, *OECD Economic Surveys: Germany, 1991/92* (Paris: OECD, 1992); and Manfred Wegner, *Bankrott und Aufbau* (Baden-Baden, Germany: Nomos, 1995).

35. The point, in fact, has recently been made with some econometric rigor. See Marcus Noland, Sherman Robinson, and Li-Gang Liu, "The Costs and Benefits of Korean Unification: Alternative Scenarios," *Asian Survey*, vol. 38, no. 8 (1998), pp. 801–14.

That study uses a computable general equilibrium model to simulate the economic consequences of Korean unification under a variety of circumstances and policies. Its findings are worth quoting in some detail:

> We find there is a scenario in which the present discounted value of South Korean income is higher with unification than without it. Although lower income groups in South Korea experience reduced incomes under this scenario, with redistribution of the gains, everyone can be better off. Indeed, this scenario, which involves relatively low levels of South Korean private investment in the North with relatively high levels of North-South migration, is also the one which generates the highest level of total peninsular income as well. The latter point is critical as it suggests there is no necessary conflict between the economic interests of the North and South Koreans after unification.

Economic modeling, of course, is just one of many forms of economic analysis; like all other forms, its results depend on the assumptions and premises of those who employ it. But since that form of economic analysis requires an especially rigorous specification of the assumptions embodied, and since the results it generates are perforce internally consistent, the exercise and its implications may be of particular interest.

36. Aaron L. Friedberg, "Ripe for Rivalry: Prospects for Peace in a Multipolar Asia," *International Security*, vol. 18, no. 3 (1993–1994), pp. 5–33.

37. Those trends have been extensively discussed. For some recent and informative commentary, see Kent E. Calder, *Asia's Deadly Triangle: How Arms, Energy, and Growth Threaten to Destabilize Asia-Pacific* (Sonoma, Calif.: Nicholas Brealey, 1997); and Zalmay Khalilzad and David A. Ochmanek, eds., *Strategic Appraisal 1997* (Santa Monica, Calif.: RAND Corporation, 1997).

38. Organization for Economic Cooperation and Development, *Financial Market Trends*, no. 69 (February 1998), p. 5; and Organization for Economic Cooperation and Development, *Financial Market Trends*, no. 70 (June 1998), p. 96.

39. That typology is drawn from Friedberg, "Ripe for Rivalry."

40. That point was initially raised in Henry Sokolski, "The Korean Nuclear Deal: How Might It Challenge the United States?" *Comparative Strategy*, vol. 14, no. 4 (1995), pp. 443–51.

41. For a succinct analysis of the situation in mid-1998, see Organization for Economic Cooperation and Development, *OECD Economic Surveys 1997/*

98: Korea (Paris: OECD, 1998).

42. Adding insult to injury is the intended symbolism in the program. The most recent addition to the South Korean submarine fleet, for example, was named *Chung Un-ho*—after a Korean admiral who directed some successful sea battles against Japan four hundred years ago! *Yonhap*, May 7, 1996 (reprinted in *FBIS/EA* as "ROK Launches Sixth Naval Submarine 7 May," May 7, 1996, p. 43).

43. For an excellent "inside" account of those diplomatic exertions, see Philip Zelikow and Condoleezza Rice, *Germany Unified and Europe Transformed: A Study in Statecraft* (Cambridge: Harvard University Press, 1995).

44. The London International Institute for Strategic Studies encapsulates that new assessment in its 1998 *Strategic Survey*, where it argues:

> The economic woes of the North and the South may be beneficial in the security context. Economic difficulties may force both to rethink their policies on the [Korean peninsula]. Kim Dae Jung's willingness to open a serious dialogue with the North, coupled with the willingness of the previously insulated regime to continue talks with the South, may have created a more encouraging atmosphere. Perhaps the changes in both the North and the South in 1997 may lead to a more constructive relationship.

Available at <http://www.isn.ethz.ch/iiss/ssaisa.htm#3>.

In Washington, the new assessment is reflected in comments by Charles Kartman, special presidential envoy to the Korean peace process, who has opined that "[t]he North may feel psychologically at ease due to the ROK's financial troubles," and by Sam Nunn, former senator and current chairman of the Center for Strategic and International Studies, who has stated that "[d]ue to the ROK's financial crisis, the ROK will be perceived as less of a threat by North Korea." *Chungang Ilbo* (Internet version), June 3, 1998 (reprinted in *FBIS/EA* as "South Korea: Financial Troubles to Aid Inter-Korean Relations," Internet version, June 3, 1998).

That assessment is further represented in *Managing Change on the Korean Peninsula*, a May 1998 report by a Council on Foreign Relations task force whose membership included, among others, "all of the former U.S. assistant secretaries of state for Asia [sic] from the last four administrations." The report concludes that "[i]ncreasingly, signals between Pyongyang and Seoul suggest there could be new opportunity for North-South dialogue and some meaningful reconciliation" and that one reason for "at least a prospect of significant improvements in North-South relations" relates to the ROK's current economic troubles:

> The South's financial crisis has changed the psychological environment of North-South relations. Hard-liners in the South can no longer garner support for a policy designed to absorb the North. . . .

> The South's economic situation has also leveled the propaganda
> playing field somewhat for the first time since the North's decline
> began eight years ago. . . . [T]he fact that both Koreas face pres-
> sures from globalism helps to create an unusual connection be-
> tween North and South, a point played up in Kim Jong Il's April 18
> letter to Kim Dae Jung.

Council on Foreign Relations, *Managing Change in the Korean Peninsula.*
Available at <http://www.foreignrelations.org/studies/transcripts/manag-
ing.html>.

In Seoul, for its part, such new thinking may be seen as already fully
incorporated into and undergirding the North Korea policy of the Kim Dae
Jung administration.

Although the ROK's economic troubles per se surely did not inspire President Kim's "sunshine policy," they clearly reinforced it and just as impor-
tantly reduced resistance to it from his domestic opposition. As the *Chungang
Ilbo* recently noted,

> [M]any ROK conservative politicians agree that the ROK is not ca-
> pable of sustaining North Korea's sudden collapse or of achieving
> absorption unification led by the ROK. Thus, the fact that there is no
> justification to challenge the incumbent government's appeasement
> policy also serves as a positive variable to the reconciliation of both
> Koreas.

"South Korea: Financial Troubles to Aid Inter-Korean Relations."

45. I have already reviewed or touched upon most of those policies and
practices. For additional detail, one may consult the following studies: Nicholas Eberstadt, "North Korea: Reform, Muddling Through, or Collapse?" *NBR
Analysis Series* (Seattle, Wash.), vol. 4, no. 5 (September 1993); Nicholas
Eberstadt, "North Korea's Interlocked Economic Crises: Some Indications from
'Mirror Statistics,'" *Asian Survey,* vol. 38, no. 5 (1998), pp. 203–30; and Nicholas Eberstadt, "'Self Reliance' and Economic Decline: North Korean Trade,
1970–1995," *Problems of Post-Communism,* vol. 46, no. 1 (January/February
1999), pp. 3–13.

46. Although a variety of changes in rules and practices within the North
Korean economy can be identified—some of them dating back to the early
1990s or even earlier—we cannot as yet accurately describe that corpus of
changes as constituting a redirection of DPRK economic policy, much less a
serious movement toward *policy reform* as that term is understood in the West.

Alterations of government policy always beg the question of intent. Should
the changes observed to date in North Korea's economic framework be viewed
as the beginnings of a conscious and deliberate rethinking of policy or are they
simply concessions to exigence, as a brittle system sags under the weight of its

own troubles?

We cannot answer that question today with absolute confidence. But we can point to a number of considerations that should weigh upon our interpretation of available evidence.

For one thing, if recent changes in North Korean economic rules and practices were actually intended as efforts to redress the country's economic troubles, it is self-evident that those measures—which amount thus far to little more than modest, opportunistic tinkerings at the margin—have been woefully inadequate for the enormous task at hand.

Second, despite the episodic reshuffling of personalities within the DPRK's top leadership, North Korea's hierarchy has been marked over the past generation by fundamental continuity—most important, in the presence of Kim Jong Il. In other communist systems, by contrast, significant change in policy has typically been accompanied by significant changeovers in top-level personnel.

Finally, we should note that it is not even clear that North Korean leadership today would understand how to go about embarking on an economic redirection, even were it so inclined. Indeed, North Korea's current leadership may quite possibly be more economically naive than any other leadership configuration to govern a country in the period since the end of the Second World War. Such economic innocence tends to encourage resistance to new economic directions in the face of crisis, not least by confounding diagnosis and prescription.

47. While policy pronouncements from Pyongyang sometimes strike outside observers as delphic, contradictory, or both, that recent exposition of DPRK economic policy—published conjointly in *Nodong Sinmun* and *Kulloja* and broadcast on September 17, 1998—would seem to be a veritable model of clarity and deserves careful reading:

> It is a foolish daydream to try to revive the economy by introducing foreign capital, not relying on one's own strength. If one wants the prosperity of the national economy, he should thoroughly reject the idea of dependence on outside forces, the idea that he cannot live without foreign capital. . . .
>
> The imperialists and reactionaries are claiming that our economic difficulties of recent years are attributable to our economy itself. Their allegation is false propaganda to distort the truth and lead us to lose our faith. . . .
>
> Ours is an independent economic structure equipped with all the economic sectors in good harmony and with its own strong heavy industry at the core. It is incomparably better than the export-oriented economic structure dependent on other countries. . . .
>
> We must heighten vigilance against the imperialists' moves

to induce us to "reform" and "opening to the outside world." "Reform" and "opening" on their lips are a honey-coated poison. Clear is our stand toward "reform" and "opening." We now have nothing to "reform" and "open." . . . The best way of blocking the wind of "reform" and "opening" of the imperialists is to defend the socialist principle in all sectors of the economy.

48. One should note, incidentally, that "separating politics from business" in North-South commercial transactions augurs for a *downturn* in inter-Korean trade, at least in the short run. That is so because South Korean businesses will now be less inclined to engage in deals with the North that look questionable from a purely commercial standpoint, insofar as Seoul is less likely to compensate those businesses for any losses they incur in such ventures.

Indeed, the inauguration of the "sunshine policy" has coincided with a precipitous drop in South Korean trade with the North. In the first half of 1998, in fact, imports from the DPRK were reportedly down by 67 percent against the previous year (that is to say, by almost twice the total decline in ROK imports in the wake of its economic crisis). *Yonhap*, July 30, 1998 (reprinted in *FBIS/EA* as "South Korea: Inter-Korean Trade Down 46 Percent in Jan–Jun 1998," August 6, 1998).

49. South Korean officials anticipate prolongation of that interruption. In the words of Kim Dae Jung, "The time is not yet ripe for direct contacts between the governments of South and North Korea." "Zhu Urges Kim to Help Cut Seoul's Huge Trade Surplus with Beijing," *Japan Times*, November 15, 1998, p. 4.

50. Cf. Article III, section 3, of the "Agreed Framework": "The DPRK will engage in north-south dialogue, as this agreed framework will help create an atmosphere that promotes such dialogue." "Agreed Framework between the DPRK and the US," October 1994. Available at *People's Korea* website, <http://www.korea-np.co.jp/pk/11th_issue/971001genevaagreemnt.htm>; accessed March 30, 1999.

51. For the first time in the ROK's history, in fact, the country's 1999 defense budget is set to decline in *nominal* terms. *Yonhap*, September 21, 1998 (reprinted in *FBIS/EA* as "South Korea: ROK Reduces Defense Budget for 1st Time in 50 Years," September 22, 1998).

52. South Korea has thus far commissioned seven submarines and is slated to add another two to its fleet by the year 2001. In 1998—after the International Monetary Fund accord—Seoul announced that it would commit another 3 trillion *won* (about $1.7 billion) to the construction of six additional submarines.

For details, see *Sisa*, April 30, 1998 (translated in *FBIS/EA* as "South Korea: Weekly on ROK 'SSU' Submarine Project," May 7, 1998); *Sisa*, June 4, 1998 (translated in *FBIS/EA* as "South Korea: Weekly Discusses Launching of Seventh Submarine," June 5, 1998); *Yonhap*, December 22, 1998 (reprinted in FBIS/EA as "South Korea: Hyundai Allowed to Bid on Submarine Contracts," December 23, 1998); and *Korea Herald*, January 20, 1999 (reprinted in *FBIS/EA* as "South Korea: Daewoo, Hyundai Compete for Submarine Deal," January 21, 1999).

South Korea is also currently embarked on a program of torpedo development for its new submarine fleet. See *Korea Times* (Internet version), July 6, 1998 (reprinted in *FBIS/EA* as "South Korea: ROK Uses Own Technology to Develop Sub-Launched Torpedo," July 6, 1998); and *Sisa*, August 13, 1998 (translated in *FBIS/EA* as "South Korea: Weekly on New Torpedo for Submarines," August 16, 1998).

53. Although President Kim Dae Jung's North Korea policy and security policy differ in some important respects from those of his predecessors, he evidently shares their enthusiasm for submarines and other military vessels. He recently proclaimed that "the country should promote the modernization of the Navy with high interest." *Yonhap*, March 18, 1998 (reprinted in *FBIS/EA* as "Kim Tae-chung Stresses Need for Naval Forces," March 18, 1998).

54. Kim Dae Jung, *The Mass Participatory Society: Korea's Road to World Economic Power* (Lanham, Md.: University Press of America, 1996).

55. Cho Soon, *The Dynamics of Korean Economic Development* (Washington, D.C.: Institute for International Economics, 1994).

Index

About the Author

NICHOLAS EBERSTADT is a visiting scholar at the American Enterprise Institute for Public Policy Research and a visiting fellow at the Harvard Center for Population and Development Studies. He is a member of the Council on Foreign Relations and is a research associate and member of the board of advisers of the National Bureau of Asian Research in Seattle, Washington. He is also a member of the board of advisers of the Korea Economic Institute, the Overseas Development Network, the Environmental Literacy Council, and the Statistical Assessment Service. He has served as a consultant for the U.S. Department of State, the World Bank, the U.S. Agency for International Development, the U.S. Bureau of the Census, and the Congressional Budget Office.

At Harvard University, Mr. Eberstadt has taught courses in population and natural resources, agricultural economics, social science and social policy, and problems of policymaking in less-developed countries.

Mr. Eberstadt has published extensively in scholarly journals and is the author of many books, including *The Tyranny of Numbers* (AEI Press, 1995), *Korea Approaches Reunification* (M. E. Sharpe, 1995), *The Population of North Korea* (with Judith Banister) (University of California Institute of East Asian Studies, 1992), and *The Poverty of Communism* (Transaction Books, 1990).

Sam Peltzman
Sears Roebuck Professor of
Economics and Financial Services
University of Chicago Graduate
School of Business

Nelson W. Polsby
Professor of Political Science
University of California at Berkeley

George L. Priest
John M. Olin Professor of Law and
Economics
Yale Law School

Thomas Sowell
Senior Fellow
Hoover Institution
Stanford University

Murray L. Weidenbaum
Mallinckrodt Distinguished
University Professor
Washington University

Paul Wolfowitz
Dean, Paul H. Nitze School of
Advanced International Studies
Johns Hopkins University

Richard J. Zeckhauser
Frank Ramsey Professor of Political
Economy
Kennedy School of Government
Harvard University

Research Staff

Leon Aron
Resident Scholar

Claude E. Barfield
Resident Scholar; Director, Science
and Technology Policy Studies

Walter Berns
Resident Scholar

Douglas J. Besharov
Resident Scholar

Robert H. Bork
John M. Olin Scholar in Legal
Studies

Karlyn Bowman
Resident Fellow

Ricardo Caballero
Visiting Scholar

John E. Calfee
Resident Scholar

Charles Calomiris
Visiting Scholar

Lynne V. Cheney
Senior Fellow

Dinesh D'Souza
John M. Olin Research Fellow

Nicholas N. Eberstadt
Visiting Scholar

Mark Falcoff
Resident Scholar

Gerald R. Ford
Distinguished Fellow

Murray F. Foss
Visiting Scholar

Hillel Fradkin
Resident Fellow

Diana Furchtgott-Roth
Assistant to the President and
Resident Fellow

Suzanne Garment
Visiting Scholar

Jeffrey Gedmin
Resident Scholar; Executive Director,
New Atlantic Initiative

Newt Gingrich
Senior Fellow

James K. Glassman
DeWitt Wallace–Reader's Digest
Fellow

Robert A. Goldwin
Resident Scholar

Robert W. Hahn
Resident Scholar; Director,
AEI–Brookings Joint Center for
Regulatory Studies

Kevin Hassett
Resident Scholar

Tom Hazlett
Resident Scholar

Robert B. Helms
Resident Scholar; Director, Health
Policy Studies

R. Glenn Hubbard
Visiting Scholar

James D. Johnston
Resident Fellow

Leon Kass
W. H. Brady, Jr., Scholar

Jeane J. Kirkpatrick
Senior Fellow; Director, Foreign and
Defense Policy Studies

Marvin H. Kosters
Resident Scholar; Director, Economic
Policy Studies

Irving Kristol
John M. Olin Distinguished Fellow

Michael A. Ledeen
Freedom Scholar

James Lilley
Resident Fellow

Lawrence Lindsey
Arthur F. Burns Scholar in
Economics

Clarisa Long
Abramson Fellow

Randall Lutter
Resident Scholar

John H. Makin
Visiting Scholar; Director, Fiscal
Policy Studies

Allan H. Meltzer
Visiting Scholar

James M. Morris
Director of Publications

Joshua Muravchik
Resident Scholar

Charles Murray
Bradley Fellow

Michael Novak
George F. Jewett Scholar in Religion,
Philosophy, and Public Policy;
Director, Social and Political Studies

Norman J. Ornstein
Resident Scholar

Richard N. Perle
Resident Fellow

Sarath Rajapatirana
Visiting Scholar

William Schneider
Resident Scholar

J. Gregory Sidak
F. K. Weyerhaeuser Fellow

Christina Hoff Sommers
W. H. Brady, Jr., Fellow

Herbert Stein
Senior Fellow

Daniel Troy
Associate Scholar

Arthur Waldron
Visiting Scholar; Director, Asian
Studies

Graham Walker
Visiting Scholar

Peter Wallison
Resident Fellow

Ben J. Wattenberg
Senior Fellow

Carolyn L. Weaver
Resident Scholar; Director, Social
Security and Pension Studies

David Wurmser
Research Fellow

Karl Zinsmeister
J. B. Fuqua Fellow; Editor,
The American Enterprise